OAKS
OF CALIFORNIA

Written by

Bruce M. Pavlik, Pamela C. Muick,
Sharon Johnson, and Marjorie Popper

Published by

Cachuma Press and the California Oak Foundation

©1991 Cachuma Press, Inc.

Editor: John Evarts
Associate Editor: Marjorie Popper
Contributing Editors: Ginger Wadsworth and Robert C. Pavlik
Editorial Assistants: Katey O'Neill and Cynthia Anderson
Designers: Adine Maron, Christine Flannery, and Sue Irwin
Illustrator: Allison Atwill
Cartography: Bruce Appleyard
Typesetting: Graphic Traffic, Santa Barbara

Printed and bound in the United States.

With permission of University of California Press, material quoted on pages 92-93 and 109 is from: William H. Brewer, *Up and Down California in 1860-1864.* Edited/translated by Francis Farquhar. Copyright ©1949 The Regents of the University of California.

Library of Congress Cataloging-in-Publication Data
Oaks of California / written by Bruce M. Pavlik ... [et al] ;
    [illustrator, Allison Atwill].
        p.   cm.
    Includes bibliographical references (p. 173) and index.
    ISBN 0-9628505-2-7 (hard) – ISBN 0-9628505-1-9 (paper)
    1. Oak—California. I. Pavlik, Bruce M.
QK495.F14O25 1991
583'.976—dc20   91-43772
                                                   CIP

Front cover/jacket cover: Oak woodland in spring, Mount Diablo State Park. CARR CLIFTON
Back cover/jacket back cover: Blue oak savanna, Temblor Range. CARR CLIFTON
Title page: Black oaks in fall, Yosemite National Park. CARR CLIFTON
Right: Valley oak leaves. ALLISON ATWILL

CONTENTS

The California Oak Foundation gratefully acknowledges the following individuals, businesses, and organizations for their sponsorship of *Oaks of California:*

Alameda–Contra Costa Regional Parks Foundation
Bedford Properties, Inc.
Blackhills Developers
DeSilva Group
Eden Development Partners
Golden Bear Arborists
Hecker Pass Specimen Trees
Sunset Development Company
Angelo and Sophia Tsakopoulos
Valley Crest Tree Company
West Coast Arborists

Above: Meadows and oaks near Liebre Mountain, Los Angeles County. CARR CLIFTON
Page vi: Wildflowers in a blue oak woodland, Henry W. Coe State Park. LARRY ULRICH
Two-page spread: Oaks and metamorphic outcrops, Sierra Nevada foothills. CARR CLIFTON

Acknowledgements

On behalf of the authors, Cachuma Press, and the book committee of the California Oak Foundation, we would like to acknowledge the many individuals who generously shared their time and expertise in reviewing the book's manuscript. We appreciated their comments and suggestions, and endeavored to incorporate them into the final text.

Among the reviewers are several individuals whose contributions of time and effort call for extra recognition. For their technical review and ideas regarding the subject of oaks and wildlife, we owe a debt of gratitude to William M. Block, William F. Laudenslayer Jr., and Samuel S. Sweet. For helping us evaluate the complex causes of poor oak regeneration, we express our appreciation to Tom Griggs and Douglas D. McCreary. For providing information on oaks in California's state parks, we extend a thank you to Jim Trumbly. For his assistance in evaluating acorn and leaf samples for the book's illustrations, we are grateful to Steve Junak. Finally, we acknowledge the important research by ecologist James R. Griffin, whose studies of oak communities since the 1970s have inspired many scientists. His work has been instrumental in promoting awareness of oak ecosystems and stimulating concern for their future.

—John Evarts and Marjorie Popper, Cachuma Press

We would also like to thank the following reviewers:

Kat Anderson, Dept. of Forestry and Resource Management, UC Berkeley; Richard A. Arnold, Entomological Consulting Services, Ltd., Pleasant Hill; Michael G. Barbour, Dept. of Botany, UC Davis; Steve Barnhardt, Biology Dept., Santa Rosa Junior College; James W. Bartolome, Dept. of Forestry and Resource Management, UC Berkeley; Craig Bates, Yosemite Museum, Yosemite National Park; Gary Bell, The Nature Conservancy, Santa Rosa Plateau Ecological Reserve, Temecula; William M. Block, Rocky Mountain Forestry and Range Experiment Station, Arizona State University, Tempe; Charles L. Bolsinger, U.S. Forest Service, Pacific Northwest Research Station, Portland; Dave Bontrager, Boneta, Oregon; Mark Borchert, U.S. Forest Service, Los Padres National Forest, Goleta; Paul W. Collins, Dept. of Vertebrate Zoology, Santa Barbara Museum of Natural History; Karen Danielson, U.S. Forest Service, Los Padres National Forest, Goleta; Jules Evens, Point Reyes Bird Observatory, Stinson Beach; James R. Griffin, Hastings Natural History Reservation, Carmel Valley; Tom Griggs, The Nature Conservancy, Hamilton City; Robert Haller, Dept. of Biological Sciences, UC Santa Barbara; Ken Hedges, San Diego Museum of Man; Robert Holland, Auburn; V. L. Holland, Biological Sciences Dept., Cal Poly State University, San Luis Obispo; Rick Hopkins, H. T. Harvey and Associates, Alviso; Steve Junak, Santa Barbara Botanic Garden; Patrick A. Kelly, Dept. of Biology, UC Riverside; Walter Koenig, Museum of Vertebrate Zoology, UC Berkeley; Earl W. Lathrop, Dept. of Biology, Loma Linda University, Riverside; William F. Laudenslayer Jr., U.S. Forest Service, Tahoe National Forest, Nevada City; Steve Laymon, Kern River Research Center, Weldon; Malcolm Margolin, Heyday Books, Berkeley; Helen McCarthy, Cultural Resource Research and Consulting, Davis; Mitchel McClaran, School of Renewable Resources, University of Arizona, Tucson; Douglas D. McCreary, Integrated Hardwood Range Management Program, Dept. of Forestry and Resource Management, UC Berkeley; Philip M. McDonald, U.S. Forest Service, Pacific Southwest Forest and Range Experiment Station, Redding; Bev Ortiz, *News from Native California,* Berkeley; V. Thomas Parker, Dept. of Biology, San Francisco State University; James L. Patton, Museum of Vertebrate Zoology, UC Berkeley; Timothy E. Payson, U.S. Forest Service, Pacific Southwest Forest and Range Experiment Station, Riverside Forest Fire Lab, Riverside; James J. Rawls, Dept. of History, Diablo Valley College, Pleasant Hill; Kevin Rice, Dept. of Agronomy and Range Science, UC Davis; Lois Reed, National Park Service, Redwood National Park, Orick; Elizabeth Ross, Museum of Vertebrate Zoology, UC Berkeley; Thomas A. Scott, Dept. of Earth Sciences, UC Riverside; Mark Stanbach, Hastings Natural History Reservation, Carmel Valley; Kelly P. Steele, Dept. of Biology, Appalachian State University, Boone, N. Carolina; William I. Stein, U.S. Forest Service, Forest Service Laboratory, Corvalis, Oregon; Richard B. Standiford, Integrated Hardwood Range Management Program, Dept. of Forestry and Resource Management, UC Berkeley; Lynn Suer, Oakland; Tedmund J. Swiecki, Plant Science Consulting and Research, Vacaville; Samuel S. Sweet, Dept. of Biological Sciences, UC Santa Barbara; William Tietje, Integrated Hardwood Range Management Program, Dept. of Forestry and Resource Management, UC Berkeley; Jan Timbrook, Anthropology Dept., Santa Barbara Museum of Natural History; Jim Trumbly, California Dept. of Parks and Recreation, Sacramento; Steven Veirs, Cooperative National Park Resources Studies Unit, UC Davis; Tom Wake, Museum of Vertebrate Zoology, UC Berkeley; Pam Williams, Kern River Research Center, Weldon.

FOREWORD

Few plants figure more prominently in California's natural and cultural history than oaks. Over millennia oaks have provided food and shelter for a rich diversity of wildlife. For countless generations oak acorns were a dietary staple of the California Indians. During two hundred years of exploration and colonization, European people marveled at the vast oak groves and savannas they encountered along the Pacific shore. In the 19th century resourceful pioneers quickly learned the value of oaks for fuel, tools, and livestock feed. Even today, no scene is more characteristic of California than rolling, grassy hills studded with oak trees.

Oaks cover millions of acres from one end of the state to the other, yet there is widespread concern that many of California's native oak landscapes are in trouble. Urbanization, conversion of wildlands to agriculture, and fragmentation of natural habitats in rural areas are some of the trends that pose a threat to oaks. In addition, at least three oak species are experiencing low rates of natural regeneration for reasons that are not fully understood.

United by a shared interest in oak conservation, a group of civic leaders, foresters, and resource managers met in Sacramento in early 1988. The participants agreed that a coordinated effort was needed to protect oaks and ensure the long-term survival of native oak communities. The outcome of this meeting was the formation of the California Oak Foundation, the first and only statewide organization devoted solely to the conservation, restoration, and management of California's native oak heritage.

The Foundation seeks to raise public awareness of oak issues by producing and disseminating news and information on oaks. It also supports and complements tree preservation efforts at the community level. Additional Foundation objectives include improving cooperation between oak preservation groups, spearheading appropriate legislative activities, and stimulating oak tree planting and habitat restoration. The Foundation's first official action was to declare 1990 the Year of the Oak. It subsequently sought and received support from the California State Legislature, which passed a Senate resolution endorsing the Year of the Oak.

More recently the Foundation sponsored a ceremonial oak planting on November 1, 1991 in Sacramento's Capitol Park. This marked California Native Oak Day, as designated by the state legislature. A resolution proclaiming November 1 as Native Oak Day was read by Senator Dan McCorquodale, who authored the legislation.

As part of the Foundation's emphasis on broadening public appreciation for native oaks, it has joined with Cachuma Press in producing Oaks of California. *We are pleased to be a partner in this project and it is our hope that this handsome and detailed book will inspire and educate. Most of all, we hope that the publication of* Oaks of California *will help engender a growing sense of stewardship for California's marvelous, but imperiled, oak landscapes.*

—Janet Santos Cobb
President Elect/Book Project Director
California Oak Foundation
November 1991

OAKS
OF CALIFORNIA

CHAPTER ONE

THE DIVERSITY
OF CALIFORNIA OAKS

CALIFORNIA HAS LONG BEEN BLESSED BY THE diversity, abundance, and beauty of oaks. At present, 18 species of oak enrich the state's native flora, each strikingly different in growth form and physiology. Some grow as tall, stately trees, while others are diminutive, ground-hugging shrubs. Some retain their foliage all year long, while others drop it at the onset of winter or drought. So many are the variations in shape, color, texture, and size that botanists have divided the 18 species into nearly 30 distinct varieties. This high diversity rivals, if not surpasses, the richness exhibited by California's magnificent pines, firs, and cypresses.

Ancient California had even more oak species in its flora, some known to us now only as fossils. The fossils reveal that oaks were as diverse and abundant in the distant past as they are today, covering millions of acres of plains, foothills, valleys, and mountains. Over geologic time, diversity and abundance permitted oaks to assume widespread ecological importance. Each species is now a prominent thread in California's complex web of plant and animal life. Humans became tangled in that web more than 100 centuries ago when they discovered that oaks could supply food, tools, fuel, and other valuable resources. But humans have also begun to appreciate oaks on their own terms, as beautiful works of nature with intrinsic value and a sovereign destiny. This appreciation continues to develop and intensify as we learn more about California oaks.

Plant scientists believe there are at least 300, and perhaps as many as 500, species of oak worldwide. All oaks have some important features in common, characteristics that constitute the essence of being an oak and living the life of an oak.

This chapter begins by discussing the essential features shared by all oaks. An understanding of California oaks, however, requires that each species be portrayed in terms of its distinctive form, physiology, geography, and relationships with humans. The tree oaks are considered first. Tree oaks are those species that tend to grow tall with large, undivided trunks. Shrub oaks, which tend to be low and densely branched from near the soil surface, are then examined.

To Be an Oak

Oaks are flowering plants belonging to the genus *Quercus*. The Latin name has always stood for oak and was derived from two Celtic words: *quer*, meaning fine and *cuez*, meaning tree. These fine trees and shrubs are set apart from all others by a

Above: Oak forest near Mt. Tamalpias. CHARLES KENNARD
Opposite: A variety of tree and shrub oaks grow in this Santa Barbara County landscape. DAVID MUENCH

unique combination of four characteristics: a fruit known as the acorn; distinctive, wind-pollinated flowers; a strong, complex wood; and an ability to live for many decades, if not centuries.

The acorn is a dry fruit that develops from the ovary of a single female flower. Its outer shell, or hull, is analogous to that of a walnut, providing a barrier between the external environment and the seed within. Both the acorn and the walnut have the same basic function: to facilitate dispersal of the seed away from the parent plant. The seed within the acorn contains the embryonic beginnings of a mighty oak, wrapped in a papery coat. The embryo has a very short root, two cotyledons that store food for the young seedling, and a shoot apex that will produce leaves and stems. The hull and seed are set within a scale-encrusted cup that is also characteristic of all oaks. The scales can be thin and shingle-like or thick and knobby, depending on the evolutionary ancestry of a particular species.

Whereas the acorn-producing female flowers are scattered singly or in small groups among the youngest twigs, the pollen-producing male flowers are clustered on pendulous threads known as catkins. Each male flower has between five and twelve stamens that actually make the pollen. Between 25 and 100 male flowers usually form a catkin, and each tree bears thousands of catkins in a single year. A single tree, therefore, is capable of enormous pollen production. This abundance is necessary because wind, and not nectar-seeking insects, distributes pollen to female flowers. Reproduction (acorn formation) is most successful when pollen from one tree makes its way to the female flowers of another tree of the same species.

Oak wood is tough and enduring. It comes in many colors, from white to yellow to reddish-brown, and has distinctive patterns of grain and stippling. These reflect the microscopic structure of oak wood and reveal something of the life of the particular tree from which it came. Grain results from alternating light and dark bands of densely aggregated wood cells. The lighter bands are mostly composed of cells with large openings for conducting water. These cells are known as xylem vessels and can be seen in cross-sections of wood with the naked eye. The vessels are surrounded by strong fibers reinforced with thick walls. Vessels and fibers are produced in the spring and early summer of each year when water is plentiful and growth is greatest. The thicker the band of spring wood, the better the growth conditions (i.e. rainfall and temperature) in that particular year. As the seasons change and conditions become less favorable, vessels are no longer produced and only fibers fill out the summer wood. This is dark-colored and separates bands of spring wood made in successive years. Rows of rectangular cells, also known as rays, impart a fine stippling pattern between the irregular swirls of spring and summer bands. Rays function like a shuttle system in living wood, moving important materials from the sapwood on the outside of the trunk or branch to the heartwood on

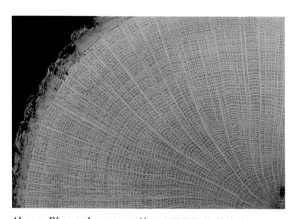

Above: Blue oak cross-section. MITCHEL McCLARAN
Left: Flowers and new leaves on black oak. BOB RONEY

the inside. Heartwood and sapwood often have different characteristics of color, hardness, and durability; these qualities are used for different purposes by experienced craftsmen in making furniture, cabinets, and panelling.

Durable, strong wood undoubtedly contributes to the great longevity of individual oaks. Trunk, limbs, and branches form the superstructure of the tree's leaf canopy, which can weigh several tons and catch wind like a sail. Evergreen oaks, which keep their leaves year-round, must be especially able to withstand the gales of winter and the Santa Ana winds of summer and fall. Under the right conditions, many California oaks resist wind, drought, fire, insect attack, and disease for 200 or 300 years. A few live for more than 600 years.

Living the Life of an Oak

An oak begins its life as a dormant embryo within the acorn. The embryo is constructed like a stubby cross, with root and shoot on opposite ends of a very short axis and two large seed leaves, or cotyledons, on the other axis. Cotyledons make up most of the embryo because they store all of the carbohydrates, proteins, and fats that the seedling will rely on after germination. These food stores attract hungry insects, birds, and mammals, few of which are deterred by the high concentrations of tannic acids that permeate the embryo tissue. Acorns that escape predation often drop where it is too shady, hot, or dry to produce a young tree. A lucky few will, by chance, land in a good spot beyond their parent's shade or end up buried in the ground by a bird or mammal that forgets to retrieve its cache. A layer of decomposing leaves or a crack in the soil provide additional refuge from predators and good contact with the fertile earth.

Germination usually occurs in response to fall or winter rains as the acorn imbibes water through its decaying husk. The embryo's root ruptures the hull and turns downward in response to gravity. Root hairs permeate the soil's smallest cracks and crevices, encountering and absorbing water. When the root is well anchored, the shoot grows out of the hull and pushes through layers of clay and leaf litter. Until the first true leaves are unfurled by the seedling, all energy and most of the materials for growth are provided by the cotyledons (and, therefore, by the parent tree). If the seedling emerges among dense grasses or in deep shade,

Top: A seedling unfurls its first leaves. DAVID CAVAGNARO
Bottom: An oak seedling grows in a shady woodland on Santa Cruz Island. RALPH CLEVENGER

This blue oak in Mariposa County long preceded the country road it borders. BILL EVARTS

it may run out of stored food before it can photosynthesize on its own. This will drastically slow or stop its growth and increase the seedling's risk of being overwhelmed by adjacent plants, fungal disease, or grazing animals. If the seedling emerges where there is adequate sunlight, it can begin photosynthesis and make the building blocks for new roots, stems, and leaves. Even under the best of conditions, however, death is the probable fate for most oak seedlings. The impact of an early spring drought, a prolonged summer heat wave, a swarm of hungry grasshoppers, or an autumn ground fire cannot be anticipated or mitigated by these young oaks. Only a few will become established in the first year of life and make the gradual transition to saplings.

Although still vulnerable, an oak sapling is much more likely to survive than a seedling because it has numerous buds and an underground reserve of food to replace damaged branches, leaves, and roots. Whole shoots of young oaks often die because of disease, browsing, or fire, but buds at the base of the stem and on the root crown are protected by the soil and can sprout and begin replacing the canopy of leaves and stems. The larger the existing root system, the more rapidly the shoots grow. Saplings of every species of California oak can sprout, and some maintain this ability even

as mature trees or shrubs.

Tree oaks tend to have a large trunk that gains most of the height and girth during maturation. Young trees may have erect, pole-like growth for many years until large, lateral branches can develop. If surrounded by a dense forest, they will continue to grow up rather than out and may never achieve the broad, rounded canopy found on trees that grow under less crowded conditions. Shrub oaks develop multiple trunks that branch from near the ground. Flower formation and acorn production may not occur until the oak is several decades old, but can continue until the end of life.

A typical oak tree will live long enough to have tens of thousands of its acorns devoured by insect larvae, birds, and mammals. Hundreds of its seedlings will wither and die among the grasses or be eaten by browsing herbivores. It will experience many onslaughts of defoliating caterpillars, twig-girdling beetles, and disease-causing fungi. Periodic droughts will cause it to become dormant and lose a whole season of photosynthesis. Wildfires will sear its bark and scorch its foliage. Floods will damage the root system, and high winds will occasionally pull away massive limbs. Despite such adversity, most tree oaks harbor the resiliency to live for centuries and provide a living heritage enjoyed by many generations.

The Diverse Shapes of Acorns

Acorns come in all shapes and sizes. Those of canyon oak are rather egg-shaped, with broad, rounded cups. Valley oak acorns are conical and cartridge-like, extending well beyond their cups. Acorns of black oak have an oval outline and are deeply set within cylindrical cups. Blue oak and leather oak acorns can vary in shape, but they still possess the distinctive characteristics of the subgenus *Lepidobalanus*—thick cup scales, smooth inner shell, and one year maturation time.

Acorns also vary greatly in size, depending on the oak species and its environment. Canyon oak probably has the largest acorns of any North American *Quercus,* especially if trees from coastal hardwood forests are measured. Other forest species—Oregon, valley, and black oak—also have large acorns when compared to species from open woodlands, savannas, and chaparrals. Huckleberry oak may have the smallest acorns, with an average volume that is ¹⁄₄₂ that of its close relative, canyon oak.

Mature valley oak acorn, in November. JOHN EVARTS

Top: Black oak acorns and leaves, Yosemite National Park. PAT O'HARA
Above: Scrub oak acorn. DEDE GILMAN

Rotund acorns on leather oak, Cuesta Ridge Botanical Area. STEVE JUNAK

Canyon oak acorns. DAVID CAVAGNARO

True and False Oaks

TRUE OAKS BELONG TO THE GENUS *QUERCUS* in the family of flowering plants called Fagaceae. The genus is set apart from most of its close relatives in the family, such as the beeches *(Fagus)* and chestnuts *(Castanea)*, by its distinctive fruit, the acorn. If a plant produces acorns, it's an oak—with one important exception. Another genus of the Fagaceae makes acorns and could rightfully be called an oak. That genus is *Lithocarpus*, otherwise known as tanbark oak, tanoak, or tanbark.

Strictly speaking, tanbark is not a true oak because its acorn cup resembles the spiny husk of a chestnut rather than the scaly cup of an oak. It also has different leaves, bark, flowers, and wood, and these distinct characteristics further justify its exclusion from the genus

Quercus. The single tanbark species found in North America, *Lithocarpus densiflora,* is not simply an oak aberration; there are 100 species of tanbark in Asia to which this one is related. Our tanbark is found in the Klamath and Coast ranges (southern Oregon to Ventura County) and scattered along the western slopes of the north and central Sierra Nevada. Throughout most of its range, tanbark acorns were an important food resource for Indian people. This book will only mention tanbark in passing, when it shares a common environment or history with the true oaks.

Outside the Fagaceae there are other plants mistakenly called oaks. The best-known of these false oaks is poison "oak," which is closely related to the cashew (family Anacardiaceae) in the genus *Toxicodendron.* The shiny, shallowly lobed leaf blades of poison oak vaguely resemble leaf features seen in *Quercus.* The leaves of true oaks, however, are always composed of a single, undivided blade while those of poison oak are compound, each divided into three separate blades (called leaflets). Unlike the true oaks, poison oak flowers are insect-pollinated and produce succulent berries as fruit. Another false oak is silk "oak" *(Grivillea robusta,* family Proteaceae), native to Australia but planted in many parts of California. Silk oak is a tall, evergreen tree with divided leaf blades and elaborate flowers bearing no resemblance to anything in the genus *Quercus.*

Above: Poison oak. CHRISTOPHER TALBOT FRANK
Top right: Tanbark with acorns. J. R. HALLER

Above: Engelmann and coast live oaks dot these rolling hills in Riverside County. BILL EVARTS
Right: Friends converse beneath the spreading limbs of a coast live oak near Sonoma. DAVID CAVAGNARO

The Tree Oaks of California

There are nine species of tree oaks in California. Collectively, they occur from the Oregon border to Baja California and are found on offshore islands, along the coast, over most of the foothills, and throughout the valleys and high mountains of the state's interior.

Depending on various ecological factors, tree oaks contribute to three structural types of natural vegetation: forest, woodland, and savanna. They often occur in forests, where their leafy canopies overlap to produce shade that is deep and constant. Forests may be associated with moist upland slopes at higher elevations or with streams and rivers at any elevation, habitats known as montane and riparian forests, respectively. Tree oaks also form woodlands, which are more open and sunlit because leaf canopies touch, but seldom overlap. Woodlands tend to occur in elevational bands below the forests, in areas that have less available soil moisture. Savannas are most spacious because trees are far apart and appear scattered over the grassland. They are usually the driest and warmest environments of any tree-dominated vegetation type.

Five of California's tree oaks—those that are described first—are deciduous. They lose their leaves at the end of the growing season (winter-deciduous) or in response to extremely dry soil (drought-deciduous). The next four species are evergreen, with leaves that remain on the tree all year long. The leaves of the deciduous species are usually thinner and less rigid than evergreen leaves. "The Key to California's Tree Oaks," which is located at the end of this chapter, uses a variety of other characteristics to identify oaks, including shape of leaves (lobed, unlobed, flat, convex), color of different leaf surfaces, and features of acorns. The key, tree oak range maps, and species descriptions are guides for understanding and appreciating the diversity of tree oaks in California.

The craggy limbs of a valley oak shade young grasses in a savanna, Santa Ynez Valley. DAVID MUENCH

Valley Oak *(Quercus lobata)*

Valley oak is the monarch of California oaks by virtue of its size, age, and beauty. The largest trees have massive trunks, sometimes six or seven feet in diameter, that support a body of great limbs and craggy branches. These may rise more than 100 feet above the ground, shielded by a thick bark that has the color of pewter and the blocky texture of alligator hide. Spherical insect galls are densely clustered on young branches within the leafy canopy. The lobed, felt-covered leaves are most active in summer, providing a kingdom of shade in a landscape drenched with hot, bright sun. The tree requires plenty of water and nutrients and thrives in a habitat with deep, rich soil where it can achieve high rates of photosynthesis and rapid growth. As a result, many rather impressive trees, with trunks three or four feet in diameter, are relatively young—only 150 to 250 years old. But under less optimal conditions, where growth is slower, yet sustained, valley oaks are able to reach ages of 400 to 600 years if they can resist the ravages of fire, wind, drought, and disease. These

are the absolute monarchs, steadfast lords of the countryside, governing the landscapes in which they reside.

Valley oak may be the largest North American oak, and descriptions of its remarkable stature appear in the diaries of many early visitors to California. Describing the open groves of the Santa Clara Valley in 1796, English explorer George Vancouver wrote:

> For about twenty miles it could only be compared to a park which had originally been closely planted with the true old English oak; the underwood, that had probably attended its early growth, had the appearance of having been cleared away and left the stately lords of the forest in complete possession of the soil which was covered with luxuriant foliage.

During the first geological survey of the state in 1861, William Brewer passed through the country near Monterey. He recorded much about the oaks he and his party encountered, including this passage:

First I passed through a wild canyon, then over hills covered with oats, with here and there trees—oaks and pines. Some of these oaks were noble ones indeed. How I wish one stood in our yard at home. . . . I measured one [valley oak], with wide spreading and cragged branches, that was 26.5 feet in circumference. Another had a diameter of over six feet, and the branches spread over 75 feet each way. I lay beneath its shade a little while before going on.

Valley oak has been given a variety of names over the years. The species reminded Spanish explorers of the majestic white oaks of Europe and so the same name *roble* was applied. Botanists were struck by the deeply sinuous outline of the leaves and formally declared the species as *lobata*. "Valley oak," the most popular common name, describes the tree's tendency to be found on fertile bottomland soils. Less dignified is "mush oak," an appellation that followed attempts to use its rot-prone sapwood for fence posts on pioneer ranches and farms. Early settlers also dubbed them "weeping oaks" because older trees, especially in the absence of browsing livestock, develop long, flowing, vine-like twigs that droop almost to the ground. "White oak," "bottom oak," "swamp oak," and "water oak" are other names that still enjoy regional use. The scientific name *Quercus lobata* is the only one with universal acceptance.

The name "white oak" carries additional significance to botanists. It not only belongs to valley oak, but also refers to a number of oak species that share some important characteristics with valley oak. Similar leaves, wood, bark, and acorns mean that these oak species form a lineage with a common evolutionary history. The white oak evolutionary lineage, formally named as the subgenus *Lepidobalanus,* consists of valley oak and a rather large number of other oak species within and beyond California's borders. This and two other lineages are discussed further in "Evolutionary Lineages of California Oaks" in this chapter.

Before extensive agricultural clearing began in the late 1880s, forests of valley oak extended for miles on both sides of the Sacramento River and along the lower reaches of its tributaries, such as the Mokelumne, Cosumnes, and American rivers. Further south, oak stands thrived along the lower San Joaquin River and trees were common on floodplains that spilled from the western slopes of the Sierra Nevada. Over the last 150 years, however,

valley oaks have been the victims of widespread agricultural and residential development on prime, lowland real estate. Where groundwater pumping has drastically lowered the water table, valley oaks have become slow growing and haggard. It is now rare to see extensive groves of this monarch species, and a regal California heritage may soon be lost.

Identifying Characteristics

GROWTH FORM: Valley oak is a large winter-deciduous tree with a round, spreading canopy of massive limbs when mature. Smaller branches on mature trees will sometimes droop or weep, extending all the way to the ground. The branches usually bear woody, spherical galls that harbor the larvae of small, native wasps. Young trees rapidly achieve a straight, pole-like form during the first 10 to 30 years of growth. The record valley oak, with a trunk 9.3 feet in diameter, stands near the town of Gridley in Butte County.

LEAVES: The two- to four-inch-long leaves are up to two inches across, with blunt, deep lobes. They

Above: Valley oak leaves and acorns. ALLISON ATWILL
Right: Valley oak bark.
DAVID CAVAGNARO

appear matte green above and pale green below, and have a soft, felt-like covering of hairs. Crushing releases a subtle, woodsy aroma.

ACORNS: Conical, cartridge-like acorns are usually one to two inches long, but shape and length may vary greatly. Warty knobs cover the base of the deep, rounded cups. They turn chestnut-brown when ripe in early autumn and can germinate immediately after falling from the tree. Large crops tend to be produced every other year.

BARK: The grayish bark is arranged in a checked pattern or has shallow, vertical fissures. Older trees develop very thick bark and deep fissures.

WOOD: The pale, dull brown or slightly yellowish wood of valley oak makes it of low commercial value except as fuel.

Habitat

If tapped into constant supplies of ground water, valley oak can grow where there is pronounced summer drought. Typically, it is found at least one ridge away from the coastal fog zone in valleys that are cool and wet in winter and hot and dry in summer. Valley oak prefers deep, rich bottomland soils at elevations below 2,000 feet, but this is not an absolute. It may range up to 5,600 feet in foothills and low mountains on shallow or stony soils if its roots can tap into sufficient moisture. Valley oak contributes to dense riparian forests, open foothill woodlands, and river valley savannas. Other trees in the vicinity often include interior live, blue, and coast live oaks, along with black walnut, sycamore, and gray pine.

Geographical Distribution

Valley oak is unique to California, where it is widely distributed in the Great Central Valley (Shasta Lake to southern San Joaquin Valley), the inner Coast Ranges from the Eel River (Mendocino County) south, and the Transverse ranges (Tehachapi Mountains to San Fernando Valley). Although remnant groves are still found in the Central Valley, the most impressive valley oak woodlands and savannas are now seen in valleys among the Coast Ranges. Round Valley (Mendocino County), the upper Salinas River drainage (San Luis Obispo County), and the Santa Ynez Valley (Santa Barbara County) provide excellent examples. Valley oaks also occur on Santa Cruz and Santa Catalina Islands.

Top: Vine-covered valley oaks dominate this riparian forest at Caswell Memorial State Park. MICHAEL FRYE
Bottom: This valley oak in Mendocino County exhibits the drooping or "weeping" branchlets that are often characteristic of the species. ROB BADGER

A black oak in Yosemite Valley displays its radiant autumn foliage. DAVID CAVAGNARO

Black Oak *(Quercus kelloggii)*

California's tree oaks often dominate their respective landscapes, but black oak is an exception. In the diverse montane communities where it is found, black oak is merely an affiliate to conifers and other broadleaf trees. Ponderosa pine is a constant companion, and white fir, incense cedar, and sugar pine are frequent associates. These evergreens are a backdrop against which black oak produces vibrant displays of seasonal color. In late spring, the oak's emerging leaves are tipped with fuchsia and pale rose; gold-green catkins of pollen-producing flowers hang from the branches. By summer black oak foliage is lustrous and deep green. Chestnut-brown acorns finish ripening in the fall as leaves turn yellow and russet. The trunk and its leafless winter branches appear black from snowmelt that trickles over the fissured platelets of dark gray bark. It was the bark that led Dr. Albert Kellogg, pioneer botanist, to first name the species "California black oak," understating the colorful contributions of its leaves, catkins, and acorns to California's montane forests.

Dense clumps of mistletoe often add splashes of yellow-green to the black oak canopy. Mistletoe is a parasitic flowering plant that sends its root-like haustoria beneath the bark of young branches. The haustoria are able to tap the oak's supply of water and mineral nutrients. Although it usurps important resources, mistletoe makes its own food through photosynthesis, stressing but seldom killing the host tree. It takes advantage of high light intensities on mild winter days, when the black oak canopy is leafless and dormant. Native Californians believed that the life-spirit of the tree retreated to the mistletoe at this harsh time; the Druids of Europe held a similar belief when worshipping their own species of deciduous oaks. Bringing mistletoe into our homes for winter holidays may have originated with these ancestors, as they celebrated the spirit of oaks in preparation for the rebirth of spring.

Black oak has a long history as a tree utilized by humans. Its acorns were considered the best tasting by Indian people throughout the state, including those of the Shasta, Miwok, and Luiseño tribes. Its acorns were also preferred because they

A black oak buds out in Sunol Regional Park, Alameda County. CARR CLIFTON

stored well and mush or pudding made from them thickened readily. Sabina Norris, a Norfolk Mono who lived in the Sierra Nevada above the San Joaquin River, said of black oak acorns:

> Acorns are everywhere, but we like the ones in the mountains, the black oak acorns. They taste the best, they cook the best—get nice and thick. That's what we ate—*ekibay* [a thick, congealed acorn pudding]—we had it everyday.

Other parts of the black oak were also used. The Miwok of Yosemite preferred young black oak branches or shoots for making household implements, such as cooking paddles and mush stirrers. Only stout black oak logs could be the support columns for roofs of Miwok ceremonial round houses. The Wintu produced rich dyes from black oak bark.

European people soon learned about the strength and utility of this wood; car axles were turned from choice logs during the early part of this century. Due to the abundance of easily harvested pines and firs, however, there was no incentive for dealing with the special problems encountered when processing black oaks for lumber. Unlike most conifers, the trunks and limbs of oaks are very crooked and cannot be processed into boards with conventional milling equipment. When only the straightest sections of trunk were hauled back to the mill, nearly 40% of the original tree was left to rot in the forest. And even the best of black oak boards warped and split upon drying. As a result, black oak was treated as a weed on forest lands until the 1960s. Much time and money were spent poisoning and girdling thousands of trees, and millions of board-feet of potential lumber were wasted.

The utility and beauty of black oak wood were rediscovered in 1965 when a mini-sawmill was developed that could handle smaller logs more rapidly and efficiently. The new mill reduced the amount of time wood spent in storage and produced fine boards from crooked trunks and limbs. Special techniques for drying were also implemented to prevent warp and splitting. Today, less than 15% of the harvested tree ends up as waste. Several mills in Northern California now produce more than six million board feet of lumber annually, including three million of the highest grade. Black oak wood, so strong and rich in color, is now made into furniture, paneling, cabinets, shipping pallets, and other valuable products. Scraps are boxed as firewood, and mountains of sawdust are sold as mulch and livestock bedding.

Identifying Characteristics

GROWTH FORM: Black oak is a tall, winter-deciduous tree with ascending limbs and an open, rounded crown. When mature, it may attain a height of 70 to 80 feet, with a trunk two to four feet in diameter. The trunk may be clear of limbs 10 to 40 feet above the ground. The largest black oak, recently found in Placer County, has a trunk 9.4 feet across and may be as old as 450 years.

LEAVES: They are deeply divided into angular lobes, each lobe with a long, soft bristle on its pointed apex. (The bristle is particularly characteristic of the red oak evolutionary lineage, which is further described on page 36.) When fully developed, the leaves are deep green, often shiny on top, and measure between two and six inches long.

ACORNS: The oblong, somewhat squat (and

Above: Black oak leaves and ripe acorns in fall.
ALLISON ATWILL
Left: Black oak bark.
DAVID CAVAGNARO

sometimes triangular) acorns are 1 to 1½ inches long and sit deep in a cup with thin, ragged scales. Papery red coats, which must be removed before the acorns are ground for eating, cover the cream-colored kernels (embryos). Maturation requires 18 to 20 months after the flowers are pollinated.
BARK: As the tree matures, the smooth gray bark becomes rough and blackish, with narrow, deep fissures.
WOOD: It is strong and reddish-brown, with significant commercial value as lumber, firewood, and mulch.

Habitat

Black oak is mostly found in mountainous areas away from the immediate coast, between 2,000 and 6,000 feet. The upland climate of this species is warm in summer and cold in winter, and typically receives more than 25 inches of precipitation. Snow and below-freezing temperatures are common. Black oak has no strict soil preference, but is usually found on coarse, well-drained soils that typify mountain slopes and ridges. Lowland valleys in the North Coast Range, such as those near Ukiah, Napa, and Santa Rosa, may also support extensive stands. The finest examples of black oak, however, are

found in Sierran mixed conifer forest, along with ponderosa pine, white fir, Douglas fir, and incense cedar. They often share the understory with dogwood, hazelnut, and western azalea. Canyon oak is also a common associate of black oak, especially in mixed evergreen forests of madrone and tanbark. Here, fire is an important habitat factor that promotes the growth of black oak and other stump-sprouting hardwoods instead of the more fire-sensitive conifers. Oregon oak woodland and northern montane forest are two other communities in which black oak is commonly found.

Geographical Distribution

Black oak is widely distributed in upland areas from central Oregon to the Laguna Mountains of southern San Diego County. Extensive stands are found throughout the North Coast, Klamath, and Cascade ranges and through most of the Sierra Nevada. Stands are smaller and more scattered in the South Coast, Transverse, and Peninsular ranges but may still harbor impressive trees. Interesting outlying populations are found on the eastern slopes of Mount Diablo (eastern Contra Costa County) and in Sierra Nevada drainages along the western edge of the Owens Valley (Inyo County). There is recent confirmation of a small stand in the Sierra de San Pedro Mártir of northern Baja California.

Above: Black oaks intermingle with a variety of conifers at Cuyamaca Rancho State Park. BILL EVARTS

Above: Spring winds ripple grasses and new leaves in a blue oak savanna, Madera County. BILL EVARTS
Right: Blue oaks, Santa Barbara County. JOHN EVARTS

Blue Oak *(Quercus douglasii)*

On the hot, dry foothills of California's interior, blue oak endures. In a landscape where midday temperatures exceed 100° F for weeks at a time, and annual precipitation is a scant 15 inches, blue oaks number in the millions. Every year, from April to October, they withstand drought and tolerate parched winds that sweep the grasslands en route to cooler elevations above.

Anyone who drives the foothill highways sees evidence of this special endurance—blue oak is usually the only tree species that extends onto the lowest, sunniest slopes and plains. This was apparent to geologist Clarence King, who rode through Madera County more than a century ago.

Riding thus in the late summer along the Sierra foothills, one is constantly impressed with the climatic peculiarities of the region. With us in the East, plant life seems to continue till the first frost; but in the Sierra foot-hills growth and active life culminate in June and early July, and then follow long months of warm stormless autumn wherein the hills grow slowly browner, and the whole air seems to ripen into a fascinating repose,—a rich, dreamy quiet, with distance lost behind pearly hazes, with warm tranquil nights, dewless and silent. This period is wealthy in yellows and russets and browns, in great overhanging masses of oak, whose olive hue is warmed into umber depth. . . . —these are the conditions of the vegetation.

How does blue oak endure? What unique features does it possess that allow establishment and growth on shallow soils in hot, dry climates? Although other oaks are resistant to drought, few of them combine all the mechanisms of opportunism, conservation, tolerance, and resiliency that are known in blue oak. Moreover, these mechanisms are integrated into all stages of the blue oak's life, from germinating acorn to mature tree.

Blue oak acorns rapidly germinate when conditions become favorable. Unlike some other oak species, blue oak embryos do not wait until spring to become active. The cool rains of late October are enough to stimulate root emergence from the just-ripened acorns. Blue oak roots grow much more rapidly than those of other oaks that inhabit deeper, more moist soils (e.g. valley and coast live oak). Despite cool soil temperatures during the winter months, growth is sustained so that the roots of blue oak seedlings have a chance to extend below the dense, competing roots of grasses and herbs.

An effective root system would be futile if seedlings also developed large, leafy shoots that used water lavishly. Water conservation mechanisms have evolved in blue oak that are similar to those observed in the hardy shrubs of chaparral and desert communities. Blue oak seedlings begin with much more root than shoot compared to other arboreal oaks, and this pattern is maintained through the sapling and adult stages of life. The mature root system is not especially deep or extensive. Rather, the canopy of leaves remains proportionally smaller in blue oak than in other, less drought-tolerant species. The leaves are also moisture conserving, covered on their upper surface by a waxy coating that gives the tree its characteristic bluish cast.

When water from the soil becomes very scarce, a remarkable array of drought tolerance mechanisms is exhibited. Leaves become reinforced with cellulose and lignin (the chemical component of wood) to withstand the physical stresses imposed by progressive dehydration. Photosynthetic cells adjust their internal salt content so that wilting is prevented even if the leaves lose up to 30% of their water to the bone-dry atmosphere. This ability surpasses that of some desert trees, such as mesquite and ironwood.

Drought-deciduous leaves are a common feature of chaparral and desert shrubs, but rare among oaks and trees in general. In extremely hot and dry years, blue oaks resort to dormancy. They drop their summer-weary leaves and take on a skeletal look. Nevertheless, drought-stricken blue oaks continue to fill their acorns with previously stored food. Under these circumstances, most of the trees do not resume growth with the arrival of fall rains; instead, they wait until spring to produce a new flush of bright-green leaves and tender shoots.

The ability to endure allows blue oak to dominate nearly half of all oak-covered lands in California. At low elevations, blue oaks are scattered in a sea of grasses and herbs, forming a distinctive savanna vegetation. Inhabited by herds of deer and other native grazers, as well as predators such as mountain lion and coyote, California's blue oak savannas have been called the Pacific Coast version of Africa's Serengeti Plain. At higher elevations, the stands of oaks are denser and include many other kinds of trees and shrubs. Known as blue oak woodland, this community is even richer in animal species than the savanna, and its fate will determine much about the future of California wildlife.

Identifying Characteristics

GROWTH FORM: Blue oak is a small or medium-sized, deciduous tree. In moist sites it may retain most of its leaves nearly year-round. It reaches a

Above: Blue oak leaves and acorns. ALLISON ATWILL
Opposite: Blue oak bark.
DAVID CAVAGNARO

maximum height of 60 feet, with a trunk that is seldom more than two feet in diameter. The canopy is compact, round, and supported by many crooked branches.

LEAVES: Leaves are one to three inches long and usually have wavy margins. Occasionally they are shallowly and irregularly lobed. The bluish-green color is most pronounced in late summer or fall and confined to the upper side of the leaf; the underside is a pale green.

ACORNS: The oval, gently tapered acorns average ¾ to 1½ inches long and nest within shallow cups with small, warty scales. They form and ripen during a single year.

BARK: The bark is light gray or whitish and arranged in narrow, shallow strips. On large trees it sometimes becomes thick with a rough, but unfissured exterior.

WOOD: Its dark brown heartwood and light brown sapwood are prone to rot and warp during drying. It has low commercial value except as fuel or fence posts.

Habitat

Blue oak is common on foothills bordering hot interior valleys. Annual rainfall ranges between 15 and 35 inches and soils are seldom well-developed. The species grows below 3,500 feet, bordering mixed chaparral and Sierran mixed conifer forest above and annual grassland below. Blue oak is the dominant species in blue oak savanna and blue oak woodland communities and may also be abundant on the margins of valley oak woodland. It is commonly associated with gray pine, buckeye, and a number of other oaks, including valley, Oregon, interior live, and coast live oak.

Geographical Distribution

Blue oak is found only in California, but manages to range into 39 of the state's 57 counties. It is a landmark species of foothills in the inner North and South Coast ranges, the Cascades, and Sierra Nevada. Its distribution around the Great Central Valley has been likened to a broad, discontinuous ring. Its main distribution ranges from Montgomery Creek (Shasta County) to Santa Ynez Valley (Santa Barbara County) and Liebre Mountain (Los Angeles County). Disjunct populations occur on the Sutter Buttes in the middle of the Sacramento Valley, at Oak Flat near Castaic (Los Angeles County), and on Santa Cruz and Santa Catalina islands.

Top: Blue oaks are the dominant native tree in the arid Cuyama Valley (shown) and thrive in similar landscapes of the inner Coast Ranges. DAVID CAVAGNARO
Bottom: The distinctive color of a blue oak's foliage stands out in this Napa County woodland. ROB BADGER

A brilliant display of lupines fills a glade in an Oregon oak woodland. LARRY ULRICH

Oregon Oak *(Quercus garryana)*

Oregon oak may be at its best in fall, when the days become shorter and cold northern air masses return to the Pacific Coast. Especially on overcast days, the rust-colored canopies of Oregon oak appear dappled against the evergreen hillsides of the inner North Coast and Klamath ranges. This happens as a tree's lobed, dark-green leaves respond to longer, chillier nights and begin a self-destructive process to prepare for the leafless winter months ahead. The living, photosynthetic machinery that worked from dawn to dusk securing food, is gradually dismantled and recycled. Amino acids, mineral nutrients, nucleotides, and other essential components are salvaged and sent back into the trunk and roots for storage until a new canopy is built next spring. Left behind in the withered, yet supple leaves are reddish pigments that had been masked by the chlorophylls of summer. Revealed beneath the festive but diminishing canopy is a green cloak of wrinkled lichens and fuzzy mosses displayed on the smaller, outer branches. These branches connect to larger, upright limbs and a stout trunk that boasts a handsome bark of fissured, ashen platelets. Any one tree, then, appears as a spreading palette of fall color, set against the backdrop of a dark forest and a long, impending winter.

Leafy branches and acorns of Oregon oak were first collected for science by Archibald Menzies during the latter half of the 18th century. Although Menzies was the first European botanist to visit the dark forests of the Pacific Northwest, he did not use the specimens to inform the Old World of Oregon oak's existence. Consequently, the Lewis and Clark Expedition "rediscovered" the species in 1806 on the plains of the Columbia River near Fort Vancouver. Another quarter of a century had to pass, however, before David

Douglas, a Scotsman who explored the botanical wilderness of America, named the species *Quercus garryanna* to honor Nicholas Garry of the Hudson Bay Company.

Douglas wrote about this lovely species in his journals, observing the characteristics of individual trees and of trees set within the landscape. The largest, most stately Oregon oaks were found on the deep, bottomland soils along the Columbia River and within the Willamette Valley of northwestern Oregon. Stumps six feet in diameter have been found near Portland and probably supported a canopy more than 90 feet high. The record for a standing individual in California is eight feet in diameter and 120 feet tall. Most Oregon oaks are not that large, but some get to be three to four feet in diameter and more than 60 feet tall. A trunk 27 inches in diameter was found to be 251 years old, so maximum ages probably exceed 400 years.

The unbranched, straight trunks with stout, upright limbs give Oregon oak a distinctive profile and allow foresters to use standard harvest techniques for obtaining timber. The pale, sandy-brown wood has excellent qualities that greatly increase its commercial value: it is close-grained, strong and hard. In the past it was used for shipbuilding, wagon parts, farm tools, railroad ties, and fuel. The heartwood of the inner trunk resists rotting when in contact with the soil and is suitable for fencing rangelands, hence its other common name, "post oak." Today, the wood is used for furniture, cabinets, and interior finish, reflecting contemporary appreciation for its color, grain, and strength.

Identifying Characteristics

GROWTH FORM: Oregon oak is a large, winter-deciduous tree with mostly upright main limbs and spreading lesser branches. Mature individuals growing in the open have a round crown, usually 50 to 80 feet tall.

LEAVES: The broad, lobed leaves measure four to six inches long and have smooth, spineless margins. The rounded or broadly angular lobes are not as deep as those of valley oak. The upper surface is shiny and dark green while the underside appears lighter due to a coating of downy hairs.

ACORNS: Large, round acorns bulge out from the small cups, which are covered with small scales. Acorns take only one year to form and mature.

Above: Oregon oak leaves and acorn. ALLISON ATWILL
Left: Oregon oak bark.
DAVID CAVAGNARO

An abundant crop is produced irregularly, perhaps every two to five years.

BARK: The bark is finely fissured, thin, and white to grayish.

WOOD: Whitish to light brown, the wood is sometimes used for lumber and has moderate commercial value (mostly in Oregon).

Habitat

Oregon oak inhabits a variety of sites away from the coastal fog belt, including upland slopes, exposed ridges, and open valley bottoms. Its main elevation range is between 1,000 and 4,000 feet. The climate is moderate, with warm summers and freezing winter temperatures, and between 20 and 50 inches of precipitation per year (in California). Oregon oak has no strict preference for soil type, being found on rocky or gravelly sites as well as on heavy clays. It is often associated with madrone, bay laurel, Douglas fir, black oak, and tanbark in northern mixed evergreen forest or sometimes at the edge of Douglas fir and redwood forest. Further inland, Oregon oak may form its own open woodland (an Oregon oak woodland community) or mingle with pines, firs, and junipers on drier volcanic soils of the inner North Coast, Klamath, and Sierra Nevada ranges.

Geographical Distribution

Oregon oak is the only California oak that extends well beyond the state's northern border. It is found throughout western Washington and Oregon and as far north as Vancouver Island in British Columbia.

In California the species is best developed in the North Coast and Klamath ranges of Humboldt, Mendocino, Sonoma, Trinity, and Shasta counties. In Humboldt County, Oregon oaks are within 15 to 25 miles of the ocean; in southwestern Sonoma County, Oregon oaks grow within 10 miles of the ocean. The easternmost stands grow in the Cascade Ranges and a large population occupies the lower half of the Pit River drainage, down to the northern arm of Shasta Lake. In the Coast Ranges, stands of Oregon oak barely extend into Marin County, but isolated groves and trees occur as far south as Santa Clara county near Gilroy. Small groves occur along most of the western Sierra Nevada and northern slopes of the Tehachapi Mountains.

Additional Varieties

Brewer oak *(Q. garryana* var. *breweri)* is unusual because it is a winter-deciduous, rather than evergreen, shrub oak. It grows up to 15 feet tall and often forms miniature "forests" that frequently exclude other shrub species. Like those of its arboreal relatives, the leaves of Brewer oak are broad with deep, rounded lobes; they are more leathery and somewhat smaller, measuring two to four inches long. They appear shiny green on the upper surface and paler underneath due to a coating of velvety hairs. Brewer oak acorns are oval and blunt, measuring less than an inch in length. The cups are shallow and have warty scales.

Although comprehensive surveys are lacking, Brewer oak is probably widely distributed between 2,000 and 6,000 feet in the Klamath and southern Cascade ranges. Here the species is associated with northern mixed evergreen and northern montane forest communities, including conifers such as Douglas fir, ponderosa pine, sugar pine, white fir, and red fir. Scattered stands may also be found along the western Sierra Nevada (Shasta to Butte counties), perhaps extending as far south as the Transverse ranges (Kern and northern Los Angeles counties). In these areas, Brewer oak is more likely to be found in woodland and chaparral vegetation, often forming dense thickets with canyon live oak. The thickets can extend up to 7,500 feet in the Tehachapi Mountains. There is some confusion, however, because populations in the Transverse Ranges and southern Sierra may in fact belong to another shrubby variety called shin oak *(Q. garryana* var. *semota).*

Above: Thickets of Oregon oak have emerged in this woodland clearing, Trinity County. DAVID CAVAGNARO
Right: Oregon oaks are best-developed north of California, such as this tree in Corvallis. RICHARD LOVETT

Above: Low, angular limbs and a somewhat open canopy are typical of Engelmann oaks. BILL EVARTS
Right: Engelmann oaks grow amid prairies of native grass at the Santa Rosa Plateau. B. "MOOSE" PETERSON

Engelmann Oak *(Quercus engelmannii)*

Engelmann oak was relatively widespread and abundant in ancient California, and prior to the formation of the modern Mojave and Sonoran deserts, it grew throughout southeastern California, Arizona, and Baja California. Along with other oaks, junipers, and madrones, it formed rich woodlands and picturesque savannas that we can only imagine from collections of leaf impressions in the fossil record. As deserts formed over great spans of geologic time, Engelmann oak disappeared from the dry interior. Today it persists in rare, scattered groves along the western edge of its previous range and is generally restricted to areas where rainfall is adequate, frosts rare, and summers relatively mild. The closest relatives of Engelmann oak, Arizona white and Mexican blue oak, still reveal the ancient pattern, as they range across Arizona and into the subtropical plateaus of the Sierra Madre Occidental

in central Mexico. Botanists consider Engelmann oak to be the northwestern outpost of these subtropical oaks in North America, cut off from its evolutionary homeland by hundreds of miles of intervening desert.

In modern California, relict populations of Engelmann oak occur on the mainland, but unlike

Silver-green foliage helps distinguish this Engelmann oak from neighboring coast live oaks. BILL EVARTS

the rare island oak, they have no oceanic moat to protect them from encroaching urban sprawl. The woodlands that once graced the foothills near Pasadena and Pomona have been overwhelmed by development, essentially eliminating the species from its northern and westernmost reaches. Although scattered trees are found in the San Gabriel Mountains and throughout the Peninsular ranges, only two strongholds support large populations of Engelmann oak in a typical woodland and savanna setting. One stronghold is around Black Mountain in central San Diego County and the other is on the Santa Rosa Plateau in southwestern Riverside County. As a result, Engelmann oak is probably the most imperiled of all tree oaks in California.

A visit to the Santa Rosa Plateau is necessary to fully appreciate the beauty of Engelmann oak within its natural setting. The plateau is an elevated landscape of gentle, undulating hills dissected by small creeks and broad, dry gullies. The surrounding hills run to the horizon, separating shallow, golden valleys from the hazy blue sky. The plateau is largely covered by prairies of native grasses and wildflowers, with chaparral on the drier slopes and pockets of riparian forest where moisture persists into the summer months. Most characteristic, however, are the globular canopies of Engelmann and coast live oak, clustered in woodlands or sprinkled across the grassy mesa. This is one of the last remaining panoramas in the hills of Southern California that Native Americans, explorers, and pioneers would recognize if they could be transported here from the past. Elsewhere, most of the oak-filled valleys that sustained and

enriched the early Californians cannot be viewed and will never be resurrected. For more information, see "Conserving Engelmann Oaks on the Santa Rosa Plateau," pages 131–132.

Identifying Characteristics

GROWTH FORM: Engelmann oaks are medium-sized, drought-deciduous trees with rounded or elliptical canopies. Mature trees rarely reach a height of more than 40 feet. The light gray or whitish trunk may be one to four feet in diameter, supporting angular limbs and branches. Trees are typically 50 to 150 years old, but some live up to 350 years.

LEAVES: The thick and leathery leaves are usually a muted blue-green color. They can be flat or wavy, with smooth, toothless margins, and are one to three inches long. They remain on the tree until replaced by next year's spring foliage, except in drought years when they may drop during the first summer or fall of their life. This pattern of leaf replacement is described as evergreen by some and as late-deciduous by others.

ACORNS: The oval to cylindrical acorns have a

Above: Engelmann oak leaves, acorns. ALLISON ATWILL
Right: Engelmann oak bark.
DAVID CAVAGNARO

Top: A single, ripening acorn extends from this Engelmann oak branchlet in Pamo Valley. BILL EVARTS
Above: White sage and other shrubs grow alongside an Engelmann oak near Ramona. B. "MOOSE" PETERSON

rounded tip and measure about one inch long. Their cups enclose about half of the nut and have light-brown, warty or pointed scales. They ripen during the fall of their first year.

BARK: The bark is thick, heavily furrowed, and light grayish-brown.

WOOD: Dark brown and strong, it splits and warps upon drying, and is of low commercial value.

Habitat

Stands of Engelmann oak are limited to sites above the dry coastal plain and below cold montane areas. In general, they do not exceed 4,200 feet in elevation. The typical habitat of the species receives at least 15 inches of precipitation per year, rarely experiences frost, and has warm or hot summers. The soil is often a deep, loamy clay, but the species also does well in rocky or shallow soils that have some source of summer moisture (e.g. a spring or intermittent stream). Engelmann oak is often known as mesa oak, perhaps due to its tendency to grow adjacent to basalt caps of mesas.

Although the seedlings are quite tolerant of fire, mature trees may be killed if trunks have prolonged contact with flame. This sensitivity may restrict the species from areas of dense chaparral that burn frequently. In areas of infrequent fire, Engelmann oak forms both woodlands and savannas, often with coast live oak. The widely spaced trees dominate a low ground cover of sagebrush, grasses, and wildflowers. Riparian woodlands of Engelmann oak are usually associated with moist sites near springs and streams. There, they tend to fringe the dense cover of willows, cottonwoods, and sycamores, rather than compete along the edge of the water or channel.

Geographical Distribution

Engelmann oak is only found in Southern California and the northern portions of Baja California; over 90% of the existing stands are located in San Diego County. The species occurs in the Santa Ana Mountains (Orange County) and is scattered in western foothills and mesas of the Peninsular Ranges in Riverside County. Two major populations are centered near the Santa Rosa Plateau (Riverside County) and around Black Mountain (San Diego County). In Los Angeles County, where it was known as Pasadena oak, there remain a few scattered groves and trees along the foothills of the San Gabriel Mountains.

This coast live oak on Mount Diablo exemplifies the species' often magnificent architecture. CARR CLIFTON

Coast Live Oak *(Quercus agrifolia)*

One way to appreciate the architecture of an old coast live oak is to stand beneath its shady, dark canopy. The dense, round helmet of leaves is elegantly structured to capture light particles (photons) that flow in the solar stream. On the outside shell of the helmet are thick, small, convex leaves that develop where light intensities are highest. These sun leaves are packed with two or three layers of photosynthetic cells, each layer acting as a net to detain and capture their luminescent "prey." Excess heat, given off by the absorbed photons, is better dissipated by the small size of these energy-drenched leaves. Photons that escape capture pass to the inner canopy where layers of thin, wide, and flat shade leaves await. Shade leaves have only one layer of photosynthetic

cells, but these are spread over a larger "target" area so that additional photons can be captured and turned into food. Deep shade is thus produced by a canopy that efficiently absorbs light. This kind of structure, best seen in coast live oak, demonstrates the subtle adjustments that a plant can make to maximize the harvest of available solar energy.

Supporting the helmet of leaves is a twisted, gray superstructure of gnarled limbs and branches. Multiple trunks, often the result of stump-sprouting after a fire, are common and may grow as much horizontally as they do vertically. This habit limits its usefulness as a timber tree and imparts a characteristic and sometimes strange appearance to the coastal woodlands. Early California visitors wrote about the mystical beauty of this tree and the enchanted landscapes that possessed it. Some felt less enchantment and more of a haunting strangeness when first encountering these unique groves along the Pacific shore. Perhaps this is what led Robert Louis Stevenson to describe the dense coast live oak forests around Monterey as "woods for murderers to crawl among." Nevertheless, coast live oak, with its curious and elegant architecture, is as much a part of western California as are the golden hills beneath its shady, dark canopy.

Despite its non-utilitarian demeanor, coast live oak has been an important resource throughout the course of human history in California. At least 12 major tribes of Indians harvested and consumed its acorns as a dietary staple. Mission builders of the San Fernando Valley reduced coast live oak wood to an excellent charcoal for firing the lime kilns that made adobe mortar. Choice trees were felled for angular timbers that could be used in ship construction. Ship captains demanded good fuel and sent small armies of cutters to the wooded shore. Live oak charcoal became important to the gunpowder, bakery, and electric power industries. Coast live oak was occasionally used by pioneers for construction, wagon parts, and farm implements. The pioneers had their greatest impact, however, as woodlands were cleared for agriculture and later for the development of rapidly spreading cities. Magnificent trees fell rapidly near the port towns of San Francisco, Monterey, and San Diego, foreshadowing the effects of a burgeoning population of settlers on the state's interior.

Identifying Characteristics

GROWTH FORM: Coast live oak is a low, evergreen tree with a dense, hemispherical crown. Its trunk divides into either erect limbs, or more commonly, into crooked, wide-spreading limbs that sometimes touch or trail along the ground. Coast live oaks commonly exceed 250 years of age. The largest known trees had trunks 8 to 12 feet across and crowns that spread nearly 130 feet across.
LEAVES: They are dark green, oval, and convex, measuring from one to three inches long. Like other evergreen oak leaves, they are tough and hard. The margins are spiny and often have short, tawny bristles. Upon close scrutiny, dense tufts of hair can usually be seen on the underside of a leaf at the intersection of the midrib and the larger, lateral veins closest to the petiole.
ACORNS: The conical acorns are ¾ to 1½ inches long, with a rich reddish-brown color. The deep

Above: Coast live oak leaves and acorns.
ALLISON ATWILL
Left: Coast live oak bark.
DAVID CAVAGNARO

cups are covered by thin, overlapping scales and lined with fuzzy hairs on the inside. Unlike acorns of other species in the red oak lineage, which require 18 months to mature, coast live oak acorns ripen 6 to 8 months after the flowers are pollinated.
BARK: On larger trunks and branches it is smooth and gray on the outside and distinctively reddish on the inside. With age it becomes brownish and shallowly furrowed.
WOOD: Brown, slightly reddish, and very fine-grained; the wood warps upon drying and has low commercial value except as fuel.

Habitat

Coast live oak is unique among the California oaks in its ability to thrive along the coast. Although probably more tolerant of salt spray than other oaks, it is not found along the immediate shore where exposure to salt-laden waves or wind is high. Proximity to the ocean provides a milder climate for coast live oak, with warmer winters (seldom encountering frost or snow) and less sweltering summers than found inland. Fog is common, providing additional relief from heat and drought. Usually, coast live oak grows on the well-drained soils of coastal plains and protected bluffs. Inland, it can be found at elevations up to 5,000 feet, with groves that spread across valleys, on steep hillsides, in rocky canyons, and along streams and intermittent watercourses. Coast live oak is an important member of many natural communities, including northern and southern mixed evergreen forests, coast live oak woodland, valley oak woodland, and Engelmann oak woodland. It is frequently associated with bay laurel, madrone, toyon, and several other native oaks.

Geographical Distribution

From Mendocino County to northern Baja, coast live oak is the most characteristic tree of California's coastal plains, valleys, and foothills. The species flourishes within a 50-mile-wide swath that borders the Pacific Ocean on the west and the Transverse, Peninsular, and inner Coast ranges on the east. It also grows on Santa Cruz and Santa Rosa islands. A few migrant trees are found in the Central Valley in Solano County and the Sacramento River Delta region.

Right: Coast live oaks are found up to about 5,000 feet in the ranges of Southern California. JOHN EVARTS
Below: Coast live oak woodlands cover much of this landscape near Cambria. ROLAND AND KAREN MUSCHENETZ

Typical of interior live oaks, this tree was as broad as it was tall. (It was cut for firewood in 1989.) DANIEL D'AGOSTINI

Interior Live Oak *(Quercus wislizenii)*

John C. Frémont made his first crossing of the Sierra Nevada in the hard winter of 1844, accompanied by a party that included scout Kit Carson and topographer Charles Preuss. Their month-long ordeal took them over a stark, white landscape of snow, ice, and barren rock en route to the "beautiful valley of the Sacramento." Indeed, when they finally descended to foothills near the south fork of the American River, it was the green of the grass and the leafiness of the oaks that caused them to celebrate. While continuing through the Great Central Valley, Frémont wrote in his log: "At every step the country improved in beauty; the pines were rapidly disappearing and oaks became the principal trees of the forest. Among these the prevailing tree was the evergreen live oak." This was the first written description of interior live oak. Specimens were later collected by German botanist Dr. F. A. Wislizenius and the tree formally named by Swiss botanist A. De Condolle.

The evergreen nature of this species impressed the snow-weary Frémont for reasons that were as much psychological as they were aesthetic, but plant scientists are impressed for reasons that are decidedly ecological. The leaves of interior live oak—and other evergreen species—have several advantages over the leaves of deciduous oaks. They can photosynthesize all year long and, therefore, generate a very large supply of food for growth and reproduction. When favorable conditions of light, temperature, and moisture occur, the leaves begin photosynthesizing immediately and require no "start-up time" for growth. Furthermore, evergreen leaves are better at retaining important mineral nutrients such as nitrogen, in part because they are not shed during the autumn of every year. These advantages allow interior live oak to occupy a large range in the foothills, low mountains, and interior valleys of California.

If these features are so obviously beneficial to interior live oak, why haven't evergreen leaves evolved in all species of California oaks?

Botanists theorize that each plant characteristic has a "cost" as well as a "benefit," and that the "cost-to-benefit ratio" varies between California's many environments. In some environments, the benefit of an all-year leaf canopy is outweighed by the cost. For example, interior live oak does well in the Coast Ranges where hard frosts and heavy snowfall are rare. Where frosts become more frequent, evergreen leaves are damaged when ice crystals form within cells and rupture internal membranes. Broad, evergreen leaves can also accumulate heavy loads of snow that send branches and large limbs crashing to the ground. The net difference between the resources gained by year-long photosynthesis and those lost in the form of damaged leaves and branches determines if interior live oak can inhabit a particular place and a particular environment. Thus, at higher elevations where frost and snow are common, interior live oak is replaced by the deciduous black oak that simply does not expose its leaves to the harsh, cold winter. (The evergreen canyon oak also extends into higher elevations, where it withstands heavy snowfall by assuming a more shrubby form and growing on exposed sites that readily shed snow.)

Other costs are associated with the evergreen leaves of interior live oak, including drought tolerance and herbivore defense. Having evolved in a region with intense summer drought, these leaves spend resources on features that conserve water and resist wilting. The leaves of interior live oak use precious carbohydrates, lipids, and mineral nutrients to construct a thick cuticle, to reinforce cell walls, and to accumulate substances for maintaining a favorable water balance. These investments are made at the expense of growth and other functions, but they allow interior live oak to maintain a dominance in drier habitats because it can ultimately produce more progeny than a drought-sensitive deciduous species such as valley oak. Interior live oak also invests more resources in producing chemicals that deter herbivores when compared to deciduous oaks because evergreen leaves are vulnerable all year long. High concentrations of tannins and lignins make interior live and other evergreen oak leaves less palatable and less rewarding to insects and mammals. Although desiccation and defoliation occasionally take their toll, interior live oaks are able to display their evergreen canopies and maintain their stature as Frémont's "principal trees of the forest."

Identifying Characteristics

GROWTH FORM: Interior live oak is a broad, densely branched evergreen tree with a full, rounded canopy of leaves. Typically, the tree is as broad or broader than tall, with numerous horizontal branches that parallel or intersect the ground.

LEAVES: The thick, leathery leaves are flat, elliptical, and one to three inches long. The upper surface is deep green and the lower surface is similar or slightly yellowish-green. The margins may be smooth, toothed, spiny or with short bristles. There are no tufts of brownish hairs on the lower surface near the midvein.

ACORNS: The narrow, conical acorns are ¾ to 1½ inches long and sit deep in their cups, which are covered with thin, overlapping scales. They require two years to mature.

Above: Interior live oak leaves and acorns.
ALLISON ATWILL
Right: Interior live oak bark. DAVID CAVAGNARO

BARK: The bark is smooth and gray on young trees, becoming darker and fissured with age.
WOOD: Light reddish-brown and strong, it is susceptible to rot and has little commercial value.

Habitat

Interior live oak is widespread on upland slopes below 5,000 feet, across low foothills, within river floodplains, and in valley bottoms away from the coast. Within the wide range of the species, summers are usually hot and dry, and winters cool and wet, but total precipitation may vary from 15 to more than 50 inches per year. Interior live oak has no apparent soil preference, but is seldom associated with serpentine. Historically, interior live oak was a dominant tree along the rivers and streams that flowed from the western Sierra Nevada into the Great Central Valley. Following dam construction during the mid-20th century, most of these floodplain populations were cleared because the land could be reliably cultivated. Today, only a few large stands of riparian forest remain, and these often include impressive examples of valley oak, black walnut, and sycamore. Interior live oak is an important species in blue oak woodland, along with gray pine and buckeye. The species is well represented in northern mixed evergreen forest, Oregon oak woodland, and, in scrub oak chaparral, as a shrubby variety.

Geographical Distribution

Interior live oak is widely distributed in the southern Klamath and southwestern Cascade ranges, and along the western slope of the Sierra Nevada, from Siskiyou County to Kern County. There is one outlying population on the east side of the Sierra in Inyo County along Oak Creek. The species is also scattered throughout the Coast Ranges and extends south along the inner Transverse and Peninsular ranges.

Additional Variety

There is a shrub form of interior live oak, *Q. wislizenii* var. *frutescens,* that grows as a tall, densely-branched shrub in chaparral. Its leaves are very much like those of the tree form: flat, shiny green on both surfaces, and lacking hairs. It is more common in Southern California, especially along the inner Transverse and Peninsular ranges. Isolated populations are also known from northern Baja California.

Top: Fall colors of a single black oak stand out amid the evergreen foliage of neighboring interior live oaks in this Calaveras County landscape. ROB BADGER
Bottom: Leaves and acorn on a shrubby form of interior live oak, Laguna Mountains. BILL EVARTS

A spreading, multi-trunked canyon oak grows at meadow's edge, Cuyamaca Rancho State Park. BILL EVARTS

Canyon Oak *(Quercus chrysolepis)*

Canyon oak ranges from Oregon to Baja California and spans elevations between sea level and 9,000 feet. It is the most widely distributed oak in the state. Canyon oak's growth form and other characteristics can vary greatly, allowing it to live in a variety of natural settings. No single description or portrait of canyon oak will suffice; instead, the species must be experienced and documented within the context of its many landscapes.

In the North Coast Ranges, for example, plentiful rainfall and mild temperatures support a rich evergreen forest of conifers and hardwoods. Soils in the canyon bottoms are well-developed, and deep leaf litter and clay help retain the water necessary to support magnificent specimens of Douglas fir, madrone, and canyon oak. The moist but shady environment drives tree growth upwards, with each overstory species competing for the light that makes additional growth possible. Here, young canyon oaks are tall, cylindrical trees with stout trunks and many large, upright branches. The high branches support dense clusters of leaves that are thrust into the shafts of light that penetrate the forest canopy. Deeply shaded, the lower limbs die and fall under their own weight, leaving the trunk free of branches for 20 or 30 feet above its base. When adjacent trees are toppled by wind or old age, the gaps are gradually filled by the horizontal growth of canyon oak branches, and the mature tree acquires a rounded, spreading crown. Under these conditions, canyon oaks may be more than 70 feet tall and four feet across at the base of the trunk. Trees of this stature can also be found in the mountains of Central and Southern California if the local environment is favorable.

Where rainfall and soil conditions are not quite as favorable and the surrounding forest is less well-developed, canyon oaks achieve the stature of a medium-sized tree. The trunks are often straight and slender, perhaps one or two feet in diameter, supporting a narrow canopy of leaves up to 60 feet tall. In the mountains of Southern California, dense forests of these trees blanket north-facing slopes above 4,500 feet.

Perhaps the most typical growth form of the species is observed in boulder-strewn canyons, and along fissured, often precipitous, rock walls. Warmer, drier conditions prevail and the shallow soil holds less water and fewer minerals. Thus the surrounding forest does not close its canopy and trees tend to grow out instead of up. The consummate tree lover, John Muir, described the canyon oaks of Yosemite Valley in this way:

> The Mountain Live Oak *(Q. chrysolepis)* is a tough, rugged mountaineer of a tree, growing bravely and attaining noble dimensions on the roughest earthquake taluses in deep cañons and yosemite valleys. The trunk is usually short, dividing near the ground into great, wide-spreading limbs, and these again into a multitude of slender sprays, many of them cord-like and drooping to the ground, like those of the Great White Oak of the lowlands *(Q. lobata)*. The top of the tree where there is plenty of space is broad and bossy, with a dense covering of shining leaves, making delightful canopies, the complicated system of gray, interlacing, arching branches as seen from beneath being exceedingly rich and picturesque.

Here the canyon oaks are usually less than 50 feet tall with slender, gnarled trunks that twist around and protrude through angular blocks of granite. They cluster around the base of Yosemite Falls, El Capitan, and Royal Arches, forming a diminutive but often continuous cover of forest. The oak's penchant for airy perches and the great strength of its wood make this wiry tree a favorite with climbers, who often ascend boughs in order to pass sections of cliff that lack hand and footholds.

Under extremely open and arid conditions, with virtually no soil development, canyon oak assumes its most subdued shape—that of a low spreading shrub. In this environment it is densely branched and leafy and may form pure stands on rocky ledges or contribute to the mosaic of chaparral species found on brushy ridges and slopes throughout the state.

Despite great variations in growth form, all canyon oaks have distinctive leaves and acorns. Some features, such as the toothed leaf margins and thickened acorn cup scales, are shared with other species in the intermediate oak evolutionary lineage *(Protobalanus)*. Other characteristics are unique to canyon oak. For example, upper surfaces of the holly-like leaves are bright green and shiny,

while lower surfaces are pale blue or grayish. A felt of minute golden or silvery hair usually overlays the blue, especially when leaves are young. This felt also covers the outer scales of the bowl-like acorn cups, hence the scientific name *"chrysolepis"* (literally "gold scale") and the older common name, "goldencup oak."

The wood, too, is a consistent feature of the species: very strong and close-grained, the hardest of any of the western oaks. It gained a favorable reputation among pioneer tool makers; a choice, well-seasoned limb sold for as much as five dollars a foot in 1882. These could be fashioned into thick, pointed wedges, fitted with iron heads and used to split redwood ties for railroad and building construction. Even hammerheads were made from young trees of canyon oak earning it the names "maul oak," "iron oak," and "hickory oak." The wood also found its way into the construction of ships, carriages, wagons, and houses.

Identifying Characteristics

GROWTH FORM: Canyon oak is an evergreen tree, typically 20 to 50 feet tall, with a dense canopy. The shape, size, and branching of the canopy vary greatly with conditions in the habitat. In moist

Above: Canyon oak leaves and acorn; oak gall on branch.
ALLISON ATWILL
Left: Canyon oak bark.
DAVID CAVAGNARO

forests canyon oaks become large, rounded, single-trunk trees; in steep, rocky canyons they form shorter, broader trees with multiple trunks; and on exposed cliffs and ridges they are densely-branched shrubs. The largest canyon oak in the state is 72 feet tall and 10 feet in diameter, and is found within a shady canyon of the Cleveland National Forest in San Diego County. Trees with trunks 12 to 18 inches in diameter are generally 100 to 150 years old, and maximum ages can exceed 300 years.

LEAVES: The elliptical leaves are 1 to 2½ inches long, shiny and dark green above, and pale blue or gray beneath with minute golden or silvery hairs. Spiny or toothed margins are common on leaves of younger trees and stump sprouts while smooth margins appear on older branches or higher on the tree. The occurrence of both forms of leaves on the same tree is common and may be confusing when attempting to identify this species.

ACORNS: The broad-based acorns are one to two inches long and light chestnut brown in color. The distinctive, saucer-shaped cup is thick and corky and covered with fine golden hairs when the acorn is green. Maturation occurs about 1½ years after the flowers are pollinated.

BARK: The gray or whitish bark is composed of smooth, shallow strips and is often covered by mosses and lichens.

WOOD: Light to dark brown, very strong and hard, it is now of low commercial value.

Habitat

Canyon oak is abundant in foothills, mountain canyons, and on upland slopes and exposed ridges throughout the state, from sea level to 9,000 feet. Climatic features of its habitat are quite variable, although large trees are seldom found in areas that experience heavy snowfall or frequent fires. Soils are just as variable, ranging from deep, rich accumulations in canyon-bottom forests to rocky veneers on exposed ridges or cliffs. It is uncommon in soils derived from serpentine rock. Canyon oak is a dominant species in northern and southern mixed evergreen forests, northern montane forest, and Sierran mixed conifer forest. Its common forest associates include madrone, bay laurel, Douglas fir, bigcone spruce, ponderosa pine, Jeffrey pine, and sugar pine. Canyon oak is also a component of Oregon oak woodland, blue oak woodland, and many kinds of chaparral where it appears with buckeye, various manzanitas, and huckleberry oak.

Geographical Distribution

Canyon oak ranges from southwestern Oregon to central Baja California and extends east into Nevada and central Arizona. It is found in virtually all major mountain ranges in California, and even occurs at high elevations in the Providence and New York Mountains of the Mojave Desert. Isolated groves are also nestled within canyons on the eastern slopes of the central and southern Sierra Nevada. It flourishes on four of California's Channel Islands, often hybridizing with the closely related island oak.

Top: Some of California's largest canyon oaks are found near Palomar Mountain State Park. BILL EVARTS
Bottom: Canyon oak leaves, acorn cups. MICHAEL FRYE

This island oak on Santa Rosa Island has persevered despite extreme soil erosion near its roots. J. C. LEACOCK

Island Oak (*Quercus tomentella*)

Island oak is the rarest of all California tree oaks, being found only on the Channel Islands and on Guadalupe Island southwest of San Diego. This narrow distribution, along with fossil evidence from the mainland, reveals that island oak is a relict of an ancient California, one that was ecologically very different from the place we know today.

The climate of ancient California was warmer and more moist, with subtropical conditions extending more than 100 miles inland from the coast. Instead of tall, rugged mountain ranges that separated very different kinds of coastal, upland, and desert landscapes, there were low hills and plains covered with a rich, often dense woodland. Among the many species in that woodland of 7 to 20 million years ago was the probable ancestor of island oak, as revealed by fossils found in the inner Coast Ranges east of San Francisco Bay and the eastern Tehachapi Mountains near the Mojave

Desert. Not only were leaves and stems of the ancestor *(Quercus declinata)* uncovered, so were those of other woody plants now known only from offshore, such as the Catalina Island ironwood and island bush poppy. These species shared a frost- and drought-free environment that was widespread across the state prior to the uplift of the modern Sierra Nevada, and Coast, Transverse, and Peninsular ranges. As great chains of mountains were thrust upward by faulting and volcanism over the last 20 million years, climate change in California was accelerated. Mountains blocked the onshore flow of moist, maritime air and so the interior of the state became drier and more extreme with respect to temperature. These changes presumably contributed to the extinction of island oak and its associated species throughout the mainland. Today island oak persists only where warm ocean waters and drenching summer fogs have maintained a fragment of ancient California—a relict species confined to a relict environment.

Although the California islands provide a refuge from frost and drought, this oak must still contend with harsh and steady winds that prune with salt spray and brute force. Even under the best of conditions, island oak is relatively small, perhaps 25 to 40 feet tall. Where the winds are harshest, these trees sometimes have elfin proportions and are resigned to propping themselves against bluffs or rock outcrops. The trunk is often swept back, naked of branches on the windward side. The evergreen canopy may be trimmed to a leafy, aerodynamic wedge on particularly exposed, windy ridges. Reproduction is also made difficult by these conditions, especially if acorns are blown into unsuitable habitat or if seedlings dehydrate in the shallow, rocky soil. Groves of island oaks are maintained, however, by sprouting new trunks from the root crowns and shoots of adult trees. The survival of these groves over the centuries is highly dependent on sprouting, rather than reproduction from acorns.

An additional difficulty of island life was added in the last century, when non-native goats, sheep, and pigs were brought from the mainland to graze. Once they began to run wild and multiply in in the absence of predators, these feral animals voraciously consumed the fragile vegetation of the islands. Acorns and oak leaves were among the preferred foods, but, before long, anything and

Winds and salt spray have pruned this exposed island oak on Santa Cruz Island. RALPH CLEVENGER

everything was stripped and devoured. Soil erosion was thus accelerated, making it more difficult for the oaks and other plants to recover. Pigs were especially responsible for increased erosion because they dug out and gnawed on the roots of island oak. Fortunately, feral animals are being removed in an effort to restore the native vegetation and to allow the islands to function once again as natural refuges from the modern world.

Identifying Characteristics

GROWTH FORM: Island oak is a small, evergreen tree, 25 to 40 feet tall with a trunk one to two feet in diameter. In sheltered areas it develops a full, round canopy but when exposed to wind and salt spray it can be dramatically pruned.

LEAVES: The leaves are two to four inches long, elliptical or egg-shaped, with 10 or 12 pairs of conspicuous, parallel veins. The tip comes to a blunt point and the margins are shallowly toothed. When new and unfolding from the bud, they are covered with fine hairs called tomentum (hence the species name *tomentella*). These hairs wear away during the life span of the leaf, revealing the dark green and shiny upper surface. The lower surface remains matted with tan hairs.

ACORNS: The oval acorns are 1 to 1½ inches long with shallow cups that are thick-walled and broad. Tawny or whitish woolly hairs conceal the cup scales. About 18 months is required for maturation after pollination.

BARK: The bark is pale gray outside, reddish-brown inside, and covers the trunk as thin, papery scales.

WOOD: It is light reddish-brown, and of low commercial value.

Habitat

Island oak grows best where climate is moderated by the ocean—not too hot, not too cold, with plenty of moisture from rain or fog. It will tolerate almost any soil condition, but attains full stature only on deeper soils in sheltered locations. Moist sites are preferred, such as steep, north-facing slopes or along streambeds; the species is also abundant on exposed ridges and hilltops. Other oaks may join island oak to form an island oak woodland community. These are most often coast live and canyon oak, but valley oak may also be found, depending on the particular island. Island oak woodland often has a closed, shady canopy with very little understory vegetation.

Geographical Distribution

The only natural stands of island oak are found on five of the Channel Islands—Santa Cruz, Santa Rosa, Anacapa, Santa Catalina, and San Clemente—and on Guadalupe Island off the coast of Baja California. On the mainland, good specimens of island oaks grow at Santa Barbara Botanic Garden. Island oak has also gained some popularity as a landscape tree in Southern California.

Above: Island oak leaves and acorns. ALLISON ATWILL
Right: Island oak bark.
CHARLES RENNIE

The Evolutionary Lineages of California Oaks

CALIFORNIA OAKS BELONG TO THREE evolutionary lineages within the genus *Quercus*. Each lineage, or subgenus, has its own distinctive set of leaf, acorn, bark, and wood characteristics, which are summarized in the accompanying table. The characteristics are often useful when identifying oaks, but more importantly, they reveal differences in genetic heritage. Each heritage is preserved because cross-pollination between species in different lineages does not produce offspring. Offspring are sometimes produced when species within a lineage cross-pollinate. These progeny, called hybrids, are discussed in "California's Hybrid Oaks" on pages 44-45.

White Oak Evolutionary Lineage (subgenus *Lepidobalanus*): The leaves of oaks in this lineage have rounded, rather than pointed leaf lobes, if they are lobed at all. The tips of the lobes and the rest of the leaf margin (edge) may have teeth or spines, but not bristles. Teeth are green leaf tissue drawn to a point along the margin. If the point is hard and very sharp it is called a spine. Bristles are dry, colorless extensions of a leaf vein that go beyond the margin. Acorns of white oaks ripen within one year and their cups have rounded, knobby scales. The wood is light brown or sandy.

Red Oak Evolutionary Lineage (subgenus *Erythrobalanus*—sometimes called the black oak evolutionary lineage): The species in this lineage may have deeply lobed leaves (like black oak) or unlobed, oval leaves (like coast live oak). The lobes or margins of the leaves are tipped with tawny bristles that extend outward beyond the green of the blade. With the exception of coast live oak, the acorns of these species take two years to ripen, so tiny, new acorns and mature acorns may be found on the same branch. Thin, flat scales cover the acorn cup like shingles on a roof, in contrast to the knobby scales of the white oak lineage. The inner wood or heartwood of red oaks is a rich reddish-brown.

Intermediate Oak Evolutionary Lineage (subgenus *Protobalanus*): Oaks in this lineage share features of both the red and white oak lineages. The leaves are unlobed and have toothed or spiny margins, but not bristles. The inside of the acorn shell may be either fuzzy or smooth. Acorns take two years to mature, and most of the acorn cups have thickened scales. The wood is light brown.

CHARACTERISTICS OF THE THREE EVOLUTIONARY LINEAGES IN *QUERCUS*

Lineage	WHITE OAKS (*Lepidobalanus*)	RED OAKS (*Erythrobalanus*)	INTERMEDIATE OAKS (*Protobalanus*)
Leaves			
lobes	lobed or unlobed	lobed or unlobed	unlobed
lobe shape	round	pointed	
margins	smooth or with blunt, green teeth or spines	tawny bristles and spines	smooth or with green teeth or spines
Acorns			
inner shell	smooth	densely hairy	smooth or hairy
cup scales	thick and knobby	thin and flat	thick, often knobby
matures in	1 year	2 years *(except coast live oak)*	2 years
Bark (mature trees)	light gray or brown, scaly or rough	dark gray, blackish or brown, smooth	light gray or brown, scaly or rough
Wood	light brown or yellowish	reddish brown	light brown
California Oaks	valley, blue, Engelmann, Oregon, scrub, leather, deer, Muller, desert scrub, coastal scrub	black, coast live, interior live, island scrub	canyon, island, huckleberry, Palmer

(from Tucker, 1979)

Above: Muller oak is a major component of this semi-desert chaparral community near the western edge of Anza-Borrego Desert State Park. BILL EVARTS
Right: Ocean spray has helped prune this coastal scrub oak at Torrey Pines State Reserve. BILL EVARTS

The Shrub Oaks of California

Although we visualize oaks as majestic, sheltering trees, half of California's oak species are shrubs. Instead of developing a single, dominant trunk that rises several feet before dividing into limbs, the shoots of shrub species form many, similar branches near the soil surface. These support a dense, interwoven canopy of smaller branches that tend to grow at right angles to each other. The leaves are evergreen, tough, and spiny, with shapes and venation patterns that are characteristic of the genus *Quercus*. Also characteristic are the acorns and acorn cups found scattered among the youngest branchlets and on the sheltered ground beneath the canopy.

Shrub oaks cover an estimated 1.5 million acres in California, and they are a common species in nearly every form of chaparral—a vegetation type that covers about 5% of the state. They thrive in a variety of environments, ranging from coastal bluffs to desert-edge canyons to subalpine ridges. In general, shrub oaks occur in drier habitats than tree oaks, and they are widespread where frequent, all-consuming fires determine much about the appearance and ecology of the landscape. The term

chaparral is derived from *chaparro,* a Spanish word for evergreen oak that was probably bestowed on the shrub oak by California's early explorers and colonists. Scrub is another, less romantic, word for the vegetation of shrub-dominated landscapes.

Nine shrub oaks are the subject of this section, and these species are divided into two categories by distribution: scrub oak, leather oak, huckleberry oak, and desert scrub oak are California's most widely distributed shrub-sized oaks; deer oak, Palmer oak, Muller oak, island scrub oak, and coastal scrub oak have more narrow distributions.

Scrub Oak (*Quercus berberidifolia*)

Scrub oak is an important member of chaparral and woodland vegetation and one of the two most common shrub oaks in California. It grows 6 to 15 feet tall, and can establish extensive, dense thickets that effectively exclude other understory plants. Scrub oak also occurs in discrete patches that are interspersed with trees, grasses, and other shrubs. Found mostly below 5,000 feet, the species ranges through the outer Coast, Transverse, and Peninsular ranges, from Tehama County to northern Baja California. Scrub oak is also found in the western foothills of the Sierra Nevada.

Leaves of scrub oak are from ¾ to 1 inch long and quite variable in shape. The margins may be smooth or toothed and sometimes quite spiny. The upper surface of the leaf is green, and the underside is a dull, grayish-green with small hairs sparsely scattered over the whole lower surface. The acorns are oval, ½ to 1 inch long, and set in a knobby cup. The regular, spiral pattern of the cup scales suggests the surface of a finely quilted blanket.

Leather Oak (*Quercus durata*)

Leather oak is largely confined to soils derived from serpentine rock. Like other shrubs restricted to this nutrient-poor, somewhat toxic substrata, leather oak tends to be small and intricately branched, with tough leaves and extensive roots. It usually grows less than 10 feet tall, and most often forms a broken cover of rounded canopies three to five feet above the ground. The species is generally found below 6,000 feet and has a scattered distribution through the Klamath and Coast Ranges (to San Luis Obispo County), and the Sierra Nevada from Nevada County to Eldorado County. An outlying southern population is found in the San Gabriel Mountains.

Leaves of leather oak are ¾ to 1 inch long, dull green, convex (almost curled), and oval, with smooth or prickly toothed margins. The undersides are pale gray and thickly coated with fine, soft hairs. The acorns are ½ to 1 inch long, variable in shape but often thick and cylindrical. The cup is bowl-shaped and decorated with warty scales.

Desert Scrub Oak (*Quercus turbinella*)

Desert scrub oak is relatively widespread on mountain slopes along the desert edge, but generally absent from hot, dry lowland desert. It occurs where cold, relatively wet winters and warm summers allow open woodlands of pinyon, juniper, and Joshua trees to flourish. Amidst these semi-desert trees, desert scrub oak forms thickets up to 10 feet tall, at elevations from 3,000 to 6,500 feet.

The species is very widely distributed between California and western Texas and from southern Colorado to northern Mexico. Two varieties are found in California. The typical form, *Q. turbinella* var. *turbinella,* grows mostly in the eastern Transverse Ranges and in the Mojave Desert's New York Mountains. The other variety, *Q. turbinella* var. *californica,* tends to occupy a separate area to the west, which extends through the inner South Coast and Transverse ranges from San Bernardino County to San Benito County. Isolated populations also occur in the Santa Rosa Mountains (Riverside County) and in northern Baja California.

The leaves of desert scrub oak are less than 1¼ inches long, oblong in outline, and yellowish-green on both sides. Margins can be toothed and spine-tipped and the apex is pointed. The leaves are semi-deciduous, often remaining on the plant through the winter but falling in spring when new leaves emerge. The mature bark on twigs and branches is gray, giving the whole shrub a similar, dull cast. Acorns are up to two inches long, usually pointed and shaped like an old-fashioned spinning top (hence the Latin name *turbinella),* but they may also be round or cylindrical. Acorn color varies from yellowish-brown to buff or light brown. The cups have thin, papery scales.

Huckleberry Oak *(Quercus vaccinifolia)*
Huckleberry oak is a low, spreading shrub of the mountains, occurring at higher elevations than any other species of California oak. The canopy is evergreen, dense with leaves, and reminiscent of the closely-related canyon oak. However, it seldom exceeds a height of three or four feet and usually forms its own peculiar type of chaparral among the conifers. It tends to be found on exposed ridges and rocky outcrops between 3,000 and 10,000 feet in the Sierra Nevada (north of Fresno County), North Coast Ranges (north of Mendocino County), and Klamath Ranges. Greenleaf manzanita, western juniper, and Jeffrey pine are common associates.

The leaves of huckleberry oak are about one inch long and have smooth margins. The top sides are shiny green and the undersides gray with sparse, golden hairs. The round to oval acorns are about ½ inch long and have shallow cups with thin, hairy scales.

Top: Huckleberry oak with a green acorn. J. R. HALLER
Bottom: A patch of huckleberry oak grows among granite outcrops along the road over Tioga Pass, Yosemite National Park. DENNIS FLAHERTY

Deer oak *(Quercus sadleriana)*

Deer oak is the most unusual shrub oak in the California flora. The species has a distinct appearance because many of its stems arise from the same region at the base of the shoot, producing a conical, vase-shaped canopy. The ancestry of the species is also different, because its closest oak relatives are in Asia rather than western North America. Deer oak resides only in the Klamath Ranges of Trinity, Del Norte, and Siskiyou counties, where it occurs on dry slopes and ridges between 3,000 and 7,000 feet. As a member of the northern montane forest, it is often found in the shade of red fir, Douglas fir, and other coniferous trees.

The evergreen leaves of deer oak are two to four inches long, oval, and prominently veined. The margins are serrated with small, coarse teeth, similar to those of alder leaves. Deer oak acorns are ½ to ¾ inch long, oval, and set in a thin-walled cup.

Palmer Oak *(Quercus palmeri)*

Palmer oak develops into a shrub or a small tree up to 10 feet tall. It typically grows in semi-desert chaparral or pinyon-juniper woodlands along desert margins in Southern California, Arizona, and northern Mexico. In California, Palmer oak is generally affiliated with chaparral communities between 3,000 to 5,000 feet in the inner Peninsular and Transverse ranges. It also occurs in the inner South Coast Ranges from Santa Barbara County to San Benito County. The northernmost population occurs on a single, windswept hill in Alameda County, east of Mount Diablo.

The evergreen leaves of Palmer oak are nearly round and usually ½ to 1½ inches long. They are a dull gray-green on the upper surface and whitish or yellowish below. Leaf margins are wavy and very spiny. Acorns are round to oval, and about 1 to 1¼ inches long. The shallow acorn cup has a distinctive, loose-fitting appearance and is covered with short, golden hairs.

Muller oak *(Quercus cornelius-mulleri)*

Muller oak has only recently been recognized as a species distinct from its close relatives, coastal scrub and desert scrub oak. Its distribution lies somewhat between the coast and desert, being centered along the crest of the Peninsular Ranges from Orange County to northern Baja California. Muller oak is found within chaparral near the desert edge, between 3,000 to 6,000 feet. Isolated populations are also known from the San Bernardino Mountains and Joshua Tree National Monument.

Muller oak has a dense canopy that is usually less than six feet tall. The thick, ½- to 1-inch-long leaves are dull grayish-green on top and densely covered with a layer of fine, pale hairs underneath. The margins are smooth but can bear a few, small teeth. The acorns are about one inch long, oblong and often pointed, and set within deep cups.

Top: Deer oak, endemic to the Klamath Ranges of northern California and southern Oregon. AL SENERES
Middle: Palmer oak. DAVID CAVAGNARO
Bottom: Muller oak in San Diego County. BILL EVARTS

Coastal Scrub Oak *(Quercus dumosa)*

Possibly the least understood species in the genus, coastal scrub oak was long thought to be the most widespread and abundant shrub oak of California. It appeared to many as a constant in almost all kinds of chaparral and woodland, spanning coast to desert, and from the North Coast Ranges to Baja California. Recent research, however, determined that the wide ecological and geographical distribution was occupied by populations of three species, not one. The common, interior populations found in chaparral are actually scrub oaks *(Q. berberidifolia)*, while the desert-edge populations are probably Muller oaks *(Q. cornelius-mulleri)*. True coastal scrub oak grows only in Southern California and northern Baja California, where it is restricted to rapidly disappearing habitats on bluffs, headlands, and hillsides within sight of the ocean. Such habitats are scheduled for development throughout the region, as slopes are leveled for housing and industry. Coastal scrub oak may now be among the rarest of the shrub oaks, although its full range and abundance have yet to be redefined.

Leaves of coastal scrub oak are borne on thin, often reddish twigs. They are cupped and small, usually less than ½ inch long. The undersides have soft, felt-like hairs and the margins are spiny. Acorns are sharply tapered and the cups rust colored.

Island Scrub Oak *(Quercus parvula)*

Island scrub oak has been recently described as a species separate from its mainland relative, interior live oak. The leaves of both species are deep green on both sides and lack small hairs near the main veins. Island oak, however, is a shrub, growing 6 to 12 feet high; the leaves are nearly twice as long as those of interior live oak. Distribution of island scrub oak is quite limited: it occurs on Santa Cruz

An island scrub oak displays new leaves and colorful blossoms, Santa Cruz Island. STEVE JUNAK

Island and a few coastal localities in Santa Barbara County. It is associated with maritime chaparral and closed-cone pine forests below 3,000 feet.

The leaves of island scrub oak are two to four inches long, oval in shape, and sometimes have a few bristles or spines along the margins. They are shiny green on both the upper and lower surfaces and completely lack hairs. The acorns are 1½ inches long, round or cylindrical, with blunt tips. The deep cups have thin, papery scales.

Island scrub oak may very well have a closer mainland relative than the interior live oak. That relative has not yet been formally recognized by science, but has been given a common name—Shreve oak. Shreve oak may be a new variety of *Quercus parvula* that grows in the form of an evergreen tree. Like island oak it has large, oblong, hairless leaves and lives close to the ocean. But in contrast, Shreve oak grows to be 15 to 50 feet tall, has convex leaves, and is associated with redwood and mixed evergreen forests, as well as coastal chaparral. In the past this tree was not linked to island scrub oak. Instead, it was thought to be an unusual form of interior live oak that just happened to thrive in a much cooler and wetter coastal environment. Although the complete story of Shreve oak has not yet been told, it seems to be abundant in the Santa Cruz and Santa Lucia mountains of the central coast.

Coastal scrub oak leaves and acorns. BILL EVARTS

Oak Identification and the Challenge of Variability

EACH OF CALIFORNIA'S 18 OAK SPECIES IS endowed with unique characteristics. Distinct physical traits, such as growth form, leaf shape, leaf color, bark texture, and acorn size, are useful in field identification and form the basis of diagnostic keys, including this book's "Key to the Tree Oaks of California." Even with the aid of a key, identifying oaks is often a challenge. Related species of oaks from the same evolutionary lineage (subgenus) can share similar characteristics. Also, individual oaks belonging to a single species may be quite variable with respect to growth form, leaves, and acorns. That variation, although it may frustrate attempts at identification, is the basis for physiological acclimation and evolutionary change.

Variation within a species of tree oak can be an expression of environmental influences and genetic programming. Many of the physical traits of an oak are "plastic" and can be molded by local conditions such as soil, light, and microclimate. In essence, these variations allow a growing individual to acclimate to its immediate environment (since plants do not have the option of migrating to a better spot). A coast live oak growing in a shady, moist woodland habitat, for example, will have larger leaves than a coast live oak stranded at the edge of a sun-drenched savanna. Environmentally induced variations that affect branching pattern, leaf size, root depth, and other characteristics allow a species to occupy a wider distribution. But these variations cannot be passed on to the next generation—

These coast live oak leaves were collected from neighboring trees; the two large leaves (left) grew in the shade, the other four in full sun. BILL EVARTS

These canyon oak leaves were picked from the same tree in Madera County. It is not unusual to find leaves with both smooth and toothed margins on the same canyon oak. The bi-colored leaves, as seen here, are a helpful identifying feature of this species. BILL EVARTS

they are not programmed by genes.

Other variations in an oak species can be inherited and, therefore, have a genetic basis. Individuals often possess variant genes that code for slight differences in their physical and physiological characteristics. In a particular environment, variant genes could permit a tree to conduct more photosynthesis, grow more, capture more resources, and leave behind more progeny than another tree with the common form of those genes. Such variations are termed "adaptive" and can lead to a new form of an old species or, over time, to an entirely new species of oak. Hybridization is one way that a species becomes genetically variable; it is discussed on the next page in "California's Hybrid Oaks."

All variability in oaks, whether induced or inherited, can present difficulty when identifying specimens in the field. Canyon oak, for example, exhibits a large degree of induced variability; it is common to find canyon oak leaves with either very spiny, toothed, or perfectly smooth margins on the same tree. To positively identify this species, it may be necessary to look at an assortment of leaves from different places on the same tree or even an assortment from adjacent trees.

The similar appearance of some species within a subgenus also presents an identification challenge. On first encounter, interior live oak and coast live oak may look essentially the same. Both are broad trees with elliptical or sometimes heart-shaped, evergreen leaves. And like all species in the red oak subgenus, their leaves have margins with bristle- or spine-tipped teeth. Their acorns are reddish-brown, conical, and with scaly cups. When examining these two species or others that look alike, knowledge about the different habitats and geographic range of oaks can augment the use of a diagnostic key. Coast live oak, for example, rarely extends into the most arid, inland

portions of the Coast, Transverse, and Peninsular ranges. Where the distributions of the two species overlap, such as valleys and ridges that traverse between coastal and interior climates, extra care must be taken to examine the specimens at hand.

Identifying oaks is best done with a diagnostic key and representative samples of leaves, acorns, and bark (preferably left on the tree). A hand lens is not necessary, but may prove helpful when examining leaves for characteristics such as tufts of hair. The text and illustrations in this chapter—especially sections that describe the identifying characteristics, habitat, and geographic distribution of each tree oak—are also valuable resources for oak identification.

Interior live oak is another evergreen species that exhibits considerable variability in its leaves; leaf margins may be smooth or toothed, as shown here. BOB RONEY

California's Hybrid Oaks

Compared to other native woody plants, oaks hybridize frequently. Within the California flora more than 20 hybrid oaks have been recognized and 11 of these are named. Hybridization is important in the evolution of oaks because it increases genetic variation within populations; the genes from one species combine with those of another, resulting in novel combinations to be selected by the environment. As many botanists have suggested, the propensity for California oaks to hybridize may indicate a potential for rapid evolution in this diverse and changing environment.

Hybrid oaks result when pollen from one species fertilizes the female flower of another species and a viable embryo is produced. Such success has only been documented between species in the same subgenus; cross-pollination between species in different subgenera, such as canyon oak *(Protobalanus)* and valley oak *(Lepidobalanus)*, does not produce viable embryos. Crosses within a subgenus, such as between interior live oak and black oak *(Erythrobalanus)*, produce embryos that grow into unusual hybrid offspring. These hybrids are often quite variable in their physical and physiological characteristics; they may vaguely resemble either parent or be perfectly intermediate. It is also possible for hybrid plants to mature and cross with a non-hybrid parent, thus complicating the patterns of inheritance and variation observed in oak species.

Hybrids are typically found where populations of two related oak species overlap, especially if one population is large and the other is not. In this case, the wind-borne pollen of the abundant species overwhelms that of the less common species, and consequently pollinates more flowers. The presence of a "hybrid habitat" is also important because it offers intermediate environmental conditions for the hybrids that differ from conditions suitable for the parent species. In some areas, such as the north San Francisco Bay counties and the Channel Islands, oak populations may be composed of many hybrids, in some cases forming a hybrid "swarm." But in most parts of California, hybrids usually occur as isolated trees or shrubs. Some of the more common hybrid oaks are introduced below and presented by subgenera.

***Lepidobalanus* Hybrids:** Epling oak is a hybrid between blue oak and Oregon oak that grows into a compact tree. Its leaf characteristics are quite variable, while its acorns usually resemble those of Oregon oak. Since both parents are deciduous, a close inspection of the leaves is required to determine its hybrid origin. This hybrid is relatively widespread in Marin, Sonoma, and Napa counties.

Another hybrid in this subgenus is Alvord oak, which is an offspring of blue oak and desert scrub oak. This large shrub is frequently

Above: Oracle oak leaf (upper right) reflects the leaf shapes of its parent trees, interior live oak (upper left) and black oak (bottom). BILL EVARTS
Opposite left: MacDonald oak. STEVE JUNAK

found in the dry, interior foothills of central California, and it ranges from Monterey County to the Tehachapi Mountains.

MacDonald oak is a hybrid that is widespread on Santa Cruz, Santa Rosa, and Santa Catalina islands. This deciduous tree develops a rounded crown and can reach over 30 feet high. While one parent is always scrub oak, its partner may be valley oak or another species in this subgenus.

***Erythrobalanus* Hybrids:** Oracle oak is the best-known California hybrid. A cross between black oak and interior live oak, it develops into a small, upright tree from 25 to 40 feet high. Like other hybrids, it can be quite variable: in Shasta County some specimens reach 70 to 80 feet; in San Diego County, where the evergreen partner is the shrubby variety *(Q. wislizenii* var. *frutescens)* it usually grows no higher than 15 to 20 feet. Oracle oak is most conspicuous in late autumn and winter when many of its deciduous leaves have turned yellow but have not dropped. This hybrid is found throughout the Sierra Nevada, the Coast Ranges south of Mendocino County, and the Peninsular and Transverse ranges.

Chase oak is another hybrid involving black oak and can easily be confused with Oracle oak. The other parental species, however, is the evergreen coast live oak. Chase oak is scattered throughout the Coast Ranges, particularly from Sonoma to Monterey counties.

***Protobalanus* Hybrids:** Even though there are currently no named hybrids within this lineage, cross-pollination is known to occur. In montane areas of the state, for example, hybrid swarms have been reported where populations of huckleberry oak and canyon oak overlap. On the Channel Islands, canyon oak genes are found in many island oaks as a result of hybridization, and pure populations of island oak may be quite rare.

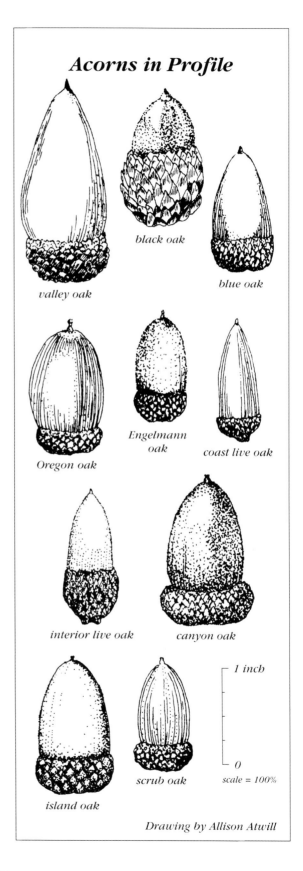

Acorns in Profile

valley oak

black oak

blue oak

Oregon oak

Engelmann oak

coast live oak

interior live oak

canyon oak

island oak

scrub oak

1 inch

0

scale = 100%

Drawing by Allison Atwill

Range Maps of Eight California Oaks

Valley Oak *(Quercus lobata)*

Black Oak *(Quercus kelloggii)*

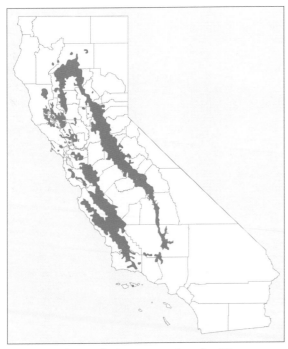

Blue Oak *(Quercus douglasii)*

Oregon Oak *(Quercus garryana)*

Coast Live Oak *(Quercus agrifolia)*

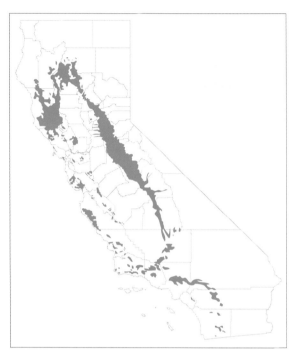

Interior Live Oak *(Quercus wislizenii)*

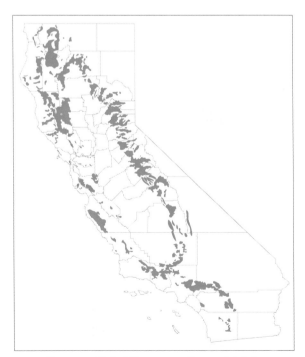

Canyon Oak *(Quercus chrysolepis)*

Engelmann Oak *(Quercus engelmanii)*

From Griffin and Critchfield, 1977

Key to the Tree Oaks of California

A. Leaves usually lobed or with wavy margins, supple, thin, and deciduous (falling in winter or during severe drought)

  B. Leaves shallowly lobed or with wavy margins, sinuses between lobes less than a finger-width deep. Upper leaf surface often with a dull gray- or blue-green cast

    C. Leaves dark green to gray-green, somewhat leathery and often retained on twigs until spring. Found south of Pasadena (central Los Angeles County) to Baja California

        ...... **Engelmann oak** *(Q. engelmanii)*

    Cc. Leaves green or bluish-green because of a waxy coating and falling from twigs by winter, especially in dry years. Found north of Valencia (north Los Angeles County) to Shasta Lake and the upper Pit River

        ...... **blue oak** *(Q. douglasii)*

  Bb. Leaves deeply lobed, sinuses between lobes usually a finger-width or more deep. Upper leaf surface green

    D. Leaf lobes pointed at tips, ending with a long, soft bristle. Bark dark gray or black

        ...... **black oak** *(Q. kelloggii)*

    Dd. Leaf lobes rounded or broadly angular at tips, lacking bristles. Bark light gray or whitish

      E. Upper leaf surface dull green with minute hairs. Lobes broadly angular with sinuses extending almost to the midvein. Buds at the ends of branches without a dense coating of hairs. Bark on mature trees gray, blocky, and deeply furrowed

        ...... **valley oak** *(Q. lobata)*

      Ee. Upper leaf surface shiny green with a waxy coat. Lobes rounded, the sinuses away from the midvein. Buds at the ends of branches densely hairy. Bark on mature trees whitish, scaly, and shallowly furrowed

        ...... **Oregon oak** *(Q. garryana)*

Key to the Tree Oaks of California, cont.

Aa. Leaves never lobed, usually thick and leathery, and evergreen

    F.   Leaves flat

        G. Upper leaf surface dark green, lower surface similar or slightly yellow-green and lacking hairs. Bark on mature trees dark gray and shallowly fissured. Acorn cup has thin, papery scales when ripening

                ...... **interior live oak** *(Q. wislizenii)*

        Gg. Upper leaf surface dark green, lower surface pale blue-green, often with a thick coat of golden or gray hairs. Bark on mature trees whitish or light gray and smooth. Acorn cup has thick, corky, hairy scales when ripening.

                ...... **canyon oak** *(Q. chrysolepis)*

    Ff. Leaves convex

        H. Lower leaf surface without hairs, yellowish-green or similar to upper surface in color. Outer South Coast Ranges, perhaps only Monterey and San Luis Obispo counties

                ...... **Shreve oak** *(Q. parvula* - tree form*)*

    Hh. Lower leaf surface with hairs, sometimes only found in small tufts

        I. Leaves with irregular pattern of veins, easier to see from below. Lower leaf surface with tufts of brownish hairs where lateral veins join the midvein. Leaf margins with spines or bristles. Widely distributed on the mainland and offshore islands

                ...... **coast live oak** *(Q. agrifolia)*

        Ii. Leaves with prominent, parallel veins, conspicuous from above and below. Lower leaf surface evenly covered with tan hairs. Leaf margins toothed but lacking spines and bristles. Occurs naturally only on the offshore islands

                ...... **island oak** *(Q. tomentella)*

CHAPTER TWO

THE OAK LANDSCAPES
OF CALIFORNIA

IMAGINE THE LANDSCAPES OF WILD CALIFORNIA: a coastal terrace fringed by dunes and bottomlands; an evergreen forest shrouded in summer fog; a warm sandstone canyon bounded by fire-scarred hills; a deep valley filled with gray winter mists; a steep range of mountains sculpted by glaciers. Despite great differences in geology, climate, soil, and animal life, each of these environments may be home to one or more species of native oak. In California, the oak-dominated landscapes include many kinds of forests, woodlands, and chaparrals. These oak landscapes comprise a rich and unusual assemblage of plant and animal life found nowhere else on the planet.

California's oak landscapes are widespread and ancient. They cover more than a third of the state and range from high-desert slopes to the Pacific shore. This widespread distribution is matched only by persistence through geological time; the relatives of modern species contributed to the landscapes of prehistoric California more than 20 million years ago. Fossils found in the Pacific Northwest show that the ancestors of coast live oak and black oak closely resembled today's species and grew in similar coastal and montane areas. Other species, such as blue oak, may be more recently evolved, having adapted to drier and warmer conditions that developed in the lowlands during the last 10 million years. As the environment changed, so did oak landscapes. Oaks migrated throughout the western portion of the continent as their acorns were dispersed to new sites where seedlings could survive. Some species became extinct as their environments were dramatically altered by climatic and geologic events, such as glacial advance and mountain uplift. Today we see the results of these dynamic processes—oak lineages and landscapes shaped by evolution, migration, and in some cases, extinction.

Over the millennia, oaks have been sculptured by the features of their landscapes; the leaves, branches, and roots of each different species have developed distinct growth forms and tolerance to environmental stress. In shady coniferous forests, for example, black oak grows as a tall tree with sunlit upper branches. In rocky, exposed areas, huckleberry oak survives icy windblast by spreading as a low shrub beneath the snowpack. Deciduous species, such as Oregon oak and valley oak, are drought sensitive and rarely thrive outside montane or riparian landscapes where soil moisture is ample.

Above: A sunlit oak stands out against a backdrop of pines on the edge of Santa Rosa Island. J. C. LEACOCK
Opposite: Coast live and blue oak intermingle on a wooded slope, Mt. Diablo State Park. PAT O'HARA

Hardy evergreen species, such as interior live and scrub oak, are able to dominate arid woodlands and chaparral due to their extensive root systems and water-conserving leaves.

Acorns too, have evolved differences. Tree species that inhabit shady forests have larger acorns than shrub species from open, sunny chaparral. Presumably, larger acorns provide more food to light-starved seedlings as they grow beneath the overstory of mature trees. The form and function of any species are reflections of the conditions in its environment. The large number of California oak species is, therefore, a reflection of the large number of California environments to which they have become adapted through time and across the changing landscape.

We can begin to understand the distribution of oaks and oak landscapes in California by examining how they are affected by factors in their natural environment. Physical factors, such as climate, soil,

fire, and light affect how an oak grows and reproduces. Individual oak species may differ in their responses to these factors, revealing differences in their autecology (self-ecology). Oaks are also affected by biological factors, such as the animals and other plants that occur in the same landscape. When considered together, oaks and other associated species form an oak community. Oak communities reflect the many kinds of interactions between their component species, including competition, herbivory, and predation. Because particular oak communities will differ in their species composition and interactions, they also have differences in their synecology (together-ecology). The term "oak landscape" is used to describe a broad panorama of communities in a geographic region, one or more of which is dominated by native oaks.

This chapter is about the ecology of oak species and oak communities. First, the autecology of oaks is examined with respect to climate, soil, fire, and light. Then, the synecology of oak communities is reviewed, emphasizing relationships between the oaks and their most commonly associated plant species. Chapter Three broadens the discussion of communities to include animals and their ecological relationships with California's oaks.

The Ecology of Oak Species

Climate

California has many climates. Some are temperate or even polar, while others nearly subtropical. The multitude of California climates is a product of a rich geography, one in which latitude, topography, and distance from the ocean influence the distribution and abundance of plant and animal life.

Although oaks are widely observed throughout this climatically complex state, they are usually found in regions that receive at least 10 to 15 inches of precipitation per year and where the annual average temperature is 57°F to 65°F. Cities such as Sacramento, Fresno, Salinas, Santa Barbara, Los Angeles, and San Diego lie in such a climate zone. Temperature appears to be less influential than rainfall in determining oak distributions. If soil moisture is available during the summer, the oaks can frequently experience temperatures exceeding 100°F without apparent damage. Evergreen oaks tend to be tolerant of temperatures below freezing, while winter-deciduous species avoid frost damage

Snow-dusted coast live oak in a southern mixed ever-green forest, Cuyamaca Peak. CHRISTOPHER TALBOT FRANK

Valley oaks thrive in the rich, moist soil of this Sierra foothill meadow, Amador County. DANIEL D'AGOSTINI

by dropping their leaves and enclosing their sensitive growing points within protective buds.

Perhaps of greater importance than annual averages of precipitation and temperature are relative seasonal patterns of weather. In California, nearly all of the yearly precipitation comes during winter and early spring; little or no rain occurs in summer and early fall. This type of climate, with cool, wet winters and hot, dry summers, is called Mediterranean and is strongly associated with oaks, both here and in the Old World.

For many plants, the harsh ecological reality of Mediterranean climates is that water is least available when it is needed most. Most annual plants avoid this problem by germinating and developing during the cool, wet winter and then flowering and dying before the onset of summer drought. Oaks and other perennials, however, survive the many summers of their lives by virtue of their specialized roots, stems, and leaves.

The structure and depth of oak root systems varies for different species and habitats. Valley oak, for example, is most often found in riparian areas with shallow water tables or in bottomlands with deep, moist, alluvial soils. A young valley oak has an unbranched tap root that can reach down 50 or 60 feet to find groundwater. As the tree matures, it develops a tiered system equipped with feeder roots that permeate each layer in the soil profile. Such a system allows the valley oak to avoid—rather than endure—drought because it is likely to find an ample supply of water during the driest years. Scrub oak, by contrast, thrives in upland areas of chaparral that lack deep soils. Growing only three to nine feet tall, a scrub oak may send its roots 25 feet deep, allowing it to effectively compete with other chaparral shrubs for small amounts of moisture. Unlike valley oak, it seldom reaches a steady supply of groundwater and must possess other stem and leaf characteristics in order to withstand aridity. Desert scrub oak, another evergreen species of the chaparral, has a dual root system: a deep tap root for obtaining groundwater and a shallow mat of feeder roots for absorbing water from the uppermost soil layer after a light rain. These kinds of root systems enable both evergreen and deciduous oaks to avoid stress and sustain photosynthesis when there has been little or no precipitation for months.

Even with an extensive root system, the oaks of Mediterranean climates must overcome tremendous forces that could damage their woody, water-conducting tissues. The evaporative power of a dry summer sky literally sucks water out of the soil through the tissues of the living plant. Vessels that conduct water in stems and roots must be able

Lichens on Oaks

LICHENS FLOURISH IN MANY OAK COMMUNITIES, where they embellish trees and rocks with their rich, colorful textures. The checked and fissured bark of large old oaks is an especially favorable substrate for lichens. These rough surfaces are readily colonized by lichen spores or fragments, and they provide a relatively stable location for their development.

A lichen grows and functions much like an individual plant, but it is actually composed of two separate organisms: a fungus and an alga. Together they thrive in a mutually beneficial and interdependent relationship that most scientists describe as symbiotic. Lichens are not parasitic. The algal partner acquires carbohydrates by conducting photosynthesis while the fungal partner absorbs water and minerals. The fungal cells also form the main body of the lichen. They protect the algal cells from desiccation during California's dry season when the fungus cannot take in enough moisture and the lichen becomes dormant.

Fishnet lichen (a foliose type) drapes a valley oak in Sonoma County.
DAVID CAVAGNARO

Lichens are separated into three groups based on their shapes: fruticose, foliose, and crustose. Fruticose lichens are shrubby or hair-like, foliose lichens resemble leaves, and crustose lichens appear flat and crusty. Two of the more common oak-associated species are fishnet lichen (fruticose) and lungwort (foliose). Both are widespread in relatively moist oak communities, such as northern mixed evergreen forest, Oregon oak woodland, and coast live oak riparian forest.

to withstand great internal tensions, just as a drinking straw must withstand the vacuum created by a child enjoying a thick malted milk. As summer drought progresses, newly formed oak vessels become progressively thicker, harder, and more compact, decreasing the likelihood of collapse as roots withdraw the last droplets of soil-bound moisture. Weak or collapsed vessels are invaded by adjacent living cells of the wood, called tyloses, which seal off the damaged sector.

The leaves of California oaks are of three kinds—evergreen, winter deciduous, and drought deciduous—and each exhibits different abilities with respect to Mediterranean drought. Evergreen leaves, such as those of canyon, coast live, and scrub oak, are tough and leathery and able to resist wilting during summer drought. Their outside surfaces are coated with a thick, waxy cuticle that minimizes uncontrolled water loss. Stomata on the leaf surface, which allow carbon dioxide to enter for photosynthesis and water vapor to escape, can shut rapidly in response to midday or seasonal aridity. The leaves of winter-deciduous oaks, however, are unable to tolerate high internal tensions. The cuticle is relatively thin and stomata are not as tightly regulated when the supply of water becomes limited. These features are typical of black, Oregon, and valley oak, species which occupy relatively moist environments (e.g. higher elevations, northern latitudes, riparian zones, deep soils) where intense, long-term drought is less common. The drought-deciduous leaves of blue and Engelmann oak have many of the drought-tolerant features of evergreen leaves but may be shed in late summer or fall to prevent further desiccation of the woody tissues.

Soil

California is a complex geologic mosaic. Its bedrock foundation comprises rock of all possible origins, chemistries, and physical properties. The rocks weather into many kinds of substrates for plant growth and are further transformed by microorganisms, roots, and burrowing animals. Some of the substrates are deep, well-developed soils while others are simply unconsolidated piles of sand or gravel. California oaks are found on a wide variety of substrates, from rich loams in the valleys to thin, rocky veneers in the mountain uplands.

Valley oak thrives in deep, nutrient-laden sediments that have been carried to the lowlands by swollen spring rivers. Over the centuries, unbridled floods filled the Sacramento, San Joaquin, Salinas, Santa Clara, San Fernando, and other valleys with thick layers of fine sand and clay that formed a loose, loamy soil. When combined with a shallow water table, these alluvial soils can sustain a riparian forest rivaling tropical rainforest in terms of canopy architecture and plant productivity. The plentiful supplies of soil-borne water, nitrogen, and phosphorous allow deciduous leaves to achieve high rates of photosynthesis, which in turn supports the rapid growth of individual trees. Some bottomland soils are prone to flooding, and in years of high rainfall, valley oaks may have to tolerate weeks of low oxygen availability in the root zone. Remnants of California's once extensive riparian forests now exist alongside levied farmlands, where orchards and row crops now thrive in the deep, rich alluvium.

In contrast to valley oak, canyon oak is commonly found among the boulders and rubble of steep mountain canyons where there is almost no soil development. Lacking fine sand and clay particles, many upland substrates have very little capacity for storing water and dissolved minerals. Although some winter rain trickles down into the deep rock crevices, it is not retained for long against the constant pull of gravity. In this harsh soil environment, canyon oak must tolerate extreme summer drought and year-round shortages of critical nutrients. Possessing evergreen leaves is essential under these conditions because they are very drought tolerant; the leaves also remain active for two or more years, which enables them to utilize scarce mineral nutrients for several growing seasons. Nevertheless, growth is slow and sometimes results in a shrubby form. Although canyon oak grows well in the developed soils of foothills and valleys, its ability to tolerate a rocky, poor substrate confers another advantage—refuge from intense fires that rage in adjacent, denser vegetation.

Certain California oaks are also tolerant of soils with unusual chemical characteristics. At mid-elevations of the Sierra Nevada, black and huckleberry oak grow on granitic soil that has been acidified by the decomposing leaf litter of associated conifers. Acid soils are often nutrient-poor and colonized by fungi, some of which can cause disease in oak roots and stems. At other locations, especially in the Coast Ranges of Central and Northern California, a few specialized oaks can be found

A moss-covered blue oak grows amid ridgetop outcrops in Fremont Peak State Park. CARR CLIFTON

growing on soils derived from a bizarre mineral called serpentine. Serpentine, which is usually slick and green-colored as a rock, weathers into coarse, infertile, brick-red soil. These soils are low in calcium, nitrogen, and phosphorous, and high in magnesium and several toxic metals, such as nickel and chromium. Among the relatively few plant species that are able to grow and reproduce on soils derived from serpentine are leather oak and locally adapted populations of huckleberry, Oregon, and deer oak. Although we do not yet understand how plants have evolved tolerance mechanisms for serpentine soils, we do know that tolerant species can escape from competitors that aggressively dominate adjacent, non-serpentine areas.

Local, often patchy variations in the soil environment commonly determine the shape and stature of individual oaks and, therefore, the structure and appearance of oak communities. Coast live oak attains its most impressive size on deep alluvium at the mouths of canyons that drain into the sea. These rich soils overlay the broad, uplifted terraces of coastal valleys such as the Russian River, Santa Clara, Salinas, Santa Ynez, and Santa Ana. The live oak woodlands of the Santa Barbara plain and the massive trees of Mission Canyon are typical of this species at its best. Coast live oak also grows on rolling hills formed from ancient coastal sand dunes. Such porous soils, however, are lower in nutrients and retain little moisture during summer. As a result, oak woodlands occur here as clumps of small trees separated by large patches of open grassland. On steep, rocky slopes above the coastal plain where there is little or no soil, coast live oak may be stunted and gnarled; here, the tree's deep roots must penetrate bedrock fissures to tap hidden seeps. If the hillsides are composed of serpentine, coast live oak may be entirely absent, despite the occurrence of favorable climate and topography. In this way, the swirling textures and colors of an oak landscape often reflect the hidden, underlying patterns of the soil environment.

Fire

Mediterranean climates are fire-prone climates. The coincidence of drought and high temperature produces ideal conditions for the spread of natural and human-set fires. Oaks that occur in savanna, woodland, and chaparral are likely to experience major fires every 30 to 50 years. In forests, major fires occur less often, with perhaps a 40 to 100 year cycle. Such conditions have existed for millennia. Furthermore, human-set fires have been a factor in the ecology of California oaks for at least 12,000 years, as Indians used them to improve plant growth for themselves and for game animals. Most oak species have thus been selected over evolutionary time to tolerate fire. In fact, fire is now viewed as an essential link between the oaks and their landscape, with beneficial as well as deleterious effects. In general, low intensity, rather infrequent fires tend to be beneficial to California oaks, especially the more resilient evergreen species.

Low-intensity fires quickly sweep across a savanna or woodland and generate relatively modest amounts of heat for a short period of time. Following a low-intensity fire, the seedlings and saplings of all oak species are capable of sending up new shoots from their buried root crowns; this type

Top: Rock outcrops are surrounded by oak woodlands in Diablo Foothill Regional Park. BOB WALKER
Bottom: Sprouts cover the limbs of this coast live oak, nine months after it burned in a wildfire. JOHN EVARTS

of growth is called "crown sprouting." In fire's aftermath, growth is vigorous, especially from the crowns of larger roots, because fire improves several key factors in the oak's environment. Plants that would compete with seedlings or saplings for water are reduced in abundance. Mineral nutrients become more available as rainwater leaches them from charred wood and ashes. Foliage-eating caterpillars, stem-girdling beetles, and bud-infesting fungi are eliminated, at least temporarily.

Mature oaks, which are rarely killed by low-intensity fires, are most vulnerable to fire around the base of their trunks. Species such as coast live,

A fast-moving summer wildfire burns through coast live oak woodland in the Santa Ynez Valley. DAVID STOCKTON

Engelmann, and valley oak have thick bark that insulates sensitive trunk tissues from short bursts of fire. If those tissues survive the passing of the flames, then dormant buds on the remaining branches can "stump sprout" and replace the once-leafy canopy. A large amount of food stored in an old oak's root system is quickly mobilized to produce new branchlets and foliage.

Fires that rage through dense chaparral and forest communities can be of such high intensity that entire shoots of trees and shrubs are incinerated beyond any prospect of recovery. The possession of thick bark is meaningless under such circumstances. Instead, coast live, scrub, canyon, and interior live oaks also maintain a large reserve of dormant buds on their root crowns. Insulated by the soil from lethal quantities of heat, the buds sprout within weeks and produce new stems and leaves below the base of the old, charred trunks. These crown-sprouting species take immediate advantage of the open, sunlit, competition-free landscape that follows the most catastrophic of fires. A profusion of new, ground-level herbage provides improved browse for wildlife.

Light

Light is of paramount importance to all plants, including oaks. Its intensity, quality, and duration affect many important life processes, especially photosynthesis. In general, all parts of California receive a similar dose of the sun's radiant energy; fog, clouds, and haze do not significantly reduce the light available to oaks for photosynthesis over long periods of time. The distribution of oaks on a large geographic scale is therefore linked to climate, soil, and fire, rather than light.

On a local scale, however, oaks can be greatly affected by the amount of available light. For example, a mature black oak growing beneath tall conifers is exposed to low levels of light that reduce photosynthesis. Some of its branches may extend up to sunlit areas in the overstory, changing the shape of the tree and providing more food in the process. For seedlings, light conditions are especially challenging on the forest floor where they must contend with heavy shade cast by overstory trees and understory shrubs. With fewer limbs and a longer way to grow before encountering a gap in the overstory, seedlings often have

A valley oak seedling develops from an acorn that was nestled in the leaf litter beneath its parent tree. DAN SUZIO

very low rates of growth. Sluggish growth can put a plant at great competitive disadvantage, since water, nutrients, and light will be less available to small, spindly, or slow-growing individuals. Death from light "starvation" would be a common fate of many oak seedlings if acclimation to deep shade did not occur.

The ability of oaks to acclimate to shade is well known to plant scientists. Coast live oak, for example, adjusts its canopy architecture and leaf anatomy in response to the local light environment. (This is discussed on page 25.) Shade leaves make physiological adjustments that allow them to conduct photosynthesis in low light conditions that would starve sun-acclimated leaves. Shade acclimation allows a seedling to grow and maintain its competitive ability until it reaches a bright, sunlit patch in the canopy. At that point, all of the leaves produced in the opening will have the characteristics of sun-acclimated leaves; equipped to utilize higher-intensity light, the sun leaves manufacture more food for the tree and thereby support higher rates of growth.

Although detailed data are lacking, it is likely that the leaves of most California oaks are capable of responding to a wide range of light availability. This is important because shady overstories occur in most oak-dominated communities, including woodlands and chaparrals. Moreover, the north-facing and interior portions of a mature oak can be in perpetual shade, even though the tree itself may stand alone on the edge of a savanna. It would not be surprising to find shade-acclimated leaves on blue, Engelmann, and other oaks that typically grow in more open, sunlit communities.

The Ecology of Oak Communities

The physical elements of an oak environment—climate, soil, fire, and light—are not the only factors which determine the presence of oaks in a landscape. Biological elements, that is, other kinds of plants and animals that share the community, are also of great importance. For example, non-native grasses successfully compete with young oak seedlings for soil water and thereby inhibit oak reproduction even though the total rainfall might otherwise be adequate. Certain species of soil-borne fungi attack oak roots as fatal diseases while others beneficially transfer soil nutrients to roots and thus promote tree growth. Gray squirrels and scrub jays are at the same time voracious predators, wide-ranging dispersers, and inadvertent planters of acorns. Bears and deer eat bark from around the main trunk and can kill well-established trees. These kinds of interactions have profound effects on the birth, growth, and death of oaks—processes that determine the size and long-term success of oak populations within the community.

Across California, oak communities vary greatly in their species composition and, therefore, in their structure and appearance. Ecologists have identified 68 different kinds of oak-containing communities in the state. Some of these communities are low, scrubby types of chaparral while others are tall, majestic forests. In 31 of the 68 communities, at least one oak species is so well represented in terms of numerical abundance, canopy coverage, or total photosynthesis that it is said to be dominant or characteristic within that particular community. Scrub oak, for example, is dominant in at least three types of chaparral communities. In each one of these, however, there is a different set of co-occurring plant species. Those species have different heights, growth rates, response to fire, and other features which distinguish one scrub oak community from another. Animals perceive these differences in terms of food supply, nesting sites, and predator cover and respond according to their own ecological requirements.

We will not be able to consider all of the known variations in California oak communities. Instead, we examine those which are the most wide-spread and characteristic, as if on a grand tour of the state. The tour will sweep over three major California landscapes, each with four to six oak-dominated communities. We begin with the coastal ranges and plains, cross to the Great Central Valley and its foothills, and end high on the slopes of California's interior mountains.

Coastal Ranges and Plains

The natural communities along California's immediate shore are not dominated by oaks. The beaches, dunes, wetlands, coastal coniferous forests, and bluff-edge prairies that cover the westernmost edge of the land are constantly exposed to wind, waves, and sea spray. Such harsh conditions are tolerated only by ecological specialists that possess unique structures or physiologies for coping with these kinds of stresses. Oaks have different tolerance mechanisms, such as those related to drought, that are not suited to conditions along the immediate coast.

Behind the dunes and above the wetlands, however, oak communities are an important feature of the coastal landscape. They experience a pronounced Mediterranean climate that is moderated by the ocean's proximity. As a result, winter temperatures seldom drop below freezing, and summer heat is tempered by fog and onshore breezes. In many coastal areas, especially in the central and northern parts of California, fog contributes significant amounts of moisture to the soil as it condenses and drips from vegetation.

Northern Mixed Evergreen Forest

In the North Coast Ranges, forests of redwood and Douglas fir are found near the ocean and at relatively low elevations. Where steep slopes rise above and to the east of these foggy, needle-leaved forests, a broad-leaved forest with oaks becomes prevalent. Comprising a rich assemblage of evergreen hardwood tree species, this community is generally referred to as mixed evergreen forest. Where it includes canyon oak, interior live oak, and tanbark, along with madrone, giant chinquapin, and bay laurel, the community is named northern mixed

evergreen forest. Although the dominant trees tend to have thick, leathery, evergreen leaves, there are also deciduous species with thin, soft leaves, such as Oregon oak, black oak, and bigleaf maple. Conifers are present but not abundant in this forest; towards the ocean, moisture-loving redwood and Douglas fir start to dominate, while the inland margins are invaded by ponderosa, sugar, and knobcone pine.

Northern mixed evergreen forest is a tall, dense community with few shrubs or low-growing herbs. Where the soil is deep and remains moist throughout the spring, no single tree species dominates the overstory canopy. Canyon oak, interior live oak, Douglas fir, madrone, tanbark, and

Top: Oak landscapes in the Coast Ranges southeast of Mt. Diablo, Contra Costa County. BOB WALKER
Bottom: Deer near oak woodland at dusk. PAT O'HARA.

Mist shrouds the vegetation in a northern mixed evergreen forest, Point Reyes National Seashore. FRANK BALTHIS

bay laurel contribute equally to the structure of the community. The bases of their massive trunks are often covered with bright-green mosses and lichens, living indicators of the wet, often foggy climate. Although the community's dominant hardwoods are capable of stump-sprouting, wildfire is not a common event in northern mixed evergreen forest. Thick accumulations of leaf litter and duff hold dampness to the soil, and provide an ideal home for many types of salamanders and mushroom-producing fungi. In the steepest, rockiest canyons, northern mixed evergreen forest can be completely dominated by canyon oak, madrones, and several other associated trees. Lichens, mosses, and mushrooms are less abundant under these drier conditions. This form of the community extends east into portions of the Cascade Range and northern Sierra Nevada. Another variation of northern mixed evergreen forest extends south along the coast into the greater San Francisco Bay Area and contains coast live oak in areas with warmer temperatures and less rainfall.

Leather Oak Chaparral

Serpentine outcrops are a common geologic feature in many of California's foothill landscapes. Found in the Coast Ranges, Klamath Ranges, and Sierra Nevada, serpentine weathers into an infertile soil that is inhospitable to most conifers, oaks, and other plants. Where this rock occurs, the vegetation is

Leather oak chaparral near San Luis Obispo. J. EVARTS

composed of low, spartan patches of serpentine-tolerant plants. Among these is leather oak, the dominant shrub in leather oak chaparral.

Serpentine-tolerant shrubs, such as Congdon's silktassel, Jepson's ceanothus, and some species of manzanita, join leather oak to form a compact overstory that is only three or four feet tall. A few species of annual grasses and herbs may grow in the shade of the shrubs, but the soil surface is otherwise barren and even lacks leaf litter. Serpentine-tolerant trees, such as Sargent cypress, incense cedar, or gray pine, occasionally protrude from the chaparral. Unlike other chaparrals, this community is very slow to recover in the wake of fire because of the harsh conditions imposed by the soil.

Oregon Oak Woodland

The Klamath and inner North Coast ranges rise and extend east of the moist slopes that typically support northern mixed evergreen forest. Dense stands of fir and pine clothe the high ridges, interrupted by a woodland community of deciduous Oregon and black oak. This Oregon oak woodland is more open than the surrounding forest and supports an occasional incense cedar, ponderosa pine, or madrone in the overstory; the understory consists of a few scattered shrubs, such as snowberry and poison oak. It is a community that readily develops in the wake of fire or logging and can maintain itself to the exclusion of conifers when exposed to periodic, low-intensity burns. The moist leaves and thick bark of Oregon oak are fairly fire resistant, and black oak stump-sprouts profusely after being burned or cut.

Pure stands of Oregon oak, called "opens" or "oak balds," are often found on shallow, volcanic soils of plateaus and ridges within mid-elevation coniferous forests. Set against an evergreen backdrop, these ridgetop woodlands produce striking displays of autumn color when the clustered oak canopies turn a rusty brown. Oregon oak woodland also occurs at lower, drier elevations where the soil is relatively deep; here, the oaks often grow amid intervening carpets of perennial grasses and broad-leaved herbs.

Coast Live Oak Woodland

Toward the southern end of the North Coast Ranges, northern mixed evergreen forest and Oregon oak woodland gradually become restricted to higher elevations and moister, north-facing

Top: Fall mist swirls through an Oregon oak woodland near the Eel River. GALEN ROWELL/MOUNTAIN LIGHT
Bottom: Swaths of coast live oak woodland are clustered along drainages on slopes of the Santa Lucia Range, above Morro Bay. DAVID MUENCH

slopes. At lower elevations they are replaced by coast live oak woodland, especially on the deeper soils of the coastal plain. One the state's most widespread oak communities, this woodland extends south to Baja California and is well-developed in the South Coast and outer Transverse and Peninsular ranges.

Coast live oak is the dominant overstory tree in this woodland, and is often joined by valley and canyon oak in the inner Coast Ranges. North of Monterey Bay, where this community receives more precipitation, bay laurel usually contributes to the dense overstory. Farther to the south, coast live oak, buckeye, and bay laurel may be forced to cluster along drainages or in moist folds between the grass-covered hills. Tall shrubs, such as coyotebush, toyon, and coffeeberry form an occasional understory, while poison oak is ubiquitous. A wide variety of flowering herbs mix in sunny openings and margins. Fires often surge through these coastal woodlands, racing between trees where there is plenty of dry grass, but halting on shady barrens beneath the oldest oak canopies.

Engelmann Oak Woodland

Toward the interior of the Peninsular Ranges, in the low hills and mesas of western Riverside and San Diego counties, there exists an oak community restricted to a small area of Southern California: Engelmann oak woodland. Where Engelmann oak grows on shallow soils, it is accompanied by an understory of aromatic shrubs, including white sage, buckwheat, and sagebrush. In valleys and mesas with deeper soils, the understory consists of introduced annuals, such as oats, barley, filaree, and native plants, such as lupine, California poppy, and purple needlegrass. Sometimes the oak overstory is so open and spacious that an Engelmann oak savanna is formed.

Engelmann oak may account for 90% of all trees in this distinctive woodland community, especially if the soil is a deep, loamy clay. Areas of deep soil with rocky outcrops, however, support an even mixture of Engelmann and coast live oak. Evidently, the soil along the shady north-facing sides of the outcrops supplies the essential extra moisture required by coast live oak acorns for germination and establishment. Of equal importance, however, is that many acorns are dispersed to these favorable sites by ground squirrels, which are attracted to the rocky habitat. Seedling survival of both oak species is enhanced in these areas because cattle and deer prefer a firm, even footing and are deterred from grazing among the outcrops. Due to the impacts of urbanization, agricultural conversion, and livestock grazing, Engelmann oak woodland is one of the most endangered natural communities in California.

Scrub Oak Chaparral

Where the soil is shallow, especially on steep hillsides and ridges, coast live oak woodland is replaced by a scrub oak chaparral. This community of evergreen, drought-tolerant shrubs is widespread in the South Coast, Transverse, and Peninsular ranges. Many different shrubs contribute to this chaparral in which scrub oak and the shrubby form of interior live oak are prominent. Associate species

Above: Annual grasses flourish beneath Engelmann oaks at Mesa Grande, San Diego County. BILL EVARTS
Right: Scrub oak chaparral covers a north-facing slope in Los Peñasquitos Canyon, San Diego. BILL EVARTS

include toyon, ceanothus, chamise, manzanita, and laurel sumac; they often join the oaks in forming an impenetrable wall of stiff stems and leathery leaves.

In the absence of fire, shrub development is slow and few herbs grow in the chaparral's accumulations of leaf litter and duff. Following a fire, however, the oaks and other shrubs vigorously crown-sprout to produce the next woody canopy. After the first winter storms, a carpet of herbs erupts from long-dormant seeds; they flower profusely, sending new seeds back to the soil to await the next fiery episode in the life of this community.

The Great Central Valley

Crossing the last interior ridges of the Coast Ranges, the eastbound traveler arrives at the edge of a seemingly endless basin—the Great Central Valley. Drained by the Sacramento River in the north and the San Joaquin River in the south, the valley is more than 400 miles long and 50 miles wide. It includes the entire central basin and the surrounding foothills of the Coast Ranges and Sierra Nevada.

The valley's climate is extreme when compared with that of the coast; it is hot and dry from April to October, cold and wet from November to March. Scorching winds draw out the moisture held within plants and soils during summer and fall. Tule fog settles in the floodplains and depressions during winter, saturating the landscape with a cold gray mist. The spring season is soothing and pleasant, but this too depends on the year-to-year vagaries of weather. The underground environment is equally diverse. Riparian soils are light and deep, while foothill soils tend to be dense clay, layered just above the bedrock. Despite the variable nature of its climate and soils, the Great Central Valley's lowlands and foothills are dominated by oak communities set among vast grasslands and agricultural fields.

Valley Oak Riparian Forest

Magnificent remnants of valley oak riparian forest border some of the last unchannelized rivers and freshwater basins of the Great Central Valley. Although this community was once widespread in riparian areas, only a handful of isolated examples exist today. This forest has the most complex structure of any vegetation type in California and, as a result, is among the most diverse in terms of animal life.

In areas where the water table is 30 to 40

Majestic oaks form a dense canopy above this trail through valley oak riparian forest at the Cosumnes River Preserve, Sacramento County. MARY ANN GRIGGS

feet deep, valley oaks form a majestic overstory that often includes sycamores. The tangle of their massive limbs in the upper canopy is revealed in fall when leaves turn dull yellow, wither, and are released to the dry wind. An understory of deciduous trees gathers beneath the giants, including black walnut, Oregon ash, and box elder. Tall shrubs, such as wild rose, California blackberry, poison oak, and willow form an impenetrable understory. There is also an herbaceous layer of nettles, grasses, and sedges where a few bright patches of sun manage to infiltrate the dense superstructure of leaves. Lianas of wild grape transcend all of the canopy layers, extending from forest floor to ceiling and back again.

Close to the river, where the water table is only 5 to 20 feet deep, the overstory of valley oak and sycamore is often replaced by cottonwood and alder, but species in the other canopy layers remain. On long summer days, the trees literally breathe the river's water into the balmy, warm air. Such lush, humid conditions retard the frequency and intensity of fires, allowing trees to reach great ages and forest architecture to be stable over long periods of time.

Valley Oak Woodland

In a few places beyond the riparian forest, valley oak woodland rises like a Gothic cathedral on rich floodplain and low foothill soils. Here the ashen trunks of valley oak, some six to eight feet across, are steadfast buttresses with a maximum age of about 500 years. A typical trunk culminates in a capitol of branches, each the size of a lesser tree. The limbs ascend 100 or more feet to form a vaulted canopy above a living mosaic of grasses and herbs. These woodlands were once a common feature of the Great Central Valley landscape. Near Cache Creek, in what is now Yolo County, a member of the 1854 railroad survey party wrote:

> The timber belt is composed of the most magnificent oaks I have ever seen. They are not crowded as in our forests, but grow scattered about in groups or singly, with open grass-covered glades between them. . . .There is no undergrowth beneath them, and as far as the eye can reach, when standing among them, an unending series of great trunks is seen rising from the lawn-like surface.

Although valley oak woodland still occurs in the Great Central Valley, the best examples of this community are now found in the inner Coast Ranges and several of the Transverse Ranges. Near its northern limit, in Mendocino County, valley oak woodland may be mixed with elements of Oregon oak woodland; to the south, in Los Angeles County, it blends with coast live oak woodland in the San Fernando Valley, Santa Clarita Valley, and Santa Monica Mountains. Superb stands extend up into the lower montane zones of the Santa Lucia Range in Monterey County and the Tehachapi Mountains in Kern and Los Angeles counties.

Woodlands of valley oak, such as this site in Sacramento County, once covered vast acreages in the Central Valley. WILLIAM M. SMITHEY, JR.

Blue Oak Savanna

A "halo" of foothill savannas and woodlands circles the Great Central Valley between 500 and 3,000 feet. Where soils are well-developed, the lower margins of this halo may consist of valley oak woodland broken by ribbons of riparian forest; otherwise, the low foothills rimming the valley are covered by a blue oak savanna that grades upslope into blue oak woodland. The inner Coast Ranges also contain well-developed blue oak savannas and woodlands, such as those seen in the Russian River Valley in the north and the upper Salinas Valley in the south.

Blue oak savanna is most common on low hillocks and exposed, south-facing slopes. Where the soil is shallow and punctured by bedrock outcrops, an occasional buckeye or interior live oak may join blue oak in the open overstory. The trees are scattered in a sea of grasses and spring wildflowers, with few or no shrubs growing in between. Probably the driest and hottest of all

*Above: December sun streams into a blue oak wood-
land in the Sierra foothills, Butte County.* JEFF GNASS
*Right: Blue oak savanna rims the Central Valley floor
at Dye Creek Preserve, Tehama County.* GEORGE STROUD

tree-dominated communities in California, blue oak
savanna is a drought-deciduous indicator of the
year's climate. If winter rains are plentiful, blue oaks
appear in summer as leafy, steel-green canopies,
surrounded by the yellow straw of desiccated
grasses and forbs. But following relatively dry
winters, blue oaks shed many of their leaves by
summer's end.

Blue Oak Woodland

Moving upslope from the undulating savanna,
other tree species are able to join the foothill
landscape and create a more continuous overstory
canopy. Where there is additional rainfall, or cool
north-facing slopes are present, blue oak savanna
makes a gradual transition to blue oak woodland.
Blue oak remains dominant, but the community is
more dense and structurally complex. Throughout
this woodland, the wispy, irregular canopies of gray
pine jut above the dense, round canopies of blue
oak. Interior live oak is another common associate,
especially in the northern and central periphery of
the Great Central Valley. At its highest reaches, this
foothill woodland may also include canyon oak.

In the Tehachapi Mountains and inner South Coast
Ranges, juniper may also be present.

A great variety of shrubs are present in blue
oak woodland. Many species extend downslope
from adjacent chaparral and ponderosa pine
communities, contributing to a scattered understory that includes whiteleaf manzanita, redbud,
coffeeberry, poison oak, and several species of
ceanothus. Annual grasses and wildflowers occur
in discontinuous patches among the shrubs and
trees. As the complexity of the foothill community
increases from savanna to woodland, so does the
diversity of animal life. Overall, the variety of
animals in blue oak savanna and woodland is higher
than in adjacent grasslands or coniferous forests.

Wildflowers
of Oak Landscapes

THE BEAUTY OF THE CALIFORNIA FLORA IS OFTEN EXPRESSED among the oaks. More than 1,400 species of native flowering plants are associated with the lowland forests, woodlands, savannas, and chaparrals of the California Floristic Province—that portion of the state which lies west of the Cascade, Sierra Nevada, and Peninsular ranges. Almost half of these species are herbs with an annual life history. Annual herbs, such as California poppy and Chinese houses, germinate, grow, flower, set seed, and die during the winter and spring. These two species, which are geographically widespread, frequently contribute to valley oak woodland and blue oak savanna. Perennial herbs also abound in oak landscapes, growing from long-lived bulbs and corms that lie beneath the soil surface. Pink globe lily thrives in the partial shade of blue oak woodland and the lower margins of Sierran forest. Some of the showiest and most persistent native wildflowers in the California Floristic Province belong to woody shrubs. Bush monkeyflower, fuchsia-flowered gooseberry, and purple nightshade are especially common in coast live oak woodland, scrub oak chaparral, and coast live oak riparian forest.

Top: California poppies. RON SANFORD
Above: Bush monkeyflower in Southern California. DEDE GILMAN

Chinese houses.
ROLAND AND KAREN
MUSCHENETZ

Purple nightshade. DEDE GILMAN

Fuchsia-flowered gooseberry. KAREN MUSCHENETZ

The High Mountains

California's high mountains form a nearly continuous chain of peaks, ridges, and upland river valleys extending from the Klamath and Cascade ranges near the Oregon border to the Peninsular Ranges in the extreme south, a distance of more than 750 miles. Abrupt changes in elevation cause these upland climates to contrast dramatically with lowland climates just a few miles away. The Mediterranean patterns so common below are not strictly applied at higher elevations; montane plants grow during the warm, mild summer and lie dormant during the cold, snow-bound winter. Upland soils are thin, porous, acidic, and as far as roots are concerned, bone dry during the freezing winters because water is immobilized in the form of ice. The tree oaks endure winter's bitter cold and. frozen soil and carry heavy loads of snow on barren branches. Shrub oaks with evergreen leaves may be able, upon occasion, to photosynthesize in winter when shallow snowpacks have been melted from their exposed, rocky habitats.

Oaks seldom dominate California's montane landscapes, where they grow as low shrubs or understory trees. They do, however, provide important food and cover resources for wildlife, protection for steep, erodible slopes, and an aesthetic complement to forests that John Muir called "the grandest and most beautiful in the world."

Northern Montane Forest

The high mountain forests of northwestern California are grand and beautiful, and they are also unique for several reasons. First of all, portions of the Klamath bedrock upon which the forests grow came from across the Pacific basin, having rafted on the Earth's crust for millions of years until colliding and fusing with the North American continent. Secondly, the forests are home to a diverse and unusual group of conifers, some of which are found in the Oregon Cascades or the distant Rocky Mountains but not the nearby Sierra Nevada. Finally, and of greatest importance here, is that these northern montane forests are the habitat of deer oak, a species unlike any other oak in western North America.

Northern montane forest has a diverse over-story of conifers: as many as 13 different and sometimes unusual species are found, including knobcone pine, Engelmann spruce, Port Orford cedar, and Alaska yellow cedar. Deer oak often forms a shrubby, evergreen understory that is best de-veloped beneath tall stands of red fir at about 5,000 feet. Canyon, black, and Oregon oak are common overstory associates in this community. On exposed slopes and ridges that are too sunny, hot, and dry for

Black oaks dominate this open woodland near the crest of the Laguna Mountains. BILL EVARTS

Top: Deer oak forms the understory of this northern montane forest in Trinity County. AL SENERES
Bottom: Acorns ripen on huckleberry oak in the high Sierra near the Mokelumne River. CHARLES KENNARD

tall conifers and oaks, deer oak and manzanita form a unique, high-elevation version of chaparral. Relatively little is known about the ecology of these montane communities as a result of their remote and often inaccessible locations.

Huckleberry Oak Chaparral

Just as scrub oak is a characteristic species in lowland chaparral, huckleberry oak distinguishes montane chaparral in the Sierra Nevada and Klamath Ranges. Huckleberry oak chaparral

typically grows among the granite boulders and glacier-polished slabs that interrupt mixed conifer forests. Low-growing huckleberry oak, along with greenleaf and pinemat manzanita, mountain whitethorn, and dwarf chinquapin, forms a dense tangle of woody stems and evergreen leaves. It maintains itself on sites usually too dry in summer or too windswept in winter to support the growth of trees.

Huckleberry oak chaparral also develops on sites with deeper soil where an avalanche, fire, or logging operation has destroyed the existing forest cover. Conifers do not readily establish themselves in disturbed areas that are exposed to intense sun and strong winds; huckleberry oak chaparral, however, tolerates such conditions and serves as an important stabilizer of slopes that would otherwise be eroded by winter runoff and summer thundershowers. Here, huckleberry oak and its associates are temporary residents, slowly giving way to pines and firs that grow up through the protective, shady tangle.

Sierran Mixed Conifer Forest

Although black oak is associated with woodland and forest communities throughout California, it probably reaches its best development on the western slopes of the Sierra Nevada, where it is a prominent member of Sierran mixed conifer forest. This community extends from about 2,500 feet, just above blue oak woodland, to around 6,500 feet. A rich mixture of pines and firs share the evergreen overstory, including ponderosa pine, sugar pine, white fir, incense cedar, and Douglas fir. Where soil moisture is ample, black oak is joined in a broad-leaved understory by hazelnut, dogwood, and bigleaf maple. This forest is especially colorful in fall when the deciduous species turn vivid shades of yellow, orange, and red.

Nearly pure stands of black oak are found in some areas. The trees often exhibit multiple trunks from stump-sprouting, and fire scars are common. The other broadleaf species usually present, such as madrone and canyon oak, are also good sprouters. A few scattered ponderosa, knobcone, or sugar pines may emerge from the canopy, but they are not dominant as in typical Sierran mixed conifer forest. Clearly, this black oak forest is a special kind of Sierran forest that is maintained by periodic fire. Prior to the establishment of strict fire suppression policies, such forests were common throughout the low elevations of the range.

Black oaks grow among ponderosa pines in this Sierran mixed conifer forest, Plumas County. CARR CLIFTON

Southern Mixed Evergreen Forest

At higher elevations in the mountains of Southern California, above the coast live oak woodlands, Engelmann oak woodlands, and scrub oak chaparral, another form of mixed evergreen forest is encountered. Southern mixed evergreen forest is generally found above 3,000 feet in the Transverse and Peninsular ranges. It is a dense vegetation that forms a transition zone to the montane forests of ponderosa pine, incense cedar, and sugar pine. Broadleaf evergreen trees are dominant, but deciduous hardwoods and lowland conifers can also be abundant.

Canyon oak is the most common tree in southern mixed evergreen forest, especially on drier slopes adjacent to chaparral or the upper reaches of coast live oak woodland. Depending on proximity to the ocean, coast live or interior live oak share dominance with canyon oak. The winter-deciduous black oak may also be a member of this community, but mostly on cooler, moister slopes at higher elevations. Madrone, bay laurel, and tanbark, so common in northern mixed evergreen forest, are rare or absent in the southern mixed evergreen forest. Coulter pine and bigcone spruce add their canopies to the overstory. The understory is usually an open, shrub-dominated layer, comprising species which extend upslope from the chaparral such as manzanita, buckbrush, and mountain mahogany.

Compared to northern mixed evergreen forest, this community records lower precipitation and higher temperatures; wildfires burn hotter and occur with greater frequency. Dense thickets of sprouted oaks may form in the aftermath of repeated fires, which transform the forest cover over wide areas. Although Coulter pine and bigcone spruce are better adapted to fire than many other conifers, they may be replaced by overstory oaks and understory chaparral shrubs in landscapes that regularly experience fires.

A large coast live oak shades this hiking trail through southern mixed evergreen forest near Pine Valley Creek, Cleveland National Forest. JERRY SCHAD

Fungi Among the Oaks

Fungi play a prominent role in the life and death of California oaks and fill several important niches within oak communities. Some fungi are highly beneficial to oaks, whereas others are extremely destructive. In fact, fungi are probably the most important agents involved in the natural decline and death of mature oaks in undisturbed woodlands.

Fungi are a diverse group of mostly microscopic organisms, somewhat similar in structure to algae and other primitive plants. Unlike plants, which produce their own food through photosynthesis, fungi obtain their food by absorbing it from living or dead organisms and organic matter. The fungal body, or mycelium, is made up of many interconnecting filaments known as hyphae. The hyphae grow through their food supply, secreting enzymes that break down larger organic molecules into smaller molecules which are then absorbed as food. The mushrooms that are commonly seen in oak woodlands during the wet months are especially large spore-bearing structures known as fruiting bodies. Although most mushrooms are ephemeral, the mycelium they arise from may live for decades within the soil or wood of living or dead oaks.

Mycorrhizal fungi form a symbiotic or mutually beneficial relationship with many plant species, including oaks. These fungi colonize living oak roots, forming mycorrhizae (literally "fungus-roots") and extracting food from the host roots. In return, mycorrhizal fungi absorb essential mineral nutrients, particularly phosphorus, and transport them to the root for use by the host plant. These fungi also protect their host roots against various diseases. A wide variety of fungi can form mycorrhizal associations with oaks, and many of the mushrooms that pop up throughout the oak woodlands during the winter and spring months belong to these mycorrhizal species.

Pathogenic or disease-causing fungi also colonize the tissues of living oaks, but the relationship is decidedly detrimental to the tree. Nearly 200 species of fungi are known to cause disease in California oaks. Different fungi attack virtually every part of the oak, from leaves and acorns to the woody stems and roots. Relatively few of these fungi, however, seriously damage or actually kill established oaks. Powdery mildews, for example, obtain their food by parasitizing living cells; since these pathogens rely on living

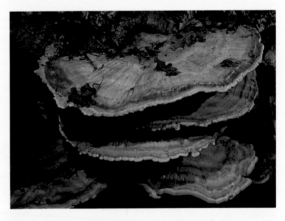

Above: This shelf fungus on a valley oak is a pathogen that causes heart rot in oaks. BILL FILSINGER
Top left: Jack-O-Lantern fungus grows on an Oregon oak, Sonoma County. DAVID CAVAGNARO

host tissues for their own existence, the damage they cause is usually minor. Other oak pathogens, ranging from relatively benign leaf-spotting fungi to highly destructive wood-decay fungi, kill host tissues in the process of breaking them down.

Infecting the host tree through fire scars, broken branches, and other wounds, a number of fungi decay wood in the branches, trunks, and roots of living oaks. In California, species of the fungal genera *Inonotus*, *Ganoderma*, and *Laetiporus* are among the most widespread fungi that cause the collapse and death of mature oaks. Many of these fungi form bracket- or sheet-like fruiting bodies that emerge from beneath the bark or the exposed wood of old wounds. These fruiting bodies sometimes arise only after the passage of many years; by then decay is quite extensive or the tree has already died.

Like other trees, oaks defend themselves from wood-decaying fungi by forming barriers of live and dead wood cells. If the invading fungus is able to breach these defenses, the oak responds with new barriers. This battle between host and pathogen may continue for years or decades. Oak limbs are lost in the fight, and as time goes on, opportunistic insects and other pathogens join in the fray against an increasingly craggy and enfeebled tree. The oak's slow decline is reflected in the observation that oaks seem to "live for about a hundred years, and then die for a hundred years." To the casual observer, it may seem that ancient oaks simply die of old age, but this is not the case. More often than not, the relentless attack of decay fungi is ultimately responsible for conquering the mighty oak.

Death does not end the relationship between oaks and fungi. The saprophytic fungi make their living by decaying dead oaks and oak cast-offs such as leaves, twigs, branches, and acorns. These fungi are the recyclers of the oak communities, breaking down dead oak tissues and other organic materials and releasing their mineral nutrients. In this way, fungi complete the nutrient cycle and help perpetuate the life of the oak community.

—Tedmund J. Swiecki

Top: The mycelium (visible here as white filaments) of a fungus help decompose the leaf litter in this coast live oak woodland. LARRY JON FRIESEN
Bottom: Oak conk, coast live oak stump. DEDE GILMAN

CHARACTERISTIC OAK COMMUNITIES OF CALIFORNIA

This table summarizes the distribution and ecological features of 18 natural communities dominated by California oaks. The oak communities summarized in this table are described in the text of this chapter, except for Coast Live Oak Riparian Forest, Semi-Desert Chaparral, Island Oak Woodland, and Engelmann Oak Savanna. The table is based on the work of Dr. Robert Holland (1986).

OAK COMMUNITIES AND OAK SPECIES [Secondary oak species in brackets]	CALIFORNIA GEOGRAPHIC REGION	VEGETATION TYPE AND ITS TYPICAL LANDFORMS	ASSOCIATED HARDWOODS AND CONIFERS
FOREST COMMUNITIES			
Valley Oak Riparian Forest: valley [and interior live oak]	central: Great Central Valley and inner Coast Ranges	riparian: valley bottoms	box elder, black walnut, sycamore, sandbar willow, cottonwood, Oregon ash
Coast Live Oak Riparian Forest: coast live [and canyon oak]	central, southwestern: Coast, Transverse, and Peninsular ranges		bigleaf maple, bay laurel, sycamore
Northern Mixed Evergreen Forest: canyon, interior live, [coast live, black, and Oregon oak]	northern: Klamath and North Coast ranges	mixed evergreen: upland slopes	madrone, tanbark, bay laurel, bigleaf maple, chinquapin, Douglas fir, redwood
Southern Mixed Evergreen Forest: canyon, coast live, [interior live, and black oak]	southwestern: Transverse and Peninsular ranges		bay laurel, bigcone spruce, Coulter pine, Jeffrey pine
Northern Montane Forest: canyon, black, deer, [Oregon, and interior live oak]	northwestern: Klamath Ranges	mixed conifer: upland slopes	tanbark, bay laurel, incense cedar, red fir, Douglas fir, white fir, ponderosa pine
Sierran Mixed Conifer Forest: black, canyon [and interior live oak]	central: Sierra Nevada		dogwood, bigleaf maple, incense cedar, sugar pine, Jeffrey pine, ponderosa pine, white fir, Douglas fir
CHAPARRAL COMMUNITIES			
Leather Oak Chaparral: leather oak	widespread: Sierra Nevada, Klamath, and Coast ranges	serpentine: upland slopes	chamise, manzanita, gray pine, Sargent cypress, California juniper, toyon
Huckleberry Oak Chaparral: huckleberry oak	northern, central: Sierra Nevada and Klamath Ranges	non-serpentine: upland slopes	ceanothus, greenleaf manzanita, bush chinquapin, western juniper, Jeffrey pine
Scrub Oak Chaparral: scrub, [coast live, and interior live oak]	widespread: Transverse, Peninsular, and inner Coast ranges	non-serpentine: coastal plains, foothills, upland slopes	manzanita, ceanothus, toyon, silktassel, coffeeberry, foothill ash, yucca, poison oak
Semi-Desert Chaparral: desert scrub, [Muller, and Palmer oak]	desert margins: inner Transverse and Peninsular ranges	non-serpentine: upland slopes	California juniper, buckwheat, opuntia, chamise

OAK COMMUNITIES AND OAK SPECIES [Secondary oak species in brackets]	CALIFORNIA GEOGRAPHIC REGION	VEGETATION TYPE AND ITS TYPICAL LANDFORMS	ASSOCIATED HARDWOODS AND CONIFERS
WOODLAND AND SAVANNA COMMUNITIES			
Oregon Oak Woodland: Oregon, interior live, coast live, [black, canyon, and blue oak]	northern: Klamath and North Coast ranges, Cascade Range	woodland: valleys, foothills	madrone, bay laurel, incense cedar, Douglas fir, ponderosa pine
Blue Oak Woodland: blue, interior live, [valley, canyon, coast live, and scrub oak]	central: inner Coast Ranges and Sierra Nevada		buckeye, whiteleaf manzanita, redbud, coffee-berry, gray pine
Coast Live Oak Woodland: coast live, [valley, interior live, canyon, and Engelmann oak]	widespread: Coast, Transverse, and Peninsular ranges	woodland: coastal plains, valleys, foothills	buckeye, California walnut, bay laurel, madrone
Valley Oak Woodland: valley, coast live, [canyon, and blue oak]	widespread: northern and central interior valleys	woodland: valleys, foothills	gray pine, Coulter pine
Island Oak Woodland: island, coast live, [MacDonald oak (hybrid), and canyon oak]	islands: Channel Islands		Catalina ironwood, Bishop pine, Santa Cruz Island pine
Engelmann Oak Woodland: Engelmann [and coast live oak]	southwestern: Peninsular Ranges		white sage, buckwheat
Blue Oak Savanna: blue, [interior live, and valley oak]	central: inner Coast Ranges and Sierra Nevada	savanna: valleys, foothills	gray pine, buckeye
Engelmann Oak Savanna: Engelmann oak [and coast live oak]	southwestern: Peninsular Ranges		

THE STRUCTURE OF OAK VEGETATION

Forest Community

Chaparral Community

Woodland–Savanna Community

Photos by JOHN EVARTS

CHAPTER THREE

WILDLIFE AND OAKS

NATIVE OAKS AND OAK COMMUNITIES PROFOUNDLY affect the variety and abundance of California wildlife. The 18 oak species figure significantly in producing food and providing shelter on more than 30 million acres (30%) of the state's land. Hundreds of vertebrate species and thousands of invertebrate species are associated with California's oak landscapes.

Oak acorns, leaves, wood, and sap are sustenance for a myriad of insects, birds, and mammals. Among these animals are insects so specialized that they feed only on the photosynthetic cells of blue oak leaves. Other insects dine on almost anything that is *Quercus*. Some vertebrates, such as bear and deer, depend on the nutritious acorn crop for food while others have an indirect dependence on oaks. Reptiles and amphibians, for example, do not consume oak products but prey heavily on insects that do.

While food is a primary resource produced by oaks, of greater overall significance is the fact that oak communities contain the nooks, crannies, perches, and passages where animals live, breed, or rest. The physical structure of those communities, especially the way different plant species are arranged in time and space, determines the availability of shelter, nesting sites, and corridors for travel. An oak woodland with complex structure—an overstory of old, middle-aged, and young trees, along with understory canopies of shrubs and herbs—forms a wealth of micro-habitats for animals to occupy. Such an oak woodland can support far more wildlife species than simpler communities with few plant species and canopy layers.

The branch of synecology dealing with plant-animal interactions is relatively young, and so there are many gaps in our knowledge of oaks and wildlife. Drawing upon a recent body of studies, this chapter describes how wildlife utilize native oaks and oak communities for food and shelter. The discussion then summarizes specific ways that insects, amphibians, reptiles, birds, and mammals interact with California's oaks. The text also profiles several animals closely associated with oaks.

Oaks as a Food Resource

Oaks produce a cornucopia of wildlife foods, including acorns, leaves, twigs, sap, roots, and pollen. They form the basis of an elaborate food web, with herbivores eating the oak products, and carnivores eating the herbivores. Enriching the

Above: A baby dusky-footed woodrat. BILL FILSINGER
Opposite: A great horned owl and her chick perch in their nest high in a valley oak. MICHAEL SEWELL

bounty of oak-associated foods are fungi, lichens, and mistletoe, all of which are relatively abundant in oak communities.

Acorns are the most widely recognized food resource identified with oaks. Consumed by insects, mammals, and birds, they are a seasonal, high-energy food, rich in carbohydrates and fats. While insects feed on both immature and ripe acorns, mammals and birds strongly prefer the latter. Acorns ripen in late summer and autumn, and depending on the species, mature at slightly different times. In communities with more than one oak species, the harvest may last from August to November. Because different species produce "bumper crops" during different years, a diverse oak woodland or forest rarely experiences a year without acorns.

The fall acorn crop comes when many animals must put on fat for the long winter. Other sources of food, such as grasses and deciduous leaves, are usually dry and of low nutritional value at this time of year. A mule deer, for example, may eat over 300 acorns per day during October; for weeks this single source may constitute over half of its daily food intake. The deer's heavy consumption of acorns, which helps it accumulate a fatty layer for insulation and energy, may confer additional benefits as well. Studies of deer and other mammals

Acorn woodpecker and granary tree. TIM DAVIS

suggest that the size of the mast crop—a term that includes all acorns, nuts, and berries in a community—is linked to reproductive success during the following year.

Harvest season allows black bears, feral pigs, and band-tailed pigeons to feast on the available acorns. Gray squirrels, woodrats, scrub jays, and acorn woodpeckers spend much time and effort caching the nuts for later consumption. (See "The Acorn Woodpecker" in this chapter.) Acorns keep well because their hull protects the enclosed seed from desiccation and deterioration. An acorn cached in a nest, burrow, granary, or other protected site can remain edible until the next harvest.

The foliage of oaks is another important food resource. Although oak leaves may be tough and contain bitter chemicals known as tannins, many animals consume them readily. Dusky-footed woodrats gnaw off and eat the leaves of oaks. (See "The Dusky-footed Woodrat" in this chapter.) Deer and domestic livestock browse extensively on oak leaves and twigs, especially in summer and fall when green grasses and forbs are less available. California oak moth caterpillars, tent caterpillars, and western tussock moths ingest large quantities of oak leaves, sometimes denuding whole trees. Aphids, whiteflies, mites, and leafhoppers suck sap from leaves and tender shoots.

A western gray squirrel races down the trunk of a valley oak with an acorn. MICHAEL FRYE

Mule deer doe and fawns travel under the cover provided by an oak woodland. B. "MOOSE" PETERSON

Oak branches, trunks, and roots also furnish food. Western harvest mice strip the bark from saplings. Pocket gophers eat the roots of seedlings and young trees. A host of burrowing insects consume woody twigs and limbs. The oak pit scale and several species of birds imbibe sap from phloem tissue beneath the bark. Larvae of California prionus (a longhorn beetle) tunnel into food-storing roots. Even the flowers of oaks are a food resource: bees and other insects gather pollen, while larvae of at least three species of moths and two species of birds feed on whole catkins.

Oaks as Shelter

The structural diversity of California's oak communities provides many kinds of shelter to wildlife. Differences in the number and height of canopy layers, the density of branches and foliage, and the variety of plant species in the community determine many of the environmental conditions important to animals. The shady, spacious interior of northern mixed evergreen forest bears little resemblance to the dense, sun-drenched thickets of desert scrub oak chaparral. As a result, different assemblages of animals will characterize these two communities. Structural diversity within and among California's oak communities offers a wide range of sites for wildlife activity.

Nest of endangered least Bell's vireo. B. "MOOSE" PETERSON

From the treetops to the root tips, every part of an oak community is utilized for shelter. Leaf canopies moderate light, temperature, moisture, and wind to the community as a whole. Within the canopy, birds and mammals find branches for supporting nests and insects locate suitable twigs and bark for depositing their eggs. Beneath the canopy, trunk cavities are important for nesting and hiding even if the tree has long since died and fallen over. Understory shrubs shield prey from predators and form protective thickets for raising the young. A litter layer of dead leaves, twigs, and branches on the soil surface retains enough moisture for invertebrates and amphibians. Reptiles and small mammals prey upon the litter dwellers while remaining concealed from their own predators. Below ground, numerous species of arthropods and burrowing rodents are associated with the extensive root networks of a mature oak community.

Shelter is also important during the daily movements of animals from one area of the community to another. Rodents such as the western gray squirrel move through the canopies of woodlands and forests, passing from tree to tree along upper branches and limbs. This arboreal style of travel allows them to avoid predators that hunt on the ground. Larger animals, such as deer and gray fox, use the cover of oak woodlands to avoid detection by their predators as well.

Oak communities can also serve as corridors for long-distance travel by linking disjunct portions of a species' range. Bats are especially dependent upon oaks for feeding and resting during their spring and fall migrations. Millions of birds of many species move through California's oak forests, woodlands, and chaparrals while heading to northern breeding grounds or returning to wintering areas in Mexico, Central America, and even South America. These long-distance travelers may be particularly sensitive to deforestation on both ends of their journey, as tropical rain forests and temperate oak woodlands are fragmented and destroyed at alarming rates.

Just as oaks directly affect the lives of animals, animals affect the lives of oaks. Acorn dispersal, oak regeneration, the spread of disease and parasites, and mineral recycling are influenced by the activities of wildlife. Birds and squirrels are known to carry acorns away from a parent tree and cache them beneath layers of litter and soil. By "planting" acorns at new sites, animals can expand the geographic ranges of oaks and restore oaks to sites where they had been eliminated. (See "Up-Hill Planters.") Animal dispersal may also enhance oak regeneration because young seedlings, especially in the white oak lineage, may not grow well beneath the parent tree's shady canopy. Oaks can be made more susceptible to disease by woodpeckers that drill entry points for fungal spores and bacteria. Western bluebirds and phainopeplas spread the sticky seeds of parasitic mistletoe from oak to oak through their feces. Finally, mineral nutrients that are locked in leaf litter and dead wood are recycled to the oaks by insects and other soil invertebrates.

Up-Hill Planters

THE SECOND WEEK OF OCTOBER, A YEAR ago, found me nature-watching on the western slope of the southern Sierra Nevada. I was walking along the road which leads up to Sequoia National Park, when, as the morning sunshine began to increase the warmth and dryness of the atmosphere, I began to note the sounds of falling and bouncing acorns. For, at the level where I was, about 5000 feet, the black oaks were just then yielding their annual crop of seeds. . . .

Acorns are smooth-shelled, heavy objects, and those of the black oak in particular, are of rotund shape. These qualities make for insecurity of placement on any slope upon which they fall, until in their movements they reach some arresting crevice, or some sufficiently wide strip of level, or nearly level, ground on which to find lodgment.

It was clear to me that the direction of seed scattering from any one oak tree was here well-nigh directly down-hill. In that place and on that day I saw *no* acorn moving *up-hill.* Gravity alone was acting as the agency of distribution. . . . In the case of the oaks, it might therefor seem, the only possible direction of general forest spreading through time would have to be through the action of gravity and streams of water, always downhill. But how, then, could forests ever have spread, naturally, so as to gain altitude on our many mountain sides?

The next two days, October 12 and 13, my companion, Dr. Eric Hill, and I spent seeking pocket-gophers down near Three Rivers, about 1000 feet altitude, in the valley of the lower Kaweah River. Here another kind of oak, the blue oak, abounded, and we observed that there was a fairly good crop of its acorns, though not borne as uniformly as those of the black oak in the life-zone above. . . .

As we tended our trap-lines, . . . we became aware of the presence and especially the activities of California Jays. . . . These activities looked into, became of deep significance to us; for here, indeed, was the agency at this particular place, at this particular time, of transportation of acorns up-hill. . . . the birds were gathering the acorns and carrying them up the slopes, to be ensconced in various hidey-holes, some of them to be buried, after the well-known blue-jay tradition, in the ground of open spaces on the hillsides. . . .

Every bird going up-slope bore an acorn lengthwise in its bill; every bird in return course was empty-billed. If I had only thought of it, here was a chance for counting birds, and their loads, in sight, during, say, a three-hour period; and then computing the bushels of blue-oak acorns being elevated by the jays perhaps hundreds of feet each October day in that one valley.

In this same locality of observation, Dr. Hill and I saw "digger" ground squirrels busily gathering acorns that had fallen to the ground, carrying them in various directions (with these animals, however, irrespective of direction of slope) to their burrows or to their shelling stations. Twice we watched a ground squirrel climb up a blue oak to the larder of a group of California Woodpeckers, filling its cheek pouches with the acorns they had gathered and stored, even though being attacked by the resentful birds. Then the squirrel would go precipitately down the trunk and off to its own cache in the ground.

Observations of the type just cited, gathered into notebook and memory from many parts of California, have led me to generalize concerning the paramount agency of vertebrate animals in the dispersal of trees, especially of oaks. My recollections bring into this credit column, not only California Jays, woodpeckers, and ground squirrels, but also gray squirrels, chickadees, chipmunks and wood rats, and Steller Jays and Band-tailed Pigeons. In reflecting upon this matter, we can see readily that the relationship is of reciprocal benefit; all of these animal agents of seed dispersal are supplied, at

An individual scrub jay may bury several thousand acorns in one season. HUGH P. SMITH, JR.

least in part, by the oaks with food, or shelter, and (or) nursery sites. The trees produce crops of nutritious seeds—each seed nutritious either to the prospective oaklet or to the animal that eats it—in vast excess of immediate seeding needs. There is enormous seeming extravagance on the part of the trees, far and away greater production than would be needed to provide for persistence of the species, *if* the species were of fixed geographic position through time. Granting an individual longevity of 75 to 300 years for more or less mature oaks of one kind and another (I cite Jepson, *The Silva of California*, 1910, p. 57), perhaps one successful germination to only a million acorns would provide for mere *forest* replacement. Even this ratio is probably far too high. The point I wish to make is that in the long-time interests of tree species, involving locomotion of the whole forest, there is value received upon this huge rate of production. It is not extravagance, but good investment, for the oaks to provide subsistence for a continuing population of animal associates.

—Joseph Grinnell,
from *The Condor*, 1936

Insects

As many as 5,000 insect species may be associated with California's oaks. A complete census of these small animals is difficult to obtain, but a recent study documented nearly 800 species from 17 different orders that used oaks for feeding purposes alone. Sucking insects (Homoptera), moths and butterflies (Lepidoptera), beetles (Coleoptera), and wasps and bees (Hymenoptera) are the four largest associated orders. Gall wasps of the family Cynipidae (Hymenoptera) have the largest number of associated species; more than 200 kinds are known to lay eggs on some part of an oak. (See "Gall Wasps and Oaks" at the end of this chapter.)

Virtually every part of an oak is food to one or more species of insect. As an oak grows and matures, so does the diversity and abundance of its insect fauna. Insects that feed directly on the oak attract their own complement of specialized predators, forming the six-legged portion of an oak-based food web. The number of insects in the food web of a large tree during one year may range into the millions. Despite the size of these populations, native insects seldom overwhelm their host trees. Infestations of tent caterpillars, California oak moth caterpillars, and crown whiteflies cause temporary depressions of oak growth and reproduction, but damage is limited in part by predators in the native food web. (See "The California Oak Moth" in this chapter.) Introduced insects, such as the oak pit scale, have few natural enemies and are not kept in check. Their populations grow and cause lasting damage to the oak resource and its associated feeders.

In general, the type of mouthpart an insect possesses determines which portions of an oak it can eat. Moth larvae, such as tent caterpillars and fruit tree leafrollers, have chewing mouth parts and are among the most common leaf-consuming insects in oaks. Chewing mouth parts are also used by leaf-mining larvae to extract soft, green tissues from between the upper and lower epidermis. Whiteflies, aphids, leafhoppers, tree-hoppers, and scales have needle-like mouthparts to tap phloem tissues containing sugary sap. Some sucking insects, such as oak pit scales, inject toxic salivary secretions that kill or deform oak tissues. The food-diverting actions of oak pit scales are especially harmful to oaks when coupled with the stress associated with prolonged drought.

It is difficult to observe the feeding activities of insects that bore into the roots, bark, twigs, or heartwood of an oak. Boring insects use hardened, biting mouthparts to chew their way through tough, woody tissues. Beneath the bark, these

Whitefly larvae on the underside of Engelmann oak leaves. DARYL KOUTNIK

Oak treehopper nymphs and one adult cluster on a twig. DAVID STOCKTON

Insect-eaten leaves of blue oak. DAVID CAVAGNARO

insects tunnel into xylem and phloem, as well as the actively growing cambium layer. This kind of feeding adversely affects portions of the oak far beyond the area of excavation. The larvae of the oak twig girdler, for example, tunnel in a spiral pattern beneath the bark of a twig or branch, shutting off the flow of food and water. When a tree has girdlers its canopy becomes blotchy with small patches of brown, dead leaves. By contrast, insects that bore into heartwood do not disrupt the supply of food to oak branches and leaves, and the effects of their excavations may go unnoticed. A tree with tunnel-ridden heartwood, however, stands a good chance of becoming infected with fungi or being toppled in a high wind.

Insects also feed voraciously on acorns, and as much as half of a given year's crop may harbor insect larvae. The two most common types of acorn larvae are the filbertworm (a moth larva) and the filbertweevil (a beetle larva). A study in Northern California found that up to 60% of blue oak acorns were infested by filbertworms and up to 47% were infested by filbertweevils. Larval feeding may destroy the embryo or diminish its food reserves.

Seven species of gall-forming wasps deposit eggs in immature acorns; this ovipositing causes acorns to abort or lose viability. Although gall wasps are widespread, their impact on oak regeneration is considered minimal.

While the canopy, limbs, trunk, and roots of oaks provide food and shelter for many kinds of invertebrates, oak litter provides habitat for a whole other assortment. Springtails, proturans, termites, beetles, and fly larvae, as well as millipedes, sowbugs, snails, slugs, and earthworms are part of a rich and abundant micro-fauna. Springtails alone (order Collembola) can exceed 100,000 per cubic yard of surface soil. They feed on decaying plant matter, fungi, bacteria, feces, and other materials, thereby recycling mineral nutrients that support plant growth.

Ants are also part of the micro-fauna that forages and nests in the litter beneath oaks. Many of these common and familiar insects scavenge both on the ground and in the trees. Ants will often travel into oaks to retrieve honeydew, a sugary secretion excreted by aphids, scales, and some caterpillars.

A fascinating but extremely rare denizen of this habitat is the springtail-stalking ant. Believed to be a relict from a period when California's climate was warm and moist, the springtail-stalking ant is now relegated to a single remnant stand of valley oak in the northern central valley. This same stand supports a population of another rare species of ant known as the valley oak ant.

Millipedes often reside in the deep leaf litter that accumulates beneath oaks. RON WEST

The California Oak Moth

THE OAK MOTH IS PERHAPS THE BEST-KNOWN insect associated with California oaks. Its larvae are voracious leaf-eaters and rarely feed on plants other than oaks. Oak moth populations experience wide fluctuations from year to year, but when their numbers peak they are capable of denuding acres of trees. Despite the conspicuous defoliation of entire trees, foraging by the caterpillars rarely kills an oak.

Found only in California and Arizona, the oak moth is the sole member of its primarily neotropical family to inhabit the United States. The adult moth has pale brown wings and a

California oak moth pupae. NANCY BURNETT

wingspan that measures about one inch. The newly hatched larva is white with black spots, while a full-sized larva is about one inch long and olive-green with conspicuous yellow and black stripes. The oak moth larva does not spin a cocoon, and the ½-inch-long, yellowish pupa hangs from leaves, tree trunks, or other surfaces until the adult emerges.

The oak moth is sensitive to climatic extremes and is generally restricted to mild-weather regions where its larvae can over winter and repopulate the next generation. In especially favorable areas, such as coastal Southern California, up to three generations may appear in one year. The lifespan of the moth varies from 15 weeks in the warm summer months to 29 weeks during winter.

Top: An adult female California oak moth deposits its eggs. NANCY BURNETT
Bottom: A magnified view of oak moth larvae emerging from their eggs. DAN SUZIO

Oak moth larvae have a variety of natural enemies that help keep their population in check. Parasitic insects and microscopic disease organisms cause the death of many; predators such as western bluebirds and Nuttall's woodpeckers pick the caterpillars off leaves and branches; white-footed mice consume large amounts of the pupae.

Ringneck snakes often inhabit oak woodland communities. BILL FILSINGER

Amphibians and Reptiles

More than 80 species of amphibians and reptiles (collectively referred to as "herps") reside in California's oak communities. Most are found foraging in the leaf litter and soil, taking advantage of the abundant prey and protective ground cover. California legless lizards burrow in loose soil for larvae and small insects. Slender salamanders find worms and small arthropods in oak detritus. Sharp-tailed snakes, which subsist almost entirely on slugs, hunt in the humus of moist oak forests. Ringneck snakes prey on slender salamanders, lizards, insects, and worms on the woodland floor. Western toads hide during the day but emerge at night to forage under oaks. Some herps extend their territories up into trunks and branches. Arboreal salamanders, for example, hunt insects high in the limbs of coast live oaks. (See "The Arboreal Salamander" in this chapter.) Alligator lizards and striped racers climb trees and shrubs to search for insects and the eggs and young of birds.

Hollows and cavities in oak trunks provide ideal shelter for herps. They form when strong, outer sapwood surrounds devoured or decaying heartwood. Reptiles and amphibians use hollows in standing trees (living or dead) for nesting, estivation, and escaping from predators. Cavities within fallen oak trunks are of even greater importance because most herp species live at or near ground level. Blue racers, California kingsnakes, and gopher snakes, for example, bask inside sunlit fallen logs without exposing themselves to predators. Alligator lizards, skinks, ensatinas, and many others live within or beneath downed logs. Western fence lizards use such logs for territorial and feeding perches.

The availability of moisture within oak communities exerts a strong influence over the distribution of herps. Amphibians, such as salamanders, are generally found in moist oak woodlands or on north-facing slopes. A notable exception is the California tiger salamander, which favors vernal ponds in oak savannas. Although present in many oak communities, frogs and toads are usually restricted to places with free-standing water. They seek shelter in oak cavities or beneath oak leaf litter when in transit between aquatic environments. In contrast, lizards and other reptiles tolerate or even prefer drier oak communities. For example, western fence lizards and Gilbert's skinks are closely associated with drought-prone blue oak savannas and show little affinity for moist groves of canyon oak. Open oak woodlands often support relatively high densities of lizard- and rodent-eating snakes, including blue and striped racers, gopher snakes, kingsnakes, and rattlesnakes.

Top: Western skink hunts in leaf litter. DAVID STOCKTON
Bottom: Western toad in an oak woodland. BOB RONEY

The Arboreal Salamander

The arboreal salamander. IAN C. TAIT

COAST LIVE OAK WOODLANDS ARE THE PRIMARY habitat of the arboreal salamander. As its name suggests, this amphibian is an expert tree climber. It is unique among salamanders of North America because it often uses tree cavities for nesting and estivation; some have been found in cavities of coast live oaks over 30 feet up. A nocturnal animal, it forages for insects and other invertebrates in trees and on the ground. The deep leaf litter that accumulates beneath mature oaks provides an ideal micro-environment for its prey. The arboreal salamander inhabits the Coast Ranges from Northern California to Baja. It also lives in Sierran mixed conifer forest in the western Sierra Nevada foothills and on several of the Channel Islands.

The arboreal salamander is a member of the largest family of salamanders, the lungless salamanders. Dependent on moist environments for survival, all lungless salamanders absorb oxygen directly through a watery film that surrounds their thin skins. The arboreal salamander is rarely seen during California's dry summer when it estivates in humid sites such as tree cavities, rodent burrows, caves, mine shafts, and under the bark of dead trees. With the arrival of the first fall storms, the salamander emerges from its protected enclosure. Dehydrated from months without rain, it clings to the trunks of trees for several hours, soaking up water in order to rehydrate.

Cavities in oak trees provide damp chambers for salamanders, and the female often selects these protected sites to lay her eggs. She deposits 15 to 18 eggs and arranges them in grape-like clusters that are attached to the roof of the enclosure. The female tends the eggs for three to four months, moistening them with skin and bladder secretions which may also prevent the onset of mold.

An adult arboreal salamander ranges from 4 ½ to 7 ¼ inches in length and varies in color from a medium to a dark brown. Most have irregular yellow spots on their backs, and all have whitish bellies. Powerful jaw muscles, which are much larger in the male, give its head a triangular appearance and allow this salamander to defend itself with a surprisingly strong bite. The bite is often preceded by the mouse-like squeak an arboreal salamander emits when agitated.

An arboreal salamander climbs the trunk of a coast live oak. PAUL W. COLLINS

Birds

Oak landscapes provide habitat for more than 100 species of birds during the breeding season. This includes year-round residents, such as acorn woodpeckers and plain titmice, and transient species that utilize oaks during all or part of their breeding activities. Some transients are short-distance migrants that move downslope into oak communities during winter. Flickers, thrushes, red-breasted sapsuckers, and ruby-crowned kinglets are good examples. Transients can also be long-distance migrants en route from tropical latitudes to other temperate and boreal landscapes. Flycatchers, vireos, and warblers stop by to feast on the abundance of insects in an oak woodland canopy. Most species are less fleeting, and at least 75 are known to build nests and raise their young in close association with oaks. This group includes ash-throated flycatchers, black-throated gray warblers, violet-green swallows, and Lawrence's goldfinches. As a result, the number of bird species inhabiting California's oak landscapes fluctuates greatly throughout the year.

Many kinds of birds build nests in the canopies of tree oaks, but some are specialized as cavity nesters. Six species of woodpeckers make their own cavities in oaks by chipping away wood that has been weakened by fungi and boring insects. At least 20 other bird species, including swallows, nuthatches, wrens, and bluebirds are known to nest in naturally formed or abandoned oak cavities. Screech owls and pygmy owls are also among those using oak cavities for nesting and cover during periods of rest. Nesting sites, of course, are not limited to oak tree cavities or the overarching forest canopy. The structure of many oak communities includes a dense understory of shrubby plants, which attracts shrub-nesting species such as Anna's hummingbirds, Hutton's vireos, and rufous-crowned sparrows.

Acorns are consumed by at least 30 species of birds. They constitute 25 to 50% of the yearly diet of wood ducks, wild turkeys, band-tailed pigeons, and jays. Acorn woodpeckers rely on them for over half their food. Consumption by flickers, Lewis' woodpeckers, and white-breasted nuthatches is also common, but acorns seldom make up a major part of their food supply.

Of the many birds that consume acorns, only three species play an active role in the range expansion of oaks: scrub jay, Steller's jay, and the

Top: Great horned owl chicks peer out from a nest cavity in a black oak. MICHAEL FRYE
Bottom: The yellow-billed magpie is among the few bird species that "plants" acorns. IAN C. TAIT

yellow-billed magpie. All of these species cache acorns in the ground. Each season, some of the buried acorns go unrecovered, and a few of these sprout into seedlings. A scrub jay may bury as many as 5,000 acorns in one season but will relocate and consume only one-third to a half of this bounty.

The rich and varied invertebrate population of oak communities is a far more important food resource for most birds. Insectivores, such as bushtits, wrens, and warblers, glean insects directly from oak leaves, twigs, and branches. Fly-catching species, such as western kingbirds, Cassin's kingbirds, and black phoebes launch their attacks on airborne prey from exposed perches on oaks. Ground-foraging thrushes, thrashers, and towhees scour the leaf litter and understory in pursuit of insects. Woodpeckers, flickers, and creepers probe for insects in bark and other woody tissues. Raptors are attracted by the abundance of vertebrate prey; hawks perch on jutting oak limbs to scan the landscape for herps and small mammals.

Some birds utilize less obvious food resources in the community. Sapsuckers and acorn woodpeckers drill for oak sap. Plain titmice tear apart oak galls to forage on the insects nestled within. Black-headed grosbeaks and acorn woodpeckers consume oak catkins during spring. Western bluebirds, phainopeplas, and cedar waxwings use mistletoe berries as a winter food, gleaning them from plants growing high in the oak canopies.

Top: A red-shouldered hawk launches from its perch in a coast live oak woodland. BILL FILSINGER
Bottom: The western bluebird is one of many species that feed on the berries of mistletoe, a parasite often found on valley oaks. B. "MOOSE" PETERSON

The Acorn Woodpecker

A male acorn woodpecker. RON WEST

O F THE MANY BIRDS THAT CONSUME ACORNS, few are more intimately associated with California's oak communities than the acorn woodpecker. In the United States, its distribution extends from central Oregon through California, and across Arizona and New Mexico to Big Bend, Texas. Within this range it is found in virtually all habitats that contain several coexisting species of oaks.

This medium-sized, clown-faced bird has a red cap, black chin and wings, and a powerful, pointed bill. Its flight is undulating and reveals a white rump and white wing patches. The calls of the acorn woodpecker, which include a raucous *waka-waka* and *karrit-cut*, are a familiar sound in valley and coast live oak woodlands.

The acorn woodpecker harvests acorns directly from oaks and caches them individually in small holes it drills in communal storage trees known as "granaries." The holes are re-used year after year and accumulate over time as the birds excavate new storage cavities. A large granary, developed and enlarged by many generations of woodpeckers, is a spectacular sight. The tree is riddled with thousands of storage holes from its trunk to its upper limbs, and following the autumn harvest, nearly every one will contain an acorn.

The acorn woodpecker's use of granaries is a unique approach to caching acorns. Other birds and mammals that store acorns usually

An acorn woodpecker tends its cache. DENNY MALLORY

bury them in the ground—where they often cache far more than they ever recover. An individual scrub jay, for example, may bury thou sands of acorns at dispersed locations but only retrieves a portion of its extensive stockpiles. In contrast, acorn woodpeckers (at a study site in Monterey County) cache only a few hundred acorns per bird per year, yet virtually all of these granary-stored acorns are eventually consumed.

When available, pines are used for granaries, but oaks, sycamores, and redwoods are also utilized. Dead or living trees are not the only sites chosen for storing acorns; the birds may make their granaries in telephone poles, fence posts, or the wood trim of buildings. Oaks are a less preferred storage substrate than pines, probably because of the hardness of their wood. Among oaks, species with thick bark such as valley oaks are preferred over thin-barked species. Regardless of the kind of tree, storage holes are drilled in dead limbs or thick bark. By excavating only in dead tissue, the birds avoid sap that would retard the drying of stored acorns and encourage mold and premature rot. Since acorn woodpeckers rarely penetrate the cambium layer when making storage holes, granary drilling appears to have little detrimental effect on living trees.

Oaks and acorns influence nearly every aspect of acorn woodpecker ecology and behavior. Although acorn woodpeckers sapsuck and eat insects, they are highly dependent on stored acorns as a food resource, especially during periods of poor weather in winter and during the breeding season in spring. Throughout the year, the birds spend approximately one-fourth of their time in granaries, defending their stores against raids by other acorn consumers and attending their caches, a task that includes checking acorns for shrinkage and moving them to smaller holes as they dry.

Acorn woodpeckers are cooperative breeders in California and most other areas that have been studied to date. They live in complex family groups with up to 15 birds sharing a territory and one or more granaries. Groups are extended families that consist of a breeding core of four or more related males, usually brothers or a father and his sons, who share up to three related females, usually sisters or a mother and her daughters. The family may also include nonbreeding "helpers" of both sexes who are older offspring of the breeding core. The group communally raises offspring and gathers acorns. Once stored, an acorn becomes community property and can be removed and eaten by any bird in the group. Such cooperation, however, is contingent on sufficient acorn production. When the crop is a total failure, acorn woodpeckers abandon an area entirely. When the crop is poor, aggression within the group becomes intense and the social structure beaks down; more dominant birds exclude the subordinates until the group disintegrates.

The primary threat to the acorn woodpecker is habitat loss. Suitable granaries are critical for reproductive success and group survivorship, and in essence are real estate for which birds must fiercely compete. Even a small granary with 1,000 holes represents a large investment in time and energy—the cumulative work of generations of woodpeckers, each adding a few new holes per year. Conservation of our native oak resources will help ensure that future Californians have an opportunity to become acquainted with one of the most fascinating residents of oak communities, the acorn woodpecker.

—Walter D. Koening

Top: A mountain lion leaps to catch its prey in an oak woodland. MICHAEL SEWEL
Bottom: Feral pigs forage for acorns during the autumn harvest. MICHAEL SEWEL

Mammals

Of California's 169 terrestrial mammal species, at least 60 utilize oak landscapes for food or cover. From demure, insectivorous moles to imposing, carnivorous grizzly bears, oak communities were brimming with fur-bearing creatures when the first Europeans arrived. Many of these species were ruthlessly trapped, hunted, and poisoned, and some driven to extinction. The fates of large, roving mammals such as elk and mountain lion are still uncertain as oak-dominated habitats vital to their survival continue to shrink and disappear as a result of land development.

Acorns are the most important oak food utilized by mammals and are found in the diets of at least 37 California species. Squirrels, gophers, and wood rats are typical consumers, but at one time so were grizzly bears. (See "Acorns and Grizzly Bears" in this chapter.) Although no mammal depends entirely on acorns, studies have shown a correlation between acorn availability and reproductive success in western gray squirrels, bears, feral pigs, and deer. New generations of these animals are, therefore, linked to new generations of oaks.

After the year's supply of acorns has been exhausted and quality spring herbage becomes scarce, mule deers often turn to oaks for browse. At such times, foliage and twigs from black, blue, canyon, and other species constitute as much as 40% of the mule deer diet. Stump-sprouts and low-growing branches are easy to reach, but when the low browse is gone, these nimble animals stand on their hind legs, with neck and chin extended, and stretch up into the canopy.

Oak-associated plants such as mistletoe and lichens are also elements of the mule deer food supply. In feeding experiments designed to test deer preference among 31 species of browse, mistletoe and lichen occupied the top two positions. These plants offer a relatively high year-round crude protein resource and are especially important to deer during the winter.

Many carnivorous mammals spend time in oak communities searching for prey. Oak woodlands and forests often contain a higher density of animals than adjacent, non-oak communities and are very attractive to predators. The large numbers of mule deer that inhabit blue oak woodland and scrub oak chaparral, for example, attract and sustain significant populations of mountain lions. Ecologically,

A young mule deer browses on the leaves of an oak sapling. IAN C. TAIT

animals such as the mountain lion exist on the outermost edges of the oak-based food web.

Dens and nests are often located in oak communities. Raccoons and squirrels utilize cavities in standing trees, while deer mice and striped skunks reside beneath fallen trees and limbs. Overstory trees and understory shrubs help conceal den sites, reduce exposure to harsh weather, and provide cover for escaping from predators. Gray fox and bobcat seek shelter from summer heat beneath dense stands of scrub oak chaparral. Squirrels and woodrats use the network of limbs and trunks in oak woodlands for travel and escape routes.

The ecological characteristics of oaks and oak communities attract and sustain mammal populations for a variety of reasons. Researchers conducting studies on the denning behavior of black bears in the San Bernardino Mountains, for example, concluded that the bears preferred to den in southern mixed evergreen forest where canyon oak dominated. (Black bears were introduced to Southern California in the 1930s when a group of 16 bears was transported from Yosemite National Park.) They concluded that black bears chose this plant community because it was relatively un-disturbed by humans, contained a supply of acorn and berry crops, and had cool winter temperatures. The cool temperatures, required for successful denning, were maintained by the dense canopies of canyon oak on north-facing slopes and in steep canyons with cold-air drainage.

Of all the vertebrates that interact with oaks, mammals probably have the greatest impact on oak regeneration. Although there is no simple explan-ation for the lack of regeneration, introduced and native mammals may contribute to the problem. Browsing and foraging by sheep, cattle, and deer are thought to be especially detrimental. These her-bivores browse on oak leaves and twigs of mature trees and feed on young seedlings that have little or no chance of surviving frequent defoliation. Feral pigs also destroy seedlings and disturb established oaks by rooting for subterranean bulbs and fungi. All of these animals consume large quantities of acorns that might otherwise germinate and grow.

Smaller mammals, especially rodents, affect oak regeneration as well. Pocket gophers are probably the principal predators of buried acorns, and the extensive systems of underground tunnels they construct disrupt and sometimes kill the roots of young oaks. Gophers and mice also prey on sur-face acorns, seedlings, and young saplings. Some rodent activities, however, can enhance oak dis-persal and regeneration. Gray squirrels and ground squirrels consume large numbers of acorns, but their tendency to cache supplies at some distance from the parent tree is an important mechanism for oak dispersal. Acorns which end up buried beneath a layer of soft soil are less susceptible to desiccation or predation than those on the surface. Some cached acorns are not retrieved, and these will germinate with the fall rains.

Top: In many areas of California black bears rely on the fall acorn crop to put on winter fat. KENNAN WARD
Bottom: The gray fox frequently hunts and seeks shelter in scrub oak chaparral. MICHAEL SEWELL

The Dusky-footed Woodrat

Live oaks fill the needs of this mammal so well that even isolated trees house wood rats. . . . Wherever this tree can grow, the dryness is not too great for the rat. Probably the live oak comes closer than any other kind to being an ideal plant for the rat.

—J. M. Linsdale and L. P. Tevis, Jr.
The Dusky-footed Wood Rat, 1951

The DUSKY-FOOTED WOODRAT OCCURS FROM the Willamette Valley in Oregon to north-western Baja California and is closely associated with evergreen oaks throughout most of its range. This nocturnal rodent prefers a fairly moist habitat, but it is also found in drier communities such as pinyon-juniper woodlands. In all locations, it seems to favor dense brush or woodland that has an oak component.

Oak leaves and acorns are especially important staples in the woodrat's diet, which is made up of leaves, flowers, nuts, seeds, and fungi. One study demonstrated that dusky-footed woodrats can maintain their weight balance on a diet of pure coast live oak leaves. Other research indicates that acorns play a key role in the reproductive success of woodrats. A bumper crop of acorns allows woodrats to breed through the winter and is linked to population increases the following year. Woodrats gather acorns on the ground and in trees, and much of their harvest goes into storage. The resulting cache can be substantial: a single woodrat den in the San Gabriel Mountains, for example, contained nearly 20 pounds of interior live oak acorns.

Although the nocturnal habits of the dusky-footed woodrat make it difficult to spot, a casual observer can often hear evidence of the rodent. Venture into a coast live oak riparian forest on a calm evening, especially during the breeding season, and you may detect the sound of woodrat tail-rattling. A unique form of communication, tail-rattling generates a wide range of rapping or whirring sounds that vary depending on individual technique and the type of substratum the woodrat strikes with its tail.

A visual sign of woodrat presence is the large house it constructs using sticks, leaves, and other detritus. This shelter contains a number of chambers used for nests, latrines, or food stores and is usually occupied by only one adult at a time. While the woodrat life span is relatively short—two to three years—successive generations often occupy the same lodge for 20 years or more. Each new resident adds materials to the house, which can measure up to six feet wide and more than six feet high. Most woodrat houses are built on the ground, but when they are constructed in trees, they are usually located in live oaks. Quite often the woodrat is not the only denizen in its multi-roomed structure. A variety of animals, including slugs, snails, insects, salamanders, lizards, and mice, are known to take up residence in the cracks, crevices, and abandoned hallways of a woodrat house.

—Patrick A. Kelly

A dusky-footed woodrat runs to its den (lower left) carrying an oak branchlet. IAN C. TAIT

Acorns and Grizzlies

From notes made in the 1840s, James Walker created his 1876 painting of a grizzly hunt near San Diego titled "Roping the Bear." CALIFORNIA HISTORICAL SOCIETY

THE GRIZZLY BEAR WAS ONCE WIDESPREAD IN California's oak landscapes and ranged from the Pacific shore to the high mountains. This fierce and adaptable omnivore commanded the respect and awe of the California Indians, with whom it coexisted for thousands of years. By the early 1920s—barely 150 years after the arrival of the first Spanish colonists—all of California's grizzlies had been exterminated by relentless hunting and trapping.

Acorns were an important food for California's grizzlies, and a number of 19th century writers noted the activities of the bears during fall harvest. Joaquin Miller, who was known as the "poet of the Sierras," wrote of how he had seen grizzlies "feeding under the oaks in Napa Valley in numbers together. . . as composedly and as careless of danger as if they had been hogs feeding on nuts under the hickory trees of the Wabash." Reverend Walter Colton, the mayor of Monterey in the mid-1800s, described how grizzlies harvested acorns that had not yet fallen to the ground: "[I]nstead of threshing them down like the Indian, he

selects a well-stocked limb, throws himself upon its extremity, and there hangs swinging and jerking till the limb gives way, and down they come, branch, acorns, and bear together."

In his memoirs, explorer John C. Frémont provided an account of how grizzly cubs were enlisted as tree climbers during acorn harvest in the Salinas Valley in 1846: "Where we were riding on the prairie bottom, between the willow and the river hills, . . . were several of the long-acorn oaks [valley oak]. Suddenly we saw among the upper boughs a number of young grizzly bears, busily occupied in breaking off the smaller branches which carried the acorns, and throwing them to the ground."

Jesse Benton Frémont, spouse of John C. and an early California explorer in her own right, wrote about her experiences in Mariposa County in 1890: "The growth of fine deciduous oaks covered a long space, some miles, and was a famous resort for grizzly bears; their 'wallows' were all around about. With the acorns, the great spring and the fresh cool air, it was a fixed resort for them in the acorn season."

Gall Wasps and Oaks

Coast live oak with galls produced by the California gall wasp. DEDE GILMAN

OAKS HOST MORE GALL INSECTS THAN ANY OTHER native tree or shrub in the western United States. Tiny wasps of the family Cynipidae are the most abundant gall inducers and produce the majority of galls that embellish California oaks. Wasp galls range in size from pinheads to softballs and assume many different forms: tiny cups, saucers, stars, volleyballs, clubs, sea urchins, and royal crowns.

Gall formation begins when a wasp deposits its eggs into plant tissue, causing minor local swelling around the eggs. Once larvae emerge from the eggs, their chemical secretions stimulate a response from the host plant, and the oviposited site gradually develops into a tumor-like growth. Although they vary in size, shape, and color, all galls serve the same purpose: to provide a protected environment and a source of food for the developing offspring. While gall wasps appear to have little detrimental impact on oaks, some gall insects are harmful to plants, such as the grape phylloxera which causes serious damage to European varieties of grapes.

More than 200 species of cynipid wasps are associated with California's native oaks. Each species has evolved a specific dependence that restricts it to either the red, white, or intermediate oak group. Gall wasps that occur on valley oak, for example, are absent from coast live oak. Blue oak (a white oak) exhibits the greatest diversity of galls. It is not unusual for a single specimen of blue oak to be decorated with the galls of 20 to 30 species of wasps. Regardless of oak species, many gall wasps oviposit on leaves, which offer the advantage of a rapid growth rate and high nutritional content. Gall wasps also oviposit on other parts of an oak, including its roots, branches, buds, leaf petioles, flowers, and acorns.

Although wasp larvae are sheltered by their gall to some extent, this "sanctuary" is still vulnerable to parasites and predators. Several

Galls of the urchin gall wasp on a valley oak leaf. DEDE GILMAN

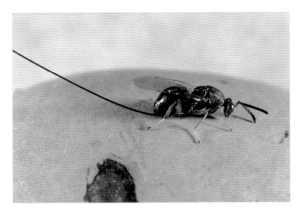

species of braconid and ichneumon wasps specialize in penetrating the exterior of the gall to parasitize the cynipid larvae within. Predaceous insects visit galls to hunt for the concealed larvae. Other insects which visit galls to feed on the gall tissues are often attacked by parasites and predators. After surviving the hazards of larval life and leaving the gall behind, a cynipid wasp may become the prey of a bird, spider, or predaceous insect. Some adults fail to find a preferred host tree; many gall wasps die without reproducing.

Much remains to be learned about the fascinating interplay between gall-inducing insects and their plant hosts. California's oak communities, where countless trees and shrubs are bedecked with colorful galls, are perhaps the finest natural laboratories for studying these unique relationships.

—Ron Russo

Top left: The California gall wasp. RON WEST
Bottom left: The oak gall chalcid oviposits in galls and its larvae parasitize the wasps within. RON WEST
Top right: Other insects induce galls on oaks, such as these button galls produced by midges. RON WEST
Bottom right: The beaked twig gall wasp produced these marble-sized galls on scrub oak. DAVID CAVAGNARO

CHAPTER FOUR

CALIFORNIA OAKS
AND THE HUMAN PAST

THE HUMAN HISTORY OF CALIFORNIA BEGAN in the shade of her native oaks. Acorn foods sustained many diverse Indian cultures that evolved and thrived among the woodlands for centuries. Widely available, nutritious, and fairly reliable from year to year, acorn was the dietary staple in most of California, just as corn was in the Southwest and buffalo in the Great Plains. In addition, Indian people knew that oak communities were rich in bear, deer, and other wildlife that thrived on the acorns and lingered within the deep shade. It is not surprising that oaks were revered by native Californians, held sacred in elaborate acorn ceremonies, and depicted as symbols of fertility, strength, and oneness with the earth.

Early Spanish explorers were awed by the park-like beauty of the oak woodlands and the sheer abundance of trees that filled the valleys and covered the endless hills. Their observations correctly led them to believe that oaks were indicators of fertile soil in this remote, uncharted land. The Franciscan padres established a chain of missions that closely followed the general distribution of the coast live oak. A rustic, European civilization emerged from the wilderness of Alta California, and its people held mass, delineated ranchos, and built new settlements beneath the massive boughs of ancient and wild oaks.

The natural wealth and beauty of California gradually attracted settlers from many countries of the Old World. Indigenous technologies, which had minimal impact on oak resources, were gradually replaced by European technologies that transformed oaks into marketable commodities: spars were turned into lumber, bark into tanning acids, wood chips into charcoal, and acorns into livestock feed. Pastoral life gave way to industry in small, isolated pockets throughout the territory, and the modern trend was thus established. Conservative and sustainable uses of oaks were replaced by expedient and consumptive uses that often led to the destruction of entire oak populations and communities. As a result, oaks were no longer sovereign symbols of a frontier coast. Instead, they were regarded as exploitable resources with great market potential, or in some cases, bulky inhabitants of otherwise productive and valuable land.

Oaks and Native Californians

The California Indians lived within a landscape as rich in natural resources as any on earth. Northern rivers were choked with salmon. Valleys of tall grass

Above: Indian ring and pin game made with canyon oak acorn cups. SOUTHWEST MUSEUM, LOS ANGELES
Opposite: Acorn grinding holes beneath canyon oaks in Palomar Mountain State Park. BILL EVARTS

Mrs. Freddie, a Hupa, leaches acorn meal in a sand basin, 1901. LOWIE MUSEUM OF ANTHROPOLOGY, UC BERKELEY

supported herds of tule elk, pronghorn, and deer. Wild plants, so abundant and diverse, were utilized as foods, building materials, clothing, medicines, and tools. Few plants, however, were as important to native Californians as the oaks. Virtually every tribe west of California's high mountains—from Mount Shasta in the north to Cuyamaca Peak in the south—harvested acorns for food. Each tribe employed specialized technologies for acorn gathering, storing, hulling, drying, leaching, pounding, and cooking. The bark, roots, wood, small branches, and galls of oaks were also part of the usable natural resource base.

Cultures of the Acorn Diet

Early in this century, anthropologist Alfred Kroeber estimated that acorns constituted the primary daily food of more than three-fourths of all native Californians. The total annual acorn crop of the Great Central Valley alone would have been measured in the millions of tons, although only a small fraction of that was ever harvested by people. Not only were acorns available throughout much of the territory, they were exceedingly nutritious. Depending on the species, acorns can contain up to 18% fat, 6% protein, and 68% carbohydrate (the rest being water, minerals, and fiber). In comparison, modern varieties of corn and wheat have 2% fat, 10% protein and 75% carbohydrate. Acorns are also good sources of vitamins A and C and many of the essential amino acids. In a semi-arid land where most herbs and seeds are available during the spring and early summer, the autumn arrival of such a satisfying and easily stored food was cause for celebration.

In places where the ranges of different oaks overlapped, resident tribes utilized acorns of nearly all available species but preferred those that were more abundant, better tasting, or easier to prepare.

Along the north coast, the Hupa and Yurok harvested tanbark acorns, which were plentiful in the redwood and mixed evergreen forests. Shortages occurred in certain years, however, and that meant that acorns from Oregon, black, and canyon oak might also be gathered. Along the south coast, the Luiseño derived up to 45% of their diet from six oak species. They relished the oil-rich, flavorful acorns of black and coast live oak. Less desirable were those of canyon oak (probably harder to grind), Engelmann oak, and interior live oak. During particularly lean years, even the small acorns of scrub oak were gathered, but not without the associated difficulties of penetrating and working in dense thickets of chaparral.

Sometimes tribes preferred acorns of species that did not grow in their home territory. Such tastes must have been acquired and sustained through trade with neighboring tribes. Acorns were second only to salt among the food items most frequently traded among native Californians. The direction of acorn trade was usually west to east: acorns from the north coast made their way to the Klamath River basin, from the San Joaquin Valley to Owens Valley, and from the Laguna Mountains into the Colorado Desert. Shasta people along the Klamath River prized the tanbark acorns they got from the coastal Yurok in exchange for obsidian and deerskin. Miwok clans gathered black oak acorns from the western Sierra Nevada, carried them over the high mountain passes, and bartered with the Mono Lake Paiute for the meaty nuts of pinyon pine. The Quechan (Yumas) along the Colorado River traded their gourd seeds for acorns from the Kumeyaay (Tipai) of western San Diego County. One notable exception to this west-to-east pattern was the flow of acorns from the mainland to Chumash groups living on the northern Channel Islands. (See the "Tribal Areas of California" map in the Appendices to locate California tribes.)

The territorial claims of tribes, villages, families, and individuals were often based upon the distribution of acorn-producing oak groves. In some cases, boundaries were clearly established in order to avoid conflict. Acorn wars between rival tribes, although rare, were not unknown. One such war took place in about 1830 just north of Healdsburg (Sonoma County) when a Pomo group stole the acorn caches of nearby Wappo villagers. The acorns had been gathered from disputed woodlands along the Russian River. A party of Wappo vigilantes

Miwok acorn granaries in the Sierra Nevada foothills near Railroad Flat, 1906. LOWIE MUSEUM OF ANTHROPOLOGY, UC BERKELEY

swiftly retaliated by destroying several Pomo villages and killing the innocent along with the guilty. Conflicts within tribes over the disposition of acorn resources were not so extreme. Patwin families were assigned collection areas by their village chief. In some tribes it was the custom for a family or group of families to claim the trees nearest to their dwellings. Otherwise, local custom dictated whether or not an individual could own a tree and lay claim to its autumn bounty.

Many cultural traditions commemorated the acorn, and religious ceremonies anticipated the arrival of each year's crop. Men and women often bore names such as "sweet acorn" and "striped acorn." The Sinkyone created unusual sounds with acorn buzzers, Luiseño children spun acorn tops, and the Cahto made music with acorns on strings. The Maidu calendar referred to our month of April as *Winuti*, ("black oak tassel") and September as *Matmeni* ("acorn bread"). Both the Yuki and the Pomo kept track of lunar cycles of the year by noting when the acorns were ripe and ready to drop (*Huwol-huntusol*) and when they actually fell (the month of *Huwol-chukmol*). The new year of the Karok began in fall, initiated by a ten-day-long ceremony in which the shaman ate only acorn porridge prepared by virgin women. As girls of the

Yuki tribe entered puberty, acorn songs (*lanl-hanp*) were sung by adults during the acorn song dance (*Lanl-hanp-wok*). If the spirits were pleased by these rituals, the tribe was assured of an abundance of acorns next fall. Solemn offerings of acorns or acorn meal were commonly made during the religious ceremonies of the Coast Miwok, Ohlone (Costanoan), Salinan, Maidu, and Chumash.

Acorns were gathered in the fall, usually by women carrying large woven baskets. Hupa gathering baskets were woven from hazelnut twigs and strong, wiry tree roots. They were conical, decorated with geometric designs, and could each hold a bushel or two of acorns. Although many tribes simply waited for the acorn drop to begin, the Chumash and Sierra Miwok used long poles to shake heavily-laden branches. Wintu men climbed the trees and rained the acorns down upon the women and children. A typical family could harvest the crop of an average-size black oak in a day and reap about 140 pounds of acorns. This was about one-fifth of what they would consume annually. In a year of plenty, families gathered a surplus in order to cover short crops during less productive years. If an industrious Nisenan family still did not have enough acorns to sustain themselves, the village headman could ask for donations on their behalf. Lazy people, however, were not helped and were forced to rely upon relatives in another village.

Most of a family's crop was dried and stored for use during the rest of the year. To hasten drying, acorns were spread in the sun or suspended in baskets above the rising heat of a low fire. The Cahuilla of Southern California built a large cache for dried acorns out of interwoven willow shoots that resembled a giant nest. The nest, two to six feet in diameter, was located outside on a raised platform of wood or rock and covered with a strong lid. In Central California, the Sierra Miwok built tall, cylindrical granaries (*chuck-ah*) that were basket-like in appearance. Willow and conifer boughs were woven around tall posts driven into the ground in a ring; strong vines of native grape circled the exterior, positioning the boughs like shingles on a roof. An inside lining was fashioned from leafy branches of wormwood, which contains a natural, aromatic insect repellant for deterring infestations of acorn worms. The bottom of the basket was about three feet above the ground, and the top was covered with slabs of incense cedar bark to discourage pilfering by rats and squirrels. A finished

Top: Gathering acorns, as depicted in Hutchings' California Magazine *in 1859.* THE BANCROFT LIBRARY
Bottom: An acorn granary near Pala, San Diego County, circa 1910. SAN DIEGO MUSEUM OF MAN

granary was about 5 feet in diameter, 10 feet high, and could hold about 50 bushels.

Elsewhere in the state, caches were not so elaborate. Large baskets were merely stored inside houses, caves, or rock crevices. Perhaps the most unusual storage technique was that of the Wintu, who buried acorns in wet, heavy soil near cold springs. Although the nuts became swollen, soft, and blackened with age, they remained fresh for years. Farmers came across many of these caches as they plowed new fields and found good acorns that had been buried up to 30 years before. The acorns were also leached of bitter tannins by the water, giving them the taste of boiled potatoes.

As needed, acorns were removed from granaries, hulled, and prepared for cooking. Each family usually stored and processed its own acorns; the women would make acorn meal, often preparing enough for several days' food. (In the case of a large feast, these tasks could occupy many women in the tribe for two or three days.) If the hulls were dry, they could be cracked by holding the acorn's pointed end against an anvil rock and striking the cup end with a small hammer-stone. If the hulls were green, they would require a hard bite and a twist in order to liberate the kernel. The reddish, papery "skin" that envelopes the kernel was removed. The raw kernels were then ready for processing into flour. Some tribes roasted acorns on hot stones before pounding.

Women of southern tribes, such as the Chumash and Gabrieleno, used stone mortars and pestles to pound acorns. The Valley Yokuts used a broad, deep mortar hewn from a circular slab of oak wood. Pomo women wove strong baskets with a hole in the bottom that were placed over stone mortars to contain the meal and nut fragments. Bedrock mortar holes, worn into massive granite slabs, were used by the Miwok and can still be seen today in the vicinity of rushing Sierra creeks. Women would sit at neighboring mortar holes, perhaps singing in rhythm with the percussive strokes of their pestles.

While acorn meal was versatile and could be used to make a wide variety of foods, acorns themselves were seldom eaten raw by the California Indians, as they usually contain bitter, unpalatable tannins. Whether roasted for eating or cooked in soup, mush, or bread, the acorns of most oak species had to be leached of their tannins prior to consumption. It was known that the kernels, if pulverized, readily gave up the tannins to large amounts of running water.

To complete the leaching process, the acorn meal was sifted, and depending on technique, mixed with water to form a paste. It was then spread into a sandy basin built on top of the ground. The basin could be more than a yard in diameter and was sometimes lined with leaves or pine needles. The meal required as many as ten applications of water, often obtained from a favorite spring. Each application, which covered the meal with a shallow layer of water, was carefully added to avoid disturbing the sandy bottom of the basin. The water was often poured through conifer boughs, which minimized agitation as it flowed into the basin. Hours later, as the coffee-colored seepage gradually turned clear, a grayish-pink flour was left behind. This was separated into fine and coarse grades; the former was best for mush while the latter was best for bread. Several days supply of leached meal for a family could take as much as seven hours of work to prepare. It is no wonder that the Cahuilla believed that tannins were the curse of an angry creator: because of the bitterness of the acorns, women would forever have to spend much of their lives pounding the nuts with mortars and leaching the meal with water.

An Indian woman pounds acorns outside her home near Warner Springs, San Diego County, 1911. SAN DIEGO HISTORICAL SOCIETY, PHOTOGRAPH COLLECTION

A Cahuilla woman fills her granary in eastern San Diego County, circa 1900. SOUTHWEST MUSEUM, LOS ANGELES

Acorn mush was eaten by nearly all tribes in California. Among the Indians that lived south of the Tehachapi Mountains, mush was usually cooked in a stone or clay pot placed over an open fire. In northern and central California, the preparation of acorn was somewhat different. A large, tightly woven basket was half filled with leached acorn flour and mixed with water. Several stones, perhaps four to eight inches in diameter, were heated until glowing and then lowered into the basket. Slow but constant stirring with a strong oak paddle or looped stirring stick was required as the mixture began to hiss, boil, and thicken. Cool stones were replaced with hot ones until the glutinous mixture was ready. The beige or sometimes reddish mush was consumed with fingers or spoons of wood, shell, or elk antler and usually eaten with other foods such as venison or salmon.

There were a great many methods for preparing acorn bread among the tribes of California Indians. In the Sacramento Valley, Indians took the fine, dry flour, added water, and kneaded it into a loaf about two inches thick. A small amount of powdered red clay was added (about 1 part in 20 parts dough), and the loaf was wrapped in a jacket of moist leaves. This was baked overnight on hot stones in a cooking hole that had been filled with an insulating layer of soil. When uncovered, the loaf was jet black and had the consistency of soft cheese. Unlike mush, acorn bread was sweet because the slow cooking converted some of the starch into sugar. In addition, the clay rendered any remaining traces of tannin undetectable to the palate. After a few days the bread became very hard, and it would keep for months. In his long journeys through the Sierra Nevada, John Muir carried his own loaves of this dry, hard acorn bread. He deemed it the most compact and strength-giving food he had ever eaten. Others have commented on the health and longevity of the California natives and attributed it to a diet derived from the strength and vitality of the oak. (Contemporary preparation of acorn is introduced in "Acorn Today" at the end of this chapter.)

Acorns at Pomo festival, Point Reyes. LEWIS KEMPER

An Acorn Feast In 1907

THE QUANTITY OF ACORN MEAL COOKED AND eaten by Indians is almost beyond belief. At a ceremony for the dead, held near Bald Rock, Tuolumne County, California, in early October, 1907, the preparation of the acorn food for the mourners and guests was begun several days in advance. Two cooking places and five leaches, each about [four] feet in diameter, were in...operation for several days.

On the opening day I counted at the cooking places about 50 huge baskets, each holding from one to two bushels, full of freshly cooked acorn mush (nup'-pah). The mush is so heavy that the services of two strong women were required to lift each basket and place it in the large conical burden basket on the back of a third woman, who slowly carried it to the roundhouse where the ceremony was held.

In addition to the mush, there were at least 50 turtle-shaped loaves of acorn bread (oo-lay'), made by dipping out the hot mush in a special basket and plunging it (turning it out of the basket) into a cold, running stream.

The action of the cold water, curiously enough, causes the loaves to contract and harden. They are then placed on rocks to drain, and in the course of a few days become dry and hard and may be carried for weeks, until consumed.

The total quantity of acorn mush and bread made for this ceremony must have exceeded a ton in weight.

—C. Hart Merriam,
from *National Geographic*, 1918

Uses Beyond Food

Oaks and acorns were also used as medicines. The bitter tannins were extracted from acorns, bark, and insect galls in order to treat a variety of ailments. Padre Ambris at Mission San Antonio de Padua noted that the Salinan people used a brew made from "western white oak" (probably valley oak) to treat bladder problems. Watery infusions of insect gall were preferred for washing open wounds. He also noted that simply by eating large quantities of acorns, effective treatment was given to "many of the ills upon which they concentrated: bowel regulation, dropsy, fistula, bladder, bile, spleen, dizziness, [and] intermittent fevers." The Luiseño made a remedy for boils and other inflammations from a particular mold that grew on acorn mush. Perhaps the mold, like many other fungi, was the source of an effective antibiotic.

Tannins were also useful for making dyes and decorating animal skins. Bark from valley oak was commonly boiled and then mixed with iron oxide until the pigment was jet black. This could be used to dye roots for weaving designs into baskets or for camouflaging the fibers in fish nets. Hides were also treated with bark extracts in order to color and soften the skin. Wintu people used black, live, or white oak bark for this purpose and obtained a variety of rich, brown shades. Oak galls, which contain large amounts of tannin when they are young and soft, were squeezed by the Lake Miwok to produce a blue-black ink for tattooing.

The material importance of oaks in California was especially reflected in the spiritual lives of the native people. The Wintu used acorns and oaks as spiritual symbols surrounding birth, puberty, marriage, and death. After the umbilical cord of a new Wintu boy had dropped off, it was tied to the limb of a live oak tree to insure that he would be alert and bold. At puberty, a girl was kept in isolation for months, eating only the acorn soup prepared by her mother or grandmother. When ready to marry, she took up residence in a man's house to help his mother pound acorns and gather seeds. At death, a corpse was always sent into the spirit world with a basket of acorn meal and water for the soul to eat and drink. Wintu mourners purified themselves after the burial by bathing in the smoke of a smoldering scrub or live oak bough. Oaks were invoked in the death rituals of other California tribes as well. A grieving Nisenan widow would paint her face with a mixture of acorn ash and pine pitch. Pomo women sprinkled acorn meal on the funeral pyre and sang mourning songs as they retraced the last footsteps of the deceased. But more than in death, oaks were summoned in celebrations of life and fertility, as revealed by this Maidu song:

> The acorns come down from heaven.
> I plant the short acorns in the valley.
> I plant the long acorns in the valley.
> I sprout; I, the black acorn, sprout; I sprout.

An Indian offering flag with acorns near Yosemite Valley, 1990. BOB RONEY

The Acorn Maidens

ONCE, ACORNS WERE IKXAREYAVS (SPIRIT-people). They were told, "You will soon have to leave the Spirit World. You are going to go. You must all have nice hats to wear. You will have to weave them." So they started to weave good-looking hats. Then all at once they were told, "You will have to go now! Human is being raised. Go quickly!"

Black Oak Acorn did not have time to finish her hat, so she picked up her big bowl basket.

Tan Oak [tanbark] Acorn did not have time to clean her hat and make it smooth.

But Post [valley] Oak Acorn and Maul [canyon] Oak Acorn finished their hats out perfectly, and even had time to clean them. Tan Oak Acorn noticed this, and said: "Though my hat is not cleaned, would that I be the best acorn soup."

Then they went. They spilled (from the Heavens) into human's place. "Human will spoon us up," they said. They were Ikxareyavs, those Acorn Maidens, they were Heavenly Ikxareyavs. They shut their eyes and then they turned their faces into their hats when they came to this earth. That is the way the Acorns did.

Tan Oak Acorn wished bad luck toward Post Oak Acorn and Maul Oak Acorn, because they had nice hats. She was jealous of them. Nobody likes to eat Post Oak Acorn. And Maul Oak Acorn does not taste good either. They do not taste good, and their soups are black. And Maul Oak Acorn is hard to pound.

They were all painted when they first spilled down. Black Oak Acorn was striped, and when one picks it up on the ground it is still striped, even nowadays. She was striped all over, that girl was. But Tan Oak Acorn did not paint herself much, because she was mad that her hat was not finished.

When they spilled down, they turned their faces into their hats. And nowadays they still have their faces inside their hats.

—John P. Harrington,
from *Bureau of American Ethnography Bulletin No. 7*, 1932

Oaks and Immigrant Californians

Prior to their arrival in California, European people had long lived among the oak landscapes of the Old World. Although the Old World species were different, they shared many characteristics with the California oaks encountered during the expeditions of Vizcaíno, Portolá, Malaspina, and others. The dominant oak of California's coastal foothills and valleys (usually coast live oak) resembled the evergreen oaks of their Mediterranean homeland and was called *encina*. The majestic valley oak was so much like the emigrant's own *roble* (*Quercus robur*) that they called it by the same name. These trees seemed so familiar to the colonists that Old World technologies—as well as attitudes regarding forest resources—were easily and rapidly deployed in the new, seemingly unlimited world of California.

The Spanish Period

Juan Rodríguez Cabrillo, a Portuguese sailor and explorer for the Spanish crown, was the first European to make landfall in Alta California (1542). Cabrillo was too busy searching for the mythical Strait of Anian, however, to pay any attention to the natural features of the coast. The first navigator to survey the California coastline for future exploration and settlement was Sebastián Vizcaíno. On December 16, 1602, Vizcaíno landed at what he considered an excellent harbor in a bay that he named for the Viceroy of New Spain, the *Conde de Monterey*. On shore, the party located a huge oak tree which served as their shelter while they celebrated mass. A large, deep cross was cut into the tree's trunk, which in effect became the Pacific coast equivalent of Plymouth Rock. Later, Vizcaíno urged that the bay become a shelter for Spanish ships sailing to and from Manila, noting that the dense forests of oak and pine could be used for repairs and fuel.

The Spanish empire would not act on his recommendations for more than 150 years, when in 1769 Gaspar de Portolá and about 60 men trekked from San Diego to San Francisco Bay in search of Vizcaíno's Monterey Bay. As they worked their way north, the explorers bestowed oak-related names on a number of locales. Two days after departing San Diego, Portolá's party passed an oak-shrouded creek in a valley they christened *Cañada de los Encinos*; a later settlement there would be named Encinitas. The diarist for the expedition, Father Juan

Crespí, indicated that San Fernando Valley was named *Valle de Santa Catalina de Bononia de los Encinos* for its sprawling groves of live oaks; the only part of the cumbersome place name that remains is that of the campsite, Encino. Crespí's journal also described the Santa Clarita Valley to the immediate north as "delightful and beautiful in the plain. . . . [W]e saw many tall and thick cottonwoods and oaks." Portolá's men were the first Europeans to travel overland through Alta California and venture through the territory's dense shrublands; perhaps they were also the first to apply the word *chaparro*, Spanish for "scrub oak," to the thick chaparral vegetation that covered many coastal slopes and headlands.

While Portolá was blazing an explorer's trail, Father Junípero Serra was busy establishing Alta California's first mission at San Diego. Between 1769 and 1823, the Franciscans founded 21 missions in coastal valleys with plentiful timber and reliable water sources. During this time oaks served as an integral part of the colonial process: Father

Father Serra celebrates mass beneath an oak near Monterey Bay in June, 1770, as depicted in an 1879 painting by artist Leon Trousset. CALIFORNIA HISTORICAL SOCIETY

Serra's first mass in Monterey was celebrated beneath the boughs of a coast live oak; the mission bell at San Antonio de Padua was hung from the branches of an oak; huge oaks were cut to provide lumber for framing doors and windows of mission buildings; smaller oak limbs fueled bonfires to produce charcoal needed for making lime. Even the corresponding distributions of oaks and native people allowed the mission system to efficiently perform one of its primary objectives: to convert the Indians to Christianity, thereby increasing the population of "citizens" and strengthening the Spanish claim to this remote, New World.

Travelers to the developing region took careful note of the oaks, as their diaries and place names indicate. Father Pedro Font, who accompanied Juan Bautista de Anza on his second California expedition in 1775-76, remarked about the oaks at Missions San Gabriel and San Antonio de Padua. He described Mission San Antonio as "situated in the Sierra de Santa Lucia . . . the mission is in a rather wide valley some ten leagues long and full of large oaks, for which reason they call the mission San Antonio de la Cañada de los Robles." Farther north, the Santa Clara Valley was known as *Llano de los Robles*, or "plain of the oaks." Font also named the southern pass over the Santa Lucia mountains *El Paso de Robles*, which was adopted as the town's name in 1889.

Recognizing the agricultural potential presented by California's virgin soils, mild coastal climate, and savannas of lush perennial grasses, the Spanish fathers were quick to introduce intensive Old World farming and animal husbandry. Gardens were grown from precious seeds of corn and beans, and near the missions small orchards began to replace the native trees. Of greatest consequence to the oaks, however, was the arrival of cattle and sheep. Heavy, year-round grazing and the rapid spread of annual European weeds began with 200 cattle at the first mission in San Diego. By 1823, all of the missions had livestock operations. Mission San Gabriel near Los Angeles had as many as 100,000 head of cattle on 17 separate ranchos. The ranchos were established around the missions, often using large, distinctive oaks as boundary markers. Perhaps one-sixth of the state's area was intensively farmed and grazed at the height of the Mission Period, as millions of sheep, horses, goats, and pigs exacted their toll on the native oaks and oak landscapes of California.

Like many California missions, La Purísima was situated near coast live oak woodlands. FRANK BALTHIS

The Mexican Era

California passed from Spanish to Mexican domination in the mid-1820s, and the missions entered a long period of decline. Huge parcels of land were granted to individuals for ranching, and the hide and tallow trade became Mexican California's dominant industry. American traders called at the ports of Yerba Buena (San Francisco), Monterey, Santa Barbara, San Diego, and points in between to pick up thousands of hides—called "California bank notes"—and barrels of tallow in exchange for manufactured goods. Some leather tanning, using bark extracts from tanbark and live oak trees, took place in the region as early as 1792. The vast majority of hides, however, were shipped east for treatment, returning in the form of finished products such as belts, shoes, saddles, harnesses, and luggage. The tanning industry would not reach its zenith in California until the late 19th century, with devastating consequences for tanbarks and oaks throughout the state. By the turn of the century, the rapacious harvest of tanbarks prompted some botanists to predict that the species would become extinct.

Spanish and Mexican control along the southern and central coast, combined with a Russian settlement at Fort Ross in Northern California, confined the Americans to explorations of the state's interior. Jedediah Smith's journeys through the Central Valley in 1826-28 revealed a startling richness of native plant and animal life. Smith wrote that he and his men rode through "groves of oak prairies and meadows of blue clover

CATTLE-DROVE, (*northward-bound for a market*) *passing the* VALLEY *of* SANTA BÁRBARA.

A cattle drive near Santa Barbara Mission, as sketched by artist Edward Vischer in 1865. THE BANCROFT LIBRARY

watered by small streams." They found and trapped abundant amounts of beaver. Their stay in the valley during the winter of 1827 was a blessed one. Water and game were plentiful and massive valley oaks provided good shelter for their camp.

Oak landscapes came to symbolize gentle refuge from the hostile climates and rugged topography encountered by the explorers. During their 1833 crossing of the Sierra Nevada near Yosemite, the men led by Lieutenant Joseph R. Walker struggled across the high, cold mountains with few provisions and much apprehension. As the party descended into the mixed forests west of Tuolumne Meadows, a hunter-scout brought a load of acorns back to camp, which were apparently dropped by a startled Indian. The diarist of the party, Zenas Leonard, wrote: "These nuts caused no little rejoicing in our camp, not only on account of their value as food, but because they gave us the gratifying evidence that a country mild and salubrious enough to produce acorns was not far distant." A similar sentiment was expressed by John C. Frémont, who led an 1844 expedition to California that first reached the Sacramento Valley near the American River. As the Sierra's cold and snowy conifer forests gave way to verdant oak woodlands, Frémont noted:

> The country is smooth and grassy; the [woodlands] had no undergrowth; and in the open valleys of rivulets, or around spring heads, the low groves of oak give the appearance of orchards in an old cultivated country.

Cattle hides, such as these displayed at La Purísima Mission State Historic Park, were a chief export product during California's Mexican era. JOHN EVARTS

Botanical Explorations

Colonization and resource exploitation were not the only objectives of expeditions to California. Scientists and naturalists explored the Pacific coast as early as 1789, collecting native plant and animal species for later analysis and description. The Malaspina Expedition (1789-94) was Spain's first and only scientific foray to the western edge of the continent. The Malaspina's officers went ashore at Monterey Bay, where they collected specimens of two oaks that were later turned over to one of the expedition's botanists, Luis Nee. Upon his return to Spain, Nee published descriptions of the coast live and valley oak, thereby introducing Europe to the oaks of California.

During a three year stay in California (1829-31), Scottish botanist David Douglas collected and described 50 kinds of trees and shrubs, including blue and Oregon oak. The extensive collections of Karl Hartweg from the Royal Horticultural Society of London included the previously unknown black oak, obtained from Sonoma County in 1846. A German physician named F. A. Wislizenius retrieved branches and acorns of interior live oak from along the Sacramento River in 1851 and sent them to the famous French botanist Alphonse de Candolle for description and naming. Throughout the 19th century, specimens literally flowed to the university botanical gardens of England, Sweden, France, and Germany—along with stories of the grand size and magnificence of these New World oaks. Reports of a huge oak near the settlement of Chico in Sacramento Valley attracted the interest of eminent British botanist Sir Joseph Hooker. Joined by American botanist Dr. Asa Gray and naturalist John Muir, Hooker journeyed to Chico's fabled valley oak in 1877 and found that the stories were true: the trunk of this immense tree was nine feet in diameter. The canopy was more than 150 feet across—enough to provide shade for 9,000 people on a summer's day. The Hooker Oak, as it became known, stood in Chico's Bidwell Park until May 1977 when its great, aged limbs were finally overcome by wind and gravity.

Early-day botanists traveled to rural areas to find new oaks. SAN DIEGO HISTORICAL SOCIETY, PHOTOGRAPH COLLECTION

The American Period

The impacts of the gold rush on California's human population are legend, with stories woven as much from fantasy as fact. The impacts on California's oaks, however, are less well known, but no less dramatic. While Richard Henry Dana was sailing the West coast during 1835-36, he landed on "Wood Island" in San Francisco Bay to collect oak fuelwood. In his log he noted that this large island was "covered with trees to the water's edge" so that only a week's worth of work provided for a year's supply. Upon his return to the region in 1859, Dana was amazed at the changes that had taken place in the ensuing 25 years. Where grizzly bears and mountain lions once roamed through oak groves, burgeoning cities and towns stood. The island where his crew had cut a few dozen coast live oaks was now "clean shorn of trees" and known as Angel Island. (Many of the oaks cut at that time must have stump-sprouted because the island's woodlands are now composed of many multiple-trunk trees.)

The first significant discovery of gold in California was made by Francisco Lopez at Placerita Canyon (Los Angeles County) in 1842. According to legend, Lopez was resting and dreamt of gold as he napped beneath a large coast live oak. He awoke and decided to gather a meal of wild onions. As he pulled the bulbs he noticed small yellow flecks sprinkled among the dangling roots. This "oak of the golden dream" was included in the mining claim soon granted to Lopez by Governor Juan Bautista Alvarado. The Placerita strike caused little excitement, however, compared with James Marshall's discovery of gold near Sacramento six years later.

The gold rush of 1849 brought tens of thousands of men to comb the hills in search of wealth. The clear-cutting of oaks on Angel Island was a fate soon shared by many other woodlands throughout the territory as the influx of settlers created large demands for energy and charcoal. Oak wood was also the principal fuel for many of the state's steam-powered locomotives; before the Central Pacific converted to coal in the early 1870s, its tenders were often filled with fuelwood harvested from blue and valley oak woodlands that lined the railroad's Central California route.

An even greater demand existed for the wood of coast live oak. Relatively easy to split and prized for its hot, slow-burning coals, it commanded a higher price per cord than any other California oak.

Butte County's "Hutchins Oak" towers above nearby orchards, a remnant of a lost oak habitat. JEFF GNASS

The magnificent groves around Santa Barbara, for example, were reduced during the Spanish and Mexican eras and further depleted during the American period when much of the area's oak wood was sent to Los Angeles. The consumption of trees went unchecked until 1855 when the Santa Barbara City Council passed an ordinance prohibiting cutting upon municipal lands. Unfortunately, most of the remaining woodlands were privately owned. In 1859 an attempt was made to regulate the cutting by levying a tax on wagon loads of wood, but this was to no avail. With many of its oak groves destroyed, Santa Barbara eventually replanted with various species of exotic trees—a pattern repeated in countless communities across the state.

Gold production in the Mother Lode peaked by the mid-1850s, but California's diverse natural resources continued to attract tens of thousands of immigrants. While oak wood was not extensively used for building materials—since long-grained redwood and pine were more suitable for construction—it was utilized for a variety of other purposes. Wedges made from canyon oak, which is also known as "maul oak," were used to split redwood. This strong hardwood also found favor among wagon makers who used it for wheels, axles, and wagon tongues. Similarly, blue oak was good for tool handles as well as firewood. Coast live, valley, and interior live oak were best suited for fuel and charcoal, which fired the blacksmith's ovens and fed the smelters that extracted mercury, silver, and copper from their parent ores. In addition, thousands of coast live oaks from the Santa Clarita Valley were cast into the ovens of Los Angeles bakeries.

Millions of acres of oak-covered land were cleared for farms and orchards in the Sacramento, San Joaquin, Salinas, Santa Clara, and San Gabriel valleys. Flood control became a high priority along the great rivers; extensive riparian forests were rapidly demolished as floodplains were graded and artificial levees constructed. Beyond the levees, families built their houses and barns beneath the shade of ancient oaks. Cattle and hogs were fed on oak seedlings and acorns, and oak limbs fed the home fires. Children of pioneer settlers cherished oak galls as toys. Clusters of settlements, road intersections, towns, cities, and other prominent landmarks, nearly 150 in all, were soon named after the native oaks. At the edges of a few of these towns, such as Second Garrote, Carpinteria, and Hangtown, old oaks with high, strong limbs were used in the administration of frontier justice.

Oak trees have shaded the graves of both the famous and obscure, and have long been associated with human burials. Perhaps they serve as long-lived monuments to the dead while offering a symbol of strength and protection to the living. One such monument is found in the Tehachapi Mountains, at what is now known as Fort Tejon State Historic Park. It is a large valley oak known as the Peter LeBeck Oak. Legend says that LeBeck was a French-Canadian trapper who was killed by one of the area's many grizzly bears and buried by his unknown companions beneath the oak that now bears his name. A carved epitaph once visible on the tree's bark succinctly stated: "Peter LeBeck killed by a X bear OctR 17 1837." A group known as the Foxtail Rangers exhumed LeBeck's remains in 1890, but further clues as to his identity and reasons for being in the area have eluded researchers. In the farmlands north of Fort Tejon, survivors of a deadly shootout mourned the dead and found comfort beneath the boughs of another valley oak near Hanford in Kings County. A long and bitter land dispute between Mussel Slough settlers and Southern Pacific Railroad officials

Large valley oaks on farm lands in the upper Salinas Valley are destoyed with the help of explosives, circa 1915. ATASCADERO HISTORICAL SOCIETY

"Oaks at Madison and 8th Streets, Oakland," painted by Ferdinand Richardt in 1869. COLLECTION OF THE OAKLAND MUSEUM, GIFT OF MR. LESTER M. HALE. PHOTO CREDIT: M. LEE FATHERREE

erupted into violence on May 11, 1880. The spreading embrace of shade from the old oak on Henry Brewer's farm provided a place of rest on that terrible day.

The serenity and beauty of the native oaks were, of course, noted under more fortunate circumstances. Individual landowners who were lucky enough to have oaks on their property came to appreciate their unique California allure. Engelmann oak became the design symbol for California's Arts and Crafts Movement of 1890 to 1930. The growing popularity of the Mission Revival and Spanish Colonial Revival styles of architecture in the teens and 1920s was enhanced by the presence of deep green *encinas* or majestic *robles* in the surrounding gardens.

Perhaps the best example of a homeowner going to great lengths to accommodate the native oaks is newspaper publisher William Randolph Hearst. (See "The Oaks of San Simeon" in this chapter.) His architect for San Simeon Castle, Julia Morgan, became known for blending architectural

and landscape elements into a new, indigenous vision of California that is also seen in her designs at Northern California's Mills College and Asilomar State Beach and Conference Center. Several of the University of California campuses, especially UC Berkeley, are graced with shady groves of native oaks.

Coast live oaks complement the Spanish Colonial style architecture of the Santa Barbara Museum of Natural History, built in 1922. JOHN EVARTS

The Oaks of San Simeon

IN APRIL 1919, NEWSPAPER PUBLISHER William Randolph Hearst met with his architect, Julia Morgan, to begin designing an elaborate estate for his rustic property in the Santa Lucia Mountains north of San Luis Obispo. As they discussed Hearst's plans, little did they know that the building project would eventually span three decades and become a California landmark and major tourist attraction: Hearst Castle.

The estate was to be situated on an oak-shaded hilltop overlooking the Pacific near the seaside community of San Simeon. As construction began, Hearst's utmost concern was the preservation of the native trees that dotted the building site. He decreed that numerous coast live oak and bay trees be incorporated into the landscaping, and under no circumstances were live oaks to be removed.

Many of the oaks were 150 to 200 years old, with huge trunks, thick, twisting branches, and massive roots. Julia Morgan had no choice but to move some of the oaks—but how? At her drafting table, she devised a method for excavating, boxing, and moving the trees, and later described the procedure in a letter to Hearst:

> The program [of moving an oak] consisted of tunneling under the tree and casting three or four parallel reinforced concrete girders under the main root area of the tree. A more or less circular trench was then dug around the tree and a reinforced concrete band was poured in this ring against the earth containing the roots. A bottom was then placed in this ring by undermining and lagging, using the concrete girders to support the lagging. Timbers and rollers were then placed under the girders and the tree was then ready for either jacking up or moving laterally.
>
> In some cases the moving was done by means of rollers, and in at least one case, where the movement was downhill, the moving was effected by means of greased skids.

Moving mature coast live oaks during construction of Hearst Castle. HEARST MONUMENT ARCHIVES

From 1926, when the first oak was moved to make way for the main building, until 1948, when construction at Hearst Castle was completed, six mature coast live oaks were relocated. Hearst also ordered an oak to be rotated so that its low-hanging branches would not disturb a walkway.

The relocation of oaks at Hearst Castle set a precedent in landscape architecture: prior to that time, oaks and other large specimen trees were rarely moved to make way for developments. Visitors to Hearst San Simeon State Historical Monument now come to enjoy the beauty of the man-made environment and the impressive art collection that Hearst used to furnish his home. They also appreciate the ancient coast live oaks that grow here, some of which were moved during construction of the castle. Four of the specimens are still alive and continue to provide shade, color, and habitat, thanks to the efforts of Julia Morgan and William Randolph Hearst.

—Robert C. Pavlik

Vineyards, such as this one in San Luis Obispo County, have replaced tens of thousands of acres of native oak woodlands. KAREN AND ROLAND MUSCHENETZ

Using Oaks in the Modern World

As California's human population exploded in the 20th century, the trend towards consumptive rather than sustained uses of oaks and oak communities was rapidly accelerated. In 1900 the total population of the state was 1.5 million people; by 1991, the number had surpassed 30 million. Most of this growth took place after 1940, during which time the oak stands throughout the state declined precipitously. In San Luis Obispo County, the reduction in hardwood (mostly oak) acreage was 27%, in Los Angeles County it ranged up to 38%, and in Tuolumne and Santa Barbara counties it was 42%. The increased demand for land to raise crops, and to build houses, commercial centers, and roads, has had a great and irreversible impact. Other uses of oak communities, such as fuelwood cutting, timbering, grazing, recreation, and scientific study, have also been important in modern California. These types of resource utilization appear to be sustainable if they do not severely inhibit oak germination and growth.

Consumptive Uses

Within this century, agricultural clearing has been the single most consumptive use of oak woodlands and riparian forests in the state. Oak communities with level topography and rich soil were among the first areas converted to large-scale farming operations by California's modern agricultural industry. The woodlands of the San Fernando, San Gabriel, and Santa Ana valleys were exchanged for vast orchards of oranges, lemons, and walnuts. More than 70% of all riparian forests in the Central Valley were cleared for plantations of stone fruits, olives, almonds, pears, and a wide variety of vegetables. Rich bottomlands in the Napa and Sonoma valleys were planted with grapes. Row crops and orchards replaced the woodlands and savannas of Tehama, Mendocino, Santa Clara, Monterey, and Riverside counties. Although there is no doubt that California farmers have built one of the most productive and profitable agricultural industries in the world, there is also no doubt that it was established at great expense to the native oaks.

Since the 1940s, more than one million acres of oak woodland, and perhaps as many as two million acres, have been cleared of trees in order to make range improvements for livestock. Rangeland clearing took place in 42 of the 58 counties, but was concentrated in and around the Central Valley. Blue oak was the species most often removed, but interior live, coast live, and canyon oak were also affected.

Following World War II, California's economy and population entered a period of unprecedented expansion. Intensive land development for homes, commercial buildings, reservoirs, roads, power transmission lines, and pipelines has consumed oak communities in both coastal and inland counties. The growth of cities such as Redding, Sacramento, San Jose, Fresno, and San Diego, and the many suburbs of Los Angeles and San Francisco, occurred in oak-covered areas or on lands previously converted from oaks to agriculture. Since the early 1970s these developments have taken place on 92,000 acres of oak woodland, averaging about 7,400 acres per year. Recent projections indicate that by early next century an additional 244,000 acres will be affected, including communities of blue oak (160,000 acres), coast live oak (50,000 acres), and valley oak (34,000 acres). Whether the oaks will be removed entirely or a few left as stately remnants amidst a sea of houses, the overall effect will be the same: a population or community of oaks will be depleted once and for all.

Sustainable Uses

Oak wood has long been recognized as a superior source of fuel and charcoal because of its density and lack of flammable resin. Commercial harvest of oak fuelwood dates back to the mid-19th century. In recent years, oak cutting—as opposed to clearing—has increased dramatically: in 1980, the California State Board of Equalization determined that more than 12,000 cords (1 cord = 128 cubic feet) of hardwoods (primarily oaks) were cut for use as fuel in homes and industry; by 1985 this figure had nearly tripled to 35,000 cords per year. This still amounts to a very small fraction of the total available wood and has involved less than 14% of California's woodland acreage. In many areas of the state, oak fuelwood commands a price that provides considerable economic incentive for commercial harvesters. Blue, interior live, and Oregon oak account for more than 75% of the productive acreage.

Until very recently, lumber production from California oaks has been insignificant when compared to lumber production from pines, firs, and cedars. In 1982 only 10 million board feet of hardwood lumber passed out of California's sawmills, or about 0.4% of the total 2.6 billion board feet produced. Despite the fact that demand for quality oak products is high and that suitable hardwoods are abundant (there are about 25 billion board feet of hardwood sawtimber in the California inventory), there have been few attempts to utilize the resource. The primary reason is that the technology of harvesting and processing timber has always been adapted to the characteristics of softwood species and communities. Softwood trees, which often grow in dense, single-species stands, have long, wide, straight trunks which can be efficiently converted into lumber. Oaks, by contrast, grow in scattered stands, which makes harvesting more difficult; the irregular trunks of oaks are also more difficult to mill. New technologies have recently been developed, however, and at least one company, Cal Oak of Oroville, has succeeded in producing oak paneling, flooring, furniture stock, and doors. In 1985 this one operation produced 3.3 million board feet of high-grade lumber, 80%

Top: Livestock grazing is one of the most important commercial uses of California's oak savannas and woodlands. DAVID CAVAGNARO
Bottom: Oak woodlands furnish much of the state's firewood. PAUL R. JOHNSON

of which was from black oak. Black oak lumber compares favorably with oak lumber from the eastern United States in terms of beauty and ease of woodworking. Having overcome some of the technical and economic problems associated with oak timber production, it is possible that some expansion of the industry is likely in the future.

One of the most important contemporary uses of oaks and oak communities is for livestock grazing. Acorns are highly regarded as a food source for domestic cattle, sheep, and pigs. They ripen and fall at a time of the year when quality forage is scarce and are, at the same time, a good source of carbohydrates and crude fiber. Sheep fed a diet of 30% blue oak acorns and 70% standard feed gained an average of 0.32 pounds per week, compared to an average loss of 0.86 pounds per week in control animals given 100% standard feed. Oak leaves are also browsed for their protein and tend to be available during a large portion of the year.

More important, however, is the fact that oak communities, especially blue oak woodland, have a productive understory of annual and perennial grasses that forms the basis of the multi-billion dollar livestock industry in California. About 60% of the state's rangelands, or 10.5 million acres, are oak woodlands that provide meat and dairy products for millions of people. From the standpoint of the oaks, however, livestock grazing is a double-edged sword. On one hand, moderate grazing acts as a substitute for wildfire, eliminating annual grasses and shrubs that compete with oak seedlings as well as with established trees. But grazers can also be detrimental to oaks by consuming acorns, browsing foliage, trampling or eating seedlings, and compacting the soil. In addition, the conversion of oak woodland into annual grassland by extensive clearing represents a consumptive use of oaks with only short-term economic benefits at best. Between 1945 and 1975, about 32,000 acres of oak woodlands were cleared every year, but the benefits to range and livestock production lasted only about 15 years at a given site. This implies that clearing for purposes of range improvement may not be as desirable as once thought and, indeed, the rate of clearing since the 1970s has declined to less than 2,500 acres per year.

Recreation is an important part of today's use of California's oak communities. Often beautiful and serene, they provide opportunities for wildlife study,

A hiker marvels at the massive limbs of a coast live oak in Crystal Cove State Park. BILL EVARTS

plant identification, hunting, camping, hiking, and quiet reflection. A great number of county, regional, state, and even national parks preserve small pieces of oak landscapes across California. Examples include Placerita Canyon Park and Nature Center near Los Angeles, the East Bay Regional Park District near Oakland, Cuyamaca Rancho State Park near San Diego, and Pinnacles National Monument near Salinas. (More than 100 places to view native oaks on public lands are described in Chapter Six.)

Finally, the scientific uses of California's oak landscapes cannot be ignored. In addition to parkland, oak reserves have been established by the Nature Conservancy, the U. S. Forest Service, the Bureau of Land Management, the State of California (Department of Forestry and the Department of Fish and Game), and the University of California. The reserves are essential for studying the basic biology of oaks and their communities and for conducting research on the preservation, use, and restoration of these invaluable California resources.

Historic Oaks of California

The Hooker Oak, circa 1900. BIDWELL MANSION S. H. P. / SPECIAL COLLECTIONS, MERIAM LIBRARY, CSU CHICO

Hooker Oak

Accounts of a gargantuan valley oak in the Sacramento Valley compelled British botanist Sir Joseph Hooker to travel halfway around the globe to investigate this tree. In autumn 1877, Hooker joined naturalist John Muir, American botanist Asa Gray, and General John Bidwell beneath the massive limbs of this arboreal landmark. Bidwell Park, Chico, Butte County.

Jack London Oak*

This stout coast live oak honors novelist Jack London. In 1904 London ran unsuccessfully for Oakland mayor as a socialist. The tree was transplanted to Oakland's City Hall Plaza on January 20, 1917, a few months after London's death. City of Oakland Parks and Recreation, City Hall Plaza (next to City Hall), Oakland, Alameda County.

Serra Mass Oak

Father Junípero Serra held the first mass at Monterey in 1770 beneath the canopy of a coast live oak—probably the same tree where Vizcaíno celebrated landfall in 1602. Venerated by pioneers for over 100 years, the tree died and was replaced by a monument in 1896. Monterey State Historic Park, Pacific Street near Scott, Monterey County.

Big Oak

Big Oak was the mascot tree for the infamous gold rush town of Big Oak Flat. This huge valley oak—at least 11 feet in diameter—graced the main street of shops, hotels, dance halls, and fraternal lodges that sprang up between 1848 and 1863. It was killed by miners who secretly removed the earth from around its roots one night in order to thoroughly extract the "metal of madness." Highway 120, Big Oak Flat, Tuolumne County.

Charter Oak*

Beneath this valley oak a party under the command of Major James D. Savage conducted the election that established Tulare County on July 10, 1852. Woodville, the county's first white settlement and its original seat of government, is located ½ mile south of this tree. Seven miles northeast of Visalia along the St. John's River, Tulare County.

Peter Lebeck Oak*

Peter Lebeck was killed by a grizzly bear in 1837 while trapping in the Tehachapi Mountains. He was buried beneath a valley oak that still bears his epitaph. Fort Tejon State Historic Park, 4201 Fort Tejon Rd. (off I-5), Lebec, Kern County.

Residents pose at the remains of Big Oak Flat's mascot tree, late 1800s. SOUTHWEST MUSEUM, LOS ANGELES

The Peter Lebeck Oak at Fort Tejon State Historic Park, 1991. BILL EVARTS

Oak of the Golden Dream*

The balmy shade of this gnarled coast live oak may have induced Francisco Lopez to dream of finding gold in Placerita Canyon. His premonition was fulfilled when he saw dull yellow flecks clinging to the roots of wild onions he collected in the vicinity. This 1842 discovery was California's first gold strike. Placerita Canyon Park, 19152 Placerita Canyon Rd., Newhall, Los Angeles County.

Oak of Peace

While encamped beside this coast live oak on January 12, 1847, General Andrés Pico sent an envoy to meet with Col. John C. Frémont. The next morning—after considering the Americans' terms for capitulation—Pico marched his troops to Cahuenga Pass where he surrendered, bringing an end to the War with Mexico. City of Glendale Parks and Community Services, 2211 Bonita Dr., Glendale, Los Angeles County.

* These trees are still standing.

Acorn Today

As for countless generations, acorn is a precious food for many California Indians today. Strong memories remain of acorn processing techniques used by a respected elder relative, a grandmother, mother, aunt, or someone else; these are a source of continued inspiration.

Acorn is eaten alone, shared during family meals, given as a gift when visiting friends, and prepared for special occasions, such as family get-togethers and community "Big Times," large gatherings which feature feasts, gambling tournaments, and ceremonies. Each fall, several Big Times are hosted throughout California to dedicate and celebrate the new harvest. As Julia Parker (Kashia Pomo) explains, "When the acorn does come, there's dances and songs. We take from the earth, we give back to the earth, and we say thank you."

It's harder to get acorns today than in the past. Many gathering places "owned" by individuals, families, or groups for as long as anyone knows are now off limits because of private property boundaries and modern laws. In many places treasured oak trees have been cut to make way for developments.

Despite the difficulties, people still find a way to gather, knowing that the interaction between the trees and themselves is an important one in which both are nourished. As Julia learned from Yosemite Miwok/Paiute elders, "They told me when it comes get out and pick and gather even if it's one basketful, so the acorn spirit will know you're happy for the acorn, and next year the acorn will come."

While some still make acorn in the old ways, most people lack the necessary baskets and old-time utensils. Instead, there are new ways that creatively blend past and present in an astonishing diversity of methods, the nuances of which vary from group to group, family to family, cook to cook.

Burlap sacks, plastic-mesh sacks, and cardboard boxes have replaced the burden baskets of old among contemporary gatherers. These

Top: Jennifer Bates (Northern Mewuk) demonstrates acorn pounding. MARTHA LEE
Bottom: Julia Parker still sifts acorn meal the old way to separate the fine from the coarse flour. BEV ORTIZ

are loaded in cars and trucks for the trip home.

Then, to prevent mold, the acorns are dried outside the home on cloths, cots, and specially built wire-mesh "tables," or inside in boxes, or on cloth near or beneath wood-burning stoves—whatever will work. Annie Fuller (Northern Mewuk) reserved four small bedrooms on the second story of her family's Twain Harte ranch to spread her acorns to dry. Dorothy Stanley (1924-1990), who was raised by Annie Fuller, recalled how, as a child, she helped mix the acorns up so they wouldn't get moldy: "You

Pomo dancers dedicate the new harvest during an acorn festival at Point Reyes National Seashore, fall 1989. LEWIS KEMPER

went up to the rooms, and you danced all over the acorn. . . . It was kind of fun to go up there and dance barefooted on the acorn. Not everybody was allowed to do this. . . .You had to be a special child to be picked to do this."

Once dried, acorns are commonly stored in boxes, sacks, and jars; again, whatever will work. Stones and hammers are widely used to shell acorns. Winnowing baskets have largely been replaced with knives for scraping away the red skins which adhere to some species' nutmeats. Olive Fulwider (Dry Creek Pomo) removes the skins of black oak by rubbing the kernels between her hands.

Such alternatives have evolved over decades, some dating to the previous century. Hand-crank grinders began to replace pounding stones early on. These were updated as gas and electric power became available. For instance, Dorothy's grandmother had a gas-powered wheat machine controlled by a pulley. "She only pounded by hand when she got angry at grandpa for not starting the machine when she asked," Dorothy recalled. The acorn went

through the machine once, then was placed in a sifting basket to separate the coarse from the fine flour.

Hand-crank grinders adapted to run on electricity provide alternatives to both pounding stones and sifting, as do electric blenders and food mills. To achieve the desired fineness, the meal is put through the grinders more than once.

As with pounding between stones, alternatives to leaching have evolved over decades. Cotton cloth has long been placed atop outdoor sand leaching basins. At times, these cloth-covered basins have been modernized still further by being placed atop a wire-mesh screen attached to a wooden framework and supported a few feet above the ground. Annie Fuller placed pine needles and broken up buck-brush leaves rather than sand atop her screen "table."

Indoors, contemporary leaching methods include placing acorn flour atop a cloth-covered winnowing basket, colander, or strainer perched in the kitchen sink below the faucet. Sometimes the acorn is placed in a cloth sack tied to a kitchen faucet, which is turned on so that water will slowly drip through the acorn throughout the night.

Once leached, freezers and refrigerators are sometimes used to store the acorn flour until cooking time. For cooking, pots, stovetops, and ovens have largely replaced baskets and heated stones.

These are but a few of the many modern ways of preparing acorn. Whatever the method chosen, old or new, the food remains to provide sustenance, enjoyment, memories, and an important expression of cultural heritage which will live on into the future. As explained by Olive Fulwider (Dry Creek Pomo), "And Grandma would say, you have to do this when I'm gone. You like it so much, you have to do this. So that's why I make my acorns. . . . I still do it. I love it."

—Bev Ortiz

CHAPTER FIVE

PRESERVING OAKS
FOR FUTURE GENERATIONS

HEN CALIFORNIA ENTERED THE 20TH century, the state's agricultural and livestock industries were expanding. Patterns of land use established in oak woodlands during the 1800s, including agricultural clearing, woodcutting, and urban expansion, continued and intensified. Cities grew with the pulse of prosperity and spread into the countryside, displacing oak landscapes with the sprawl of houses, industry, roads, and other symptoms of a burgeoning economy.

As oaks fell before the ax and the plow at the turn of the century, California's fledgling conservation movement was fighting to protect other tree species—the redwood and its cousin, the giant sequoia. Organizations such as the Save-the-Redwoods League and the Sierra Club sought new or expanded parklands to protect these majestic conifers. While battles over redwoods and sequoias captured the headlines, the first skirmishes to save oaks were beginning to take place. During the opening decade of the 20th century another concern about oaks surfaced: botanists noted an absence of oak seedlings in areas grazed by livestock. Seventy years passed, however, before the intertwining issues of oak protection and regeneration shared the agenda at scientific symposia devoted to the ecology and management of California's oaks. The symposia, publication of new research, and related public events signalled a growing interest in oaks and marked the beginning of a new era of environmental activism and research on their behalf.

This chapter explores the complex problems that face California's oaks and describes a strategy for oak conservation. It then profiles several oak preservation and habitat restoration efforts.

Oaks in Trouble

In the 220 years that followed the founding of the first Spanish mission at San Diego, California's human population increased from about 300,000 to over 30 million. This staggering growth and the concurrent introduction of ranching and farming to the state's oak-covered valleys, plains, and foothills brought dramatic and irreversible changes to the natural landscape. Among the first to recognize the relentless loss of California's oaks was botanist Willis Linn Jepson, who wrote in 1909:

> In some regions where the horticultural development has been rapid or the needs of an increasing population urgent, extensive areas have been cleared to make room for orchards or gardens, and scarcely a [valley oak] tree remains to tell the story

Above: A small remnant of valley oak riparian forest is preserved at Caswell Memorial State Park. JIM BARRY
Opposite: Homes have displaced the oaks that once graced this valley, Santa Clara County. FRANK BALTHIS

A valley oak is removed from farm land in the upper Salinas Valley, circa 1915. ATASCADERO HISTORICAL MUSEUM

of the old-time monarchs of the soil; in other regions the destruction has not been so complete.

The observations of scientists like Jepson were shared by a growing legion of citizens, some of whom mounted the first efforts on behalf of endangered oaks. Early campaigns, such as the one in Visalia to preserve a valley oak grove in 1909 or the fight in Glendale in 1927 to save a venerable coast live oak from road construction, were harbingers of the widespread concern for native oaks that began to coalesce in the 1970s and 1980s.

Researchers in California's universities and colleges, as well as biologists at state and federal agencies, had become increasingly aware of oak issues by the 1970s. This was evident in the workshops and papers offered at the first oak symposium held at Scripps College in Claremont in 1979. The proceedings of this meeting, along with those of two subsequent symposia at Cal Poly State University, San Luis Obispo (1986) and UC Davis (1990), were published by the U.S. Forest Service's Pacific Southwest Forest and Range Experimental Station in Berkeley. These reports broadened the

concern about oaks within the scientific community and helped stimulate much of the oak research that is being conducted today.

A cooperative effort to study the management, regeneration, and enhancement of oaks and other hardwood trees was launched in 1986 when the California State Legislature established the

The Giant Oak near Visalia, photographed about 1900, stood 178 feet high. ALAN GEORGE COLLECTION

Integrated Hardwood Range Management Program (IHRMP); the program is conducted by the University of California and the California Department of Forestry and Fire Protection. Provided with state funding and a mandate to study oak resources, the IHRMP sponsors oak research and disseminates oak management information to agencies and citizens throughout California.

The surging interest in oaks during the 1980s also gave rise to the California Oak Foundation. Formed in 1988, the foundation promotes the statewide protection of oaks, and stresses the "conservation, restoration, and management of our native oak heritage."

At the city and county level, proponents of urban forestry have played a growing role in oak protection. By 1991 more than 100 California municipalities had enacted oak tree preservation ordinances. In addition to citizen activism, public acquisition of lands for recreation and wildlife preservation has augmented the protected acreage of oak landscapes. In 1990, for example, Californians passed a bond measure (Proposition 117) that makes $30 million available each year for 30 years for the enhancement and purchase of wildlife habitats, including oak communities.

Despite a growing mantle of protection, California's oaks remain at risk. The vast majority of the state's oak woodlands and savannas are found on private property; many of these oak communities are located in suburban and semi-rural areas destined to be transformed by land development. Since the 1940s, California has lost more than one million acres of oak woodland as a result of rangeland clearing and agricultural conversion. Projections indicate that population growth—and the inevitable suburbanization that accompanies it—may claim another quarter million oak-covered acres by the year 2010.

The Regeneration Problem

While concern for oaks among the public has centered around the need to save individual trees or woodlands, the efforts of the scientific community have largely focused on the issue of oak regeneration. In many areas of the state, particularly in savannas or woodlands with low annual rainfall, oak populations are experiencing little or no tree replacement. Although these populations periodically have seasons of good acorn germination and seedling establishment,

Top: A plant scientist closely inspects the annual rings of a blue oak to determine the tree's age and growth characteristics. CAROLINE L. SHUGART
Bottom: Oaks are converted to firewood during range clearing in Amador County. DANIEL D'AGOSTINI

there is a persistent failure of the seedlings to be "recruited"—to make a transition into saplings and pole-size trees. Communities dominated by valley, blue, or Engelmann oaks are especially devoid of trees established in the last 75 to 125 years. In the absence of vigorous seedlings and saplings to take the place of aging and fallen monarchs, the nature and persistence of many oak landscapes is in jeopardy.

The first scientist to detect poor regeneration among oaks may have been dendrologist George B. Sudworth. In describing blue oak in his 1908 book, *Trees of the Pacific Slope*, he wrote: "Prolific periodic seeder. Seedlings scarce in ground usually

Introduced annual grasses often form a dense ground cover in valley oak savannas. JOHN EVARTS

grazed or cultivated, where much seed is destroyed or has little chance of germination; rather abundant elsewhere." For the next 60 years, however, practically no mention of the oak regeneration problem appears in print—a notable exception being the observations of rancher, botanist, and author Ernest Twisselman, who suggested in 1956 that livestock grazing and introduced annuals were both detrimental to oak recruitment on Kern County rangelands.

In 1971 research ecologist James R. Griffin published the results of his landmark study of oak regeneration in the upper Carmel Valley. Despite good acorn germination and the complete exclusion of livestock, Griffin's seedlings experienced a poor survival rate for a variety of reasons, including browsing by deer, predation by pocket gophers, and competition for soil moisture on grassy slopes. Two years later, Griffin sounded the alarm over the future of valley oaks in Central California in *Fremontia*, the journal of the California Native Plant Society. In an article titled "Valley Oaks—The End of Era?" he stated:

Where are the young trees under the big oaks? At first glance there seem to be none. One can drive through literally tens of thousands of acres and not see a single Valley Oak sapling. The alert observer can poke around and find a few young trees, to be sure, but the conclusion is clear: under present circumstances, large portions of the savanna [on the Hunter Liggett Military Reservation] will not be adequately replaced by Valley Oaks.

The lack of blue oak regeneration and the wholesale clearing of blue oaks to improve rangeland forage was addressed by plant ecologist V. L. Holland in his resonant 1976 article in *Fremontia* titled "In Defense of Blue Oaks." He began by warning: "California may be in danger of losing an important part of its biotic heritage, the picturesque blue oak trees that dot the scenic foothill woodlands." Holland implicated livestock grazing, deer browsing, acorn predation by rodents, and changes in the makeup of California's grassland vegetation as the chief reasons for low recruitment in blue oak stands. The work of researchers like Griffin and Holland raised troubling questions about the myriad causes of poor oak regeneration and set the stage for future scientific and policy debate on the issue.

The widespread lack of oak regeneration is a complex problem with origins that can be traced back to the arrival of the Spanish fathers. Although Indians altered and managed the landscape with fire for hundreds, if not thousands, of years, it was the Europeans who wrought the most profound ecologic changes to California. With permanent settlements came the weeds, livestock, predator control, and fire suppression that would impact the state's flora, fauna, and natural communities forever. We are just beginning to understand how these factors complicate and hinder the establishment of oak seedlings and relate to the problem of oak regeneration.

Since the arrival of the Spanish in the late 1700s, native grasses and wildflowers have been largely replaced by weedy plants that came from the Mediterranean Old World. The seeds of these

A herd of sheep gathers beneath a winter canopy of oaks in the Sacramento Valley. RON SANFORD

weeds, especially those of annual grasses, arrived as stowaways in the hay bales and grain sacks that supplied Spanish settlements and were casually dispersed throughout the territory on the hides and in the feces of roaming cattle and wildlife species. Other weed seeds, such as those of filaree, were sometimes intentionally sown by colonists to ensure plentiful forage for sheep. Livestock preferred to graze on the palatable and nutritious native plants that often lack the barbs, bitter juices, and ephemeral foliage of the European weeds. The weeds, thus avoided, grew with relative impunity for they evolved with these grazers in the Old World. But in the New World they have escaped the diseases, insect pests and other organisms that kept their homeland populations in check. The weedy grasses and herbs spread rapidly, forming a dense, competitive cover that now dominates the California grasslands.

This complete change in the flora of the grasslands has brought other broad ecologic changes that affect oak regeneration. Recent research has shown that introduced annual grasses, which grow rapidly during spring, deplete surface water much earlier in the season than the displaced perennial grasses. This diminishes water supplies to oak seedlings. Although the ultimate effects of grassland composition on oak regeneration are not fully understood, observations such as these suggest that grasslands dominated by introduced species do not provide an environment that is conducive to natural oak regeneration.

In addition to facilitating the spread of competitive, non-native plants, livestock grazing directly impacts oak regeneration. Stock eat leaves, acorns, seedlings, and saplings as they move through the savannas and woodlands. The growth of saplings is suppressed when branches and leaves are browsed, and these saplings may never make the transition to tall adult trees. The extent to which livestock are detrimental to oak regeneration has been the subject of heated debate. Research conducted at a number of locations in California has challenged the assumption that sheep and cattle are the sole culprits in poor oak regeneration. In some cases, sites that have been free of livestock for decades show the same low rates of oak recruitment as lands still being grazed. However, some plant ecologists feel that changes brought about by prior grazing can so alter an environment that the effects of grazing can endure well beyond

Top: Cattle browse on oak leaves, especially when grasses are dry in late summer and fall. RICK PHILLIPS
Bottom: Native bunchgrasses are scattered across this prairie in Tehama County near Corning. TOM GRIGGS

Pole-size saplings, such as the pair pictured here, are rare in many valley oak woodlands. JOHN EVARTS

the point that livestock are removed from the area.

The arrival of Europeans and the introduction of widespread grazing brought other changes to California's oak woodlands that, in aggregate, may contribute to poor oak regeneration. Rangeland soils, for example, are compacted where livestock travel, congregate, and rest, making it difficult for rainfall and oak roots to penetrate. This may be particularly critical in areas as hot and dry as those occupied by the blue and Engelmann oaks.

Domestic livestock are not the only animals that eat oaks, and dramatic changes in populations of oak and acorn predators also accompanied European settlement. Deer populations grew explosively as mountain lions were hunted to protect livestock. Abundant deer place great demands on acorn crops and on oak saplings for nutritious forage. Where herbivore browsing is intense, young oaks may take the form of shrubs or bushes. At the University of California's Hastings Reservation, for example, observations of a group of coast live oak seedlings that became established prior to 1940 showed that by 1969, less than half had begun to make the transition into saplings—the rest remained shrubby because of browsing.

Pocket gophers, mice, and ground squirrels also multiplied in the absence of bobcats, gray fox, coyotes, and badgers. Large populations of these

and other rodents voraciously consume acorns as well as the now-abundant seeds of non-native grasses and herbs. Studies in Carmel Valley have shown that even when valley oak acorns are protected from deer and cattle, fewer than 1% escape consumption by pocket gophers. Many that eventually germinate succeed only to have their fleshy roots devoured from below. In a San Luis Obispo County study less than 1% of the blue oak seedlings left unprotected from herbivores survived for three growing seasons. This research would indicate that reestablishing predator populations may be necessary in order to reduce herbivore populations in some stands of blue and valley oak.

There are some animals that clearly foster oak regeneration, including the scrub jay and western gray squirrel. These species cache acorns by burying them—and then recover only a portion of their harvest. This behavior can benefit oaks in at least three ways: first, buried acorns are less susceptible to predation by deer and other grazing animals; second, seedlings from buried acorns have much higher survival rates than those that emerge from acorns on the surface; and third, buried acorns are often placed outside the shady canopy of the parent trees in sites that may favor germination and seedling development.

Alterations in the rangeland fire cycle also influence oak regeneration. Widespread Indian burning of oak landscapes was common when the Spanish arrived. As explained by a Karok woman in 1933, her people used fire for several reasons:

> Our kind of people never used the plow. . . . All they used to do was to burn the brush at various places, so that some good things will grow up. . . . And sometimes they also burn where the tan oak trees are lest it be brushy where they pick up the acorns. They don't want to burn too hard, they fear that the oak trees might burn. . . . Some kinds of trees are better when it is burned off; they come up better ones again.

Burning was practiced by ranchers until the mid-1950s but declined dramatically due to concerns about liability and air quality. It has all but disappeared from modern-day oak communities.

If fires are suppressed over long periods of time, the non-native understory may overwhelm any seedlings that are not yet well-established. Similarly, light ground fires help control weedy annuals and favor the growth and reproduction of native perennial grasses. The fast vertical growth of oak sprouts following a wildfire may help young trees more rapidly achieve heights that put upper leaves and vulnerable shoots beyond the reach of browsing herbivores (about five to seven feet). On the other hand, if fires become too frequent the young oaks may be eliminated in spite of their ability to sprout. Although fire undoubtedly plays a critical role in the ecology of California's oak woodlands, its role is not yet well understood. A detailed study of tree ages and fire scars conducted in the Sierra foothills, for example, showed a high correlation between episodes of fire and successful establishment of blue oak saplings during the last 200 years. This relationship was associated with about 70% of the burns.

The growing body of published research on the subject of oak regeneration has identified various agents that inhibit seedling recruitment. More importantly, much of this literature proposes that successful regeneration only occurs when several natural factors coincide, such as a summer ground fire, large acorn crop, wet winter, and decline in the deer population. Seedling recruitment appears to be a somewhat irregular event, with "pulses" of regeneration taking place when and where the right combination of conditions exist. An example of such a regeneration pulse was documented at the Nature Conservancy's Kaweah River Preserve in 1983: a good acorn crop was followed by a wet winter and on-site flooding that reduced populations of ground-dwelling acorn predators. The preserve now supports an abundance of saplings that date back to that year.

While episodic regeneration may be the norm in many oak communities, it is unclear if this has always been the case. Age studies of blue oaks in Tulare and Kern counties indicate that prior to the mid-1800s some woodlands had a relatively steady rate of recruitment. Since species of *Quercus* typically live for 200 years or more, sporadic and sometimes widely spaced regeneration pulses could still be expected to produce sufficient saplings to replace the trees in aging stands. As Griffin concluded in his 1971 *Fremontia* article:

> Where grazing and browsing pressures are low during a combination of good acorn years and wet winters, new Valley Oaks may replace the veterans. These conditions seem hard to achieve, but we must remember that such a long-lived tree can afford to wait a long time for the winning combination to arrive.

Oaks of Special Concern

The combined impact of poor regeneration and habitat loss has particularly affected three tree oak species: valley, blue, and Engelmann. These are oaks of special concern.

Valley oak must compete with farmers and developers for prime lands in valley bottoms and on low foothills. Valley oaks in streamside habitats have been especially hard hit; as much as 90% of California's valley oak riparian forests were destroyed by the beginning of the 20th century. Compounding this loss of trees and habitat has been an alarming failure of valley oak seedlings to make the transition to saplings. Recruitment rates in valley oak communities, especially in savannas, are very low or nonexistent.

Blue oak is found on more than 10,000 square miles of land and therefore cannot be considered endangered. But the widespread absence of regeneration in blue oak savannas and woodlands, coupled with the escalating conversion of blue oak communities to ranchettes and subdivisions, has raised concern for the species in some parts of its range.

The growth of a blue oak sapling (left of tree trunk) has been stunted by browsing. WILLIAM M. SMITHEY, JR.

Engelmann oak occupies the smallest natural range of any mainland tree oak. Suburbanization, farming, and ranching are exerting extraordinary pressures on native plant communities in northern San Diego County, where this species is concentrated. The Engelmann oak's low rates of recruitment add to its vulnerability.

In general, California's evergreen oaks are not exhibiting serious regeneration problems. Some coast live oak woodlands in Central California appear to have low rates of recruitment, but the evergreen species that concerns most conservationists is the coastal scrub oak. Because its distribution is confined to coastal Southern California and northern Baja, most remaining stands of this shrub oak occur in areas that are rapidly being developed.

Top: Blufftop stands of coastal scrub oak are preserved within Torrey Pines State Reserve. BILL EVARTS
Bottom: Many of California's valley oak savannas are used for farming or ranching operations. JOHN EVARTS

A Strategy For Oak Conservation

Private organizations and public agencies are seeking ways to conserve California's oaks. The task is complicated by the fact that more than 80% of the state's oak woodlands and savannas are privately held. This ownership pattern contrasts with that of the state's conifers, more than 50% of which are found on public lands. Although some oak species are harvested for lumber, California has not declared any native oak a commercial species. Oaks are therefore not subject to the kind of forestry regulations that apply to most pines and firs.

California's oak heritage depends largely on resource management and policy decisions that affect private lands. The long-range goal of oak preservation requires a multi-faceted strategy that addresses the sustainability of the resource as well as the needs of property owners. The major facets of that strategy include: (1) preservation, (2) habitat restoration, (3) wildland management, (4) urban forestry, and (5) education.

Preservation

The oldest, most widely recognized method of conserving oaks is the establishment of parks, preserves, or other protected areas that safeguard the land on which oaks grow. In California most of these lands are publicly held, and their management varies from agency to agency. The California State Park System, California Department of Fish and Game, and the National Park system, for example, place a high priority on protecting natural communities within their parks and reserves. Activities that may conflict with this objective, such as grazing or firewood cutting, are excluded. In comparison, most of the oak landscapes administered by the U.S. Forest Service and Bureau of Land Management are subject to a multiple-use mandate. In addition to supporting ecological values, these lands must accommodate uses such as logging, livestock grazing, and hunting. Both of these agencies, however, are developing management plans to protect sensitive oak habitats.

City, county, and regional parks and open space districts play an important role in preserving oak landscapes. They range in size from several to thousands of acres and may embrace a single oak grove or an entire watershed. These types of preserves contain some of California's finest oak woodlands near urban areas.

Several nonprofit conservation organizations are active in oak habitat preservation. The amount of property they administer is tiny compared to the millions of acres controlled by public agencies, but their holdings are significant for other reasons. First, many private preserves embrace oak communities that are becoming increasingly rare. Second, most of these lands are managed with the primary objective of protecting and enhancing their natural communities. Finally, large tracts within some of these preserves are being transformed by ambitious habitat restoration projects.

Of particular importance for oak research and education are the natural reserves and field stations operated by the University of California. These facilities typically combine university property with adjoining private or public land. A number of important studies have been conducted in native oak communities at UC's field stations and natural reserves. The Nature Conservancy has also hosted oak research at several of its preserves.

Habitat Restoration

Habitat restoration offers one of the most exciting but still developing approaches to enhance California's oak landscapes. Restoration plans are necessarily site-specific, but where oaks are involved, they usually entail one or more of the following: planting trees or acorns; eradicating non-native vegetation and reintroducing native plant species; limiting or excluding livestock access; and conducting carefully prescribed burns.

Oak restoration projects have been initiated in most regions of the state. In the Bald Hills of Redwood National Park, ecologists have excluded cattle and reintroduced fire to help maintain existing bunchgrass prairies and Oregon oak woodlands. Along the Cosumnes River in the Sacramento Valley, Nature Conservancy volunteers have planted more than 140 acres with valley oak and other native tree species in order to expand and link the preserve's blocks of valley oak riparian forest. In Yosemite Valley, revegetation specialists have conducted prescribed burns, removed exotic plants, and planted native understory species and black oak seedlings in an effort to renew degraded black oak woodland. In Malibu Creek State Park, ecologists and members of the California Conservation Corps have planted native grasses in an attempt to improve oak regeneration in a valley oak savanna. Several of these programs are

Top: Cages protect oaks from insects and rodents in a research plot, Hopland Field Station. ROBERT SCHMIDT
Bottom: Fields planted with valley oak beside native oak forest, Cosumnes River Preserve. TOM GRIGGS

described in more detail in the "Profiles of Oak Preservation and Restoration" section that follows.

The principles and practices of ecological restoration are still in their infancy, and decades will pass before the success of current programs can be fully evaluated. The Nature Conservancy, for example, has planted more than 41,000 oaks at three of its preserves, but these seedlings won't become mature trees until the mid-21st century. Many aspects of restoration may prove too costly and labor-intensive for application on a large scale. The greatest value of today's restoration experiments may lie in their potential to reveal new techniques for managing native oak landscapes that are losing their ecological integrity.

Wildland Management

Oaks occur on at least one-third of California's 85 million acres of forests and rangelands (referred to collectively as wildlands); they are the dominant tree in woodlands and savannas that support the state's multi-billion dollar livestock industry.

Since grazing appears to be one of the factors that contributes to poor oak regeneration, the conservation of oak communities on wildlands may necessitate new methods of ranching. Reducing animal numbers, carefully timing the season and duration of grazing, and rotating pastures are three approaches to livestock management that may encourage better rates of oak recruitment. Ecologists and ranchers are just beginning to evaluate the relationships between oak regeneration and livestock operations; their work will be closely followed because of its critical importance to the livestock industry and the millions of oak-covered acres it uses.

Conservationists are also studying the role of fire as a tool for managing oak communities.

Below: A controlled burn clears the woodland understory, Folsom State Recreation Area. MITCHEL McCLARAN
Right: Cattle rely less on oaks as a source of forage when fresh grasses and forbs are plentiful. BOB RONEY

Research on the impact of both wildfires and controlled burns suggests that burning may play an important role in oak regeneration. Each oak community responds differently to fire, however, and burning is not a sure remedy for improving recruitment; for example, a hot wildfire fueled by a dense understory can readily kill some species of oaks. The effects of burning vary depending on the frequency, duration, and intensity of the fires. Additional research and experimentation will be required before management prescriptions for wildland burning can be widely applied.

Urban Forestry

In cities throughout the state, urban forestry has been instrumental in protecting old oaks and planting new ones. Oaks and other species of street, park, yard, and remnant forest trees are natural resources that greatly improve the quality of the urban environment. The value of the urban forest is evident by the fact that 70% of California's incorporated cities have enacted ordinances that regulate the planting, maintenance, and removal of street trees; at least 60% of these laws also include provisions for registering large or historic trees, known as heritage trees.

Urban foresters have championed the use of oaks and other native trees in city landscaping. Oaks are increasingly utilized in street and park plantings and are gaining newfound appreciation for their hardiness, beauty, longevity, and importance to birds and other wildlife. Volunteer plantings of oak seedlings and acorns have become annual events in many California communities.

While mature oaks in many urban areas have received some measure of protection, oaks and oak communities in and around California's fast-growing towns and suburbs have continued—for the most part—to suffer from unregulated clearing and cutting. In recent years, however, urban forestry has expanded its scope to include the conservation of suburban and semi-rural oak woodlands. Many resource managers now evaluate the impact of development on oaks, and a small but growing number of planning departments are developing "woodland" tree ordinances designed to mitigate the loss of oak resources on the urban fringe. Increasingly, land developers are encouraged to cluster houses and commercial buildings to minimize the fragmentation of oak landscapes. Undeveloped pockets and corridors of oak woodland and chaparral—especially where they adjoin existing wildlands—are critical to urban wildlife and, unlike other parts of the urban forest, hold the potential for natural oak regeneration.

Education

Education is one of the keys to promoting oak conservation. Tree-planting groups, botanic gardens, and community service agencies are among the diverse organizations that have produced publications, videos, and workshops about oaks. The California Oak Foundation and the Integrated Hardwood Range Management Program are leaders in developing materials that promote oak conservation.

Whether the information concerns the care of a backyard oak or the protection of millions of oaks on foothill rangelands, it expresses a common theme: native oaks are an invaluable and irreplaceable resource challenged by the modern era. Education will help guide the minds and hands of those who can ensure the future of California's oak heritage—citizens, landowners, and policymakers.

Top: Clustered housing, such as this residential development in Portola Valley, reduces the impact of urbanization on oak landscapes. RON SANFORD
Bottom: San Diego residents plant native oaks in Balboa Park, Earth Day 1990. BILL EVARTS

Profiles of Oak Preservation and Restoration

Throughout California, from the northern coast to the Mexican border, conservationists are working to protect and sustain oak landscapes. While habitat restoration is a relatively new part of the strategy for conserving oaks, wildland preservation has been an effective conservation tool for decades. As early as 1930, for example, landscape architect Frederick Law Olmsted recommended that natural corridors, or "scenic lanes," be created in the oak-studded hills behind Berkeley and Oakland; the East Bay Regional Park District was born four years later and today comprises more than 70,000 acres in those hills.

Most of the profiles that follow are authored by individuals who have worked on the project described. With the exception of the Visalia profile, these stories summarize preservation and restoration efforts that have been initiated in recent years; each project is still ongoing.

Young people, such as this girl scout, learn about the value of native oaks through tree planting. BILL EVARTS

Visalia: The City of Oaks

Visalia lies in the heart of what was once a vast valley oak riparian forest. Nourished by the rich, well-watered soils of the Kaweah River delta, valley oaks covered a 400-square-mile area when the first pioneers arrived. By the 1890s, however, most of this magnificent forest had disappeared, a victim of relentless agricultural clearing and timber harvest.

Alarmed by continued decimation of the area's remaining oaks, Visalia community leaders—some of whom were also working to save giant sequoias in the nearby Sierra Nevada—mounted a campaign to protect the valley oak. In 1909 they proposed that Tulare County buy 100 oak-covered acres on the Mooney Ranch near Visalia and preserve the land as a park. Residents throughout the southern San Joaquin Valley were enthusiastic about the proposal. The *Hanford Journal*, published in adjacent Kings County, editorialized:

> One of the grandest objects of nature in Tulare County, second only to the majestic forests of sequoias within its confines. . .is its oak trees, and the forests of these have been rapidly disappearing before the woodman's axe to supply the fuel of commerce. Unless the Mooney grove is. . . preserved, one of the grandest oak groves in California will be forever lost to posterity.

On August 7, 1909 the Tulare County Board of Supervisors approved the land purchase and declared Mooney Grove a park. (See "Mooney Grove Park" listing in Chapter Six.) Long after the park was established, Visalia citizens continued the effort to preserve and enhance the area's native forest; the planting of oak trees began in 1922 and continues to this day.

Despite the community's concern for its oaks, rapid urban growth during the 1960s and 1970s took a heavy toll on the trees. In 1971 the City adopted an ordinance requiring a permit for the removal of valley oaks. The ordinance was amended in 1974 to establish regulations for development among oaks and to set guidelines for oak maintenance and pruning; it also made public funds available to assist with oak maintenance on private property. This pioneering legislation has been a model for similar laws in cities throughout California. Visalia, which was once known as Oak Grove City, is justifiably proud of its legacy of providing protection for its majestic oaks.

—Ginger Strong

Engelmann oaks form woodlands and savannas on the Santa Rosa Plateau. WILLIAM M. SMITHEY, JR.

Conserving Engelmann Oaks on the Santa Rosa Plateau

The open, gentle country of the Santa Rosa Plateau, with its handsome Engelmann oaks, wide vistas, and proximity to major cities, made it a land developer's dream. Although The Nature Conservancy had already preserved 3,100 acres here in 1984, another 3,800 acres were destined to become houses, shopping centers, commercial areas, and golf courses in the 1990s. At least 2,000 additional acres on the plateau were also available for suburbanization.

As development plans moved steadily closer to approval, a storm of controversy gathered around the Santa Rosa Plateau. Advocates for the oaks and for additional parkland argued on behalf of an open, serene plateau, free from the destruction and congestion so common near the state's urban centers. Project proponents, however, felt that enough of this area had already been preserved; they commended the developer's master plan, which would spare the largest oaks by carefully designing roads and incorporating trees into yards and fairways. They asked: "Hadn't enough space already been set aside to effectively conserve the plateau and allow for new home construction in fast-growing Riverside County?"

The answer from conservation biologists was no. Engelmann oak and its habitat had been greatly diminished throughout Southern California, and remaining groves consisted of many scattered, isolated fragments. The same thing was about to happen on the Santa Rosa Plateau, one of two last strongholds of the species. Studies of nature preserves around the world have shown that fragmentation increases the probability of species extinction. Roads and fences become habitat edges with different environmental characteristics that are often adverse to native species or that allow disturbance to penetrate a preserve's interior. The effects of the edge are most pronounced in small preserves—which The Nature Conservancy's holdings would have become if surrounded by 5,800 acres of development. Such preserves are also hard to manage. Some homeowners view adjacent open space as free play areas for bicycles or dumping grounds for yard waste and motor oil. Many would object to the use of controlled burning just beyond their property lines, even though it is an essential tool for maintaining oaks, grasslands,

131

Native bunchgrasses grow in the Englemann oak savannas at Santa Rosa Plateau. TOM GRIGGS

was written in the shade of a California oak.

This is what some of the important players involved in saving the Santa Rosa Plateau had to say about the establishment of the ecological preserve:

> The business community must do their part in cooperating with nature and the environment by offering creative solutions that allow for win-win outcomes. That's what we have done here today.
> —Won Yoo, President, RANPAC Inc.

> It's a tremendous accomplishment for all of these parties to work together and come up with the resources to protect such an important place in difficult financial times.
> —Dan Silver, President, Preserve Our Plateau

> This place has so many unusual, beautiful features. Each time I go up there I discover something new. . . . I came to realize that the people who were yelling about saving this place were right all along.
> —Walt Abraham, Riverside County Supervisor

> If we can't find the will and the resources to protect the biological treasures of Southern California, the wealthiest region of the country, what hope is there for nature in the rest of the world? The protection of the Santa Rosa Plateau sets a hopeful precedent.
> —Gary Bell, Southern California Area Ecologist, The Nature Conservancy

Restoration of a Valley Oak Riparian Forest

Valley oak riparian forests exist today only as isolated fragments along the floodplains of the controlled rivers of the Great Valley. The total acreage of this type of oak community is probably less than 10% of what it was 150 years ago. The Nature Conservancy established the Cosumnes River Preserve in 1987 to protect and expand one of California's largest remnants of this environment.

There are no major dams on the Cosumnes River, and regular winter flooding of lowlands along its banks still occurs. Floods are the main ecological force that keeps the riparian forest healthy, and they are beneficial to oaks in several ways. First, flood waters import nutrients to the soil; second, they drown many rodents that are predators on acorns and oak seedlings; finally, they wash away dead trees and brush, "clearing" new sites for acorn germination and seedling establishment.

Where feasible, The Nature Conservancy is

and chaparral. Conserving the Santa Rosa Plateau and, therefore, Engelmann oak, would require a single, large reserve with minimal edge and maximal habitat protection. Local groups of citizens, such as Preserve Our Plateau, along with statewide environmental organizations, focused their efforts on convincing Riverside County supervisors and project proponents of the need for a preserve.

On Earth Day 1990, the conservationist's dream of a large Santa Rosa Plateau preserve began to move toward reality. The developer entered into negotiations with The Nature Conservancy to sell 3,800 acres of oak woodlands, native grasslands, and chaparral. A year later the deal was done: most of the $35 million needed to complete the purchase would come from Riverside County and the Metropolitan Water District as partial mitigation for the effects of other development projects in the region. Government agencies, such as the California Department of Fish and Game and the U.S. Fish and Wildlife Service, were also involved. As a result, the Santa Rosa Plateau Ecological Reserve now covers 6,925 acres, and as many as 2,000 acres could be added in the future. This cooperative effort, involving citizens, environmental groups, business interests, and government, will serve as a model for conservation well into the 21st century. It is probably no coincidence that this kind of history

enlarging the preserve's natural habitat by restoring valley oak riparian forest to adjacent acreage. The restored areas will link preexisting blocks of oaks and create wildlife corridors. These passageways allow animals to travel between forest stands during migrations or following floods, wildfires, or human-caused disasters and enhance the ecological resilience of the preserve over time.

Large tracts that were once livestock pasture border the riparian forests within Cosumnes River Preserve. Restoration of these flood-prone agricultural lands began soon after the preserve was opened. In the fall of 1987 acorns were collected from valley oaks growing on the preserve; they were planted in early winter by volunteers and given supplemental irrigation through the summer months. Other natives were also planted, including Oregon ash, box elder, arroyo willow, wild rose, and cottonwood. In late September 1988 most of the new oak seedlings were over one foot tall; about 5% had grown to over three feet tall.

By January 1991 volunteers had planted 140 acres at the Cosumnes River Preserve. When the valley oak saplings reach over five feet in height—their leaders safely above the reach of browsing deer—individual wire protectors are removed from the trees. In 20 years dense stands of 20- to 30-foot-tall saplings will cover the pastures. In 50 years, an oak forest embracing a diversity of trees, shrubs, and herbs should rise above the restored floodplain.
—Tom Griggs

Nature Conservancy staff and volunteers plant valley oaks at the Cosumnes River Preserve. MARY ANN GRIGGS

Expanding Yosemite's Black Oak Woodlands

Famous for its granite monoliths and spectacular waterfalls, Yosemite Valley is also known for its magnificent black oaks. These handsome trees shade trails and visitor facilities and serve as beacons of seasonal passage with their brilliant displays of changing foliage.

Human impact on Yosemite's native black oak stands has a long history. The Ahwahneechee (a Miwok tribe) actually aided expansion of the oak groves. They set fire to the valley floor each year to help ensure an abundant supply of acorns, their dietary staple. By burning off the understory beneath the oaks, the Ahwahneechee kept competitive shrubs and conifers in check, made acorn gathering easier, and encouraged the growth of grasses used in basket weaving. Park Guardian and long-time Yosemite resident Galen Clark described the burning in an 1896 report to the Yosemite Commissioners:

> The Valley then (1855) had been exclusively under the care and management of the Indians, probably for many centuries. Their policy of management . . . was to annually start fires in the dry season of the year and let them spread over the whole Valley to kill the young trees just sprouted and keep the forest groves open and clear . . . and to have clear grounds for hunting and gathering acorns.

The oak stands of Yosemite Valley began to suffer after white settlers arrived in the mid-1800s and introduced practices such as fire suppression, grazing, fencing, and farming. Non-native understory species and fast-growing conifers gradually began to overtake the oaks and spread into the meadows. The valley's population of mule deer, protected by a national park ban on hunting, grew large and their consumption of acorns, oak seedlings, and browse increased. Finally, the sheer number of annual visitors to the valley contributed to the lack of oak regeneration—many new seedlings were inadvertently trampled by humans.

As Yosemite begins its second century as a national park, an ambitious black oak restoration program is underway. Prescribed burning, such as that used by the Ahwahneechee Indians, was reintroduced in Yosemite Valley some twenty years ago. In 1988 the National Park Service and the California Conservation Corps began an innovative oak-protection effort: they fenced a black oak stand,

Magnificent groves of black oak add to the grandeur of Yosemite Valley. CHUCK PLACE

posted interpretive signs, removed non-native plants, and planted native understory species and black oak seedlings. This project is being carefully monitored and photo-documented. The techniques used will be applied to four other areas that hold the best remaining examples of black oak woodland in Yosemite Valley. With the aid of volunteers, the National Park Service will continue a long term effort to conserve and expand the beautiful black oak woodlands of Yosemite Valley for the enjoyment of future generations.

    —Ben Alexander

Planting Bunchgrass In a Valley Oak Savanna

The California Department of Parks and Recreation has undertaken a valley oak savanna restoration project in Malibu Creek State Park in the Santa Monica Mountains, where the valley oak reaches the southern extreme of its distribution.

    Valley oak savannas once covered thousands upon thousands of acres of fertile lowlands throughout the coastal and central valleys and on the alluvial fans of the western Sierra foothills. Immense valley oaks dotted the landscape for miles

on end, some standing magnificently alone, while others were grouped in twos and threes in an endlessly varied arrangement. The grasslands under and around the oaks supported dozens of species of native grasses and, in spring, a glorious array of wildflowers. Many people hold this image as the landscape most characteristic of California.

    Although many acres of valley oak savanna remain, most resemble the savannas of a past era only superficially. The giant monarch trees still stand in many areas, producing large crops of acorns which germinate into seedlings in favorable years. But missing from the picture are the saplings and intermediate-aged trees which would replace the large trees as they eventually die. Without establishment of new trees, California's valley oak savannas will be lost.

    A number of factors have been identified which may contribute to the failure of today's seedlings to become established as young trees. One of the most fundamental of these factors is the sweeping change that has transformed the understory of the oaks. Prior to Euro-American settlement and the advent of widespread cattle grazing, the native understory of valley oaks consisted of perennial bunchgrasses, with native annual grasses and wildflowers growing sparsely in the spaces between. Disturbances created by cattle grazing, combined with the introduction of aggressive annual grasses from the Mediterranean and changes in the frequency of fires, resulted in the wholesale conversion of the native perennial grass understory to exotic annual grasses and forbs (non-grass herbaceous plants).

Perennial native grasses are widely spaced, deep rooted, and long-lived—some up to 200 years—and thus have a completely different water use pattern and reproductive strategy from that of the introduced annual grasses. Native bunchgrasses spend their first years establishing deep root systems before putting out much above-ground growth. It is these deep root systems that enable the grasses to survive long periods of drought. Because perennial native grasses are long-lived, they have many years to reproduce; they do not need to produce large numbers of seeds right away, or in an unfavorable year, to ensure their survival as a species.

The introduced annual grasses are a different story. Annual plants have only one short growing season to flower and produce seed before dying. Their reproductive strategy of necessity includes early germination with the first rains of the season; then, rapid root and shoot growth take advantage of all available soil moisture and nutrients to ensure the production of as many seeds as possible. Compared to the natives, the annual grasses are shallow rooted, and they form dense, solid stands which allow little sunlight to penetrate to the soil surface. Unfortunately, the growth pattern of annual grasses works to the detriment of valley oak seedlings, which require a high soil moisture for uninterrupted root growth. Oak seedlings that do manage to get started are often shaded out by the rapidly growing annual grass crop. The multitude of seeds which are produced by the annuals may encourage high rodent populations by providing them with plenty of seeds to eat; these rodents also love to gnaw on young oak roots.

It thus appears that preservation of California's magnificent valley oaks requires active management of the herbaceous understory to return it to a composition which is more friendly to young oaks. This is the goal of the valley oak savanna restoration project at Malibu Creek State Park.

In the spring of 1989 all native grasses in the park were surveyed and mapped to characterize the ecological requirements of various grass species and to determine the location of seed sources within the park. State Park ecologists were aware of the importance of using locally collected seeds in restoration projects to ensure that the plants adapt to local conditions, and to avoid contamination of the gene pool which has evolved in the area. Hence, seeds were collected within the park from three species of native grass: purple needlegrass, California brome, and wild rye. These were grown into seedlings at the Napa nursery of the California Conservation Corps. Once the rainy season finally arrived in Southern California in January 1990, 20,000 grass seedlings were shipped to Malibu Creek State Park. They were planted on about ten acres, under and around seven outstanding valley oaks, by the California Conservation Corps under the direction of State Park ecologists. The grasses received supplemental water in March 1990, and as of late summer 1991, most were surviving. Three additional native plant restoration projects in the park will include additional oak understory plantings. Establishment and reproduction of the grasses will be monitored in the coming years, and it is hoped that successful native grass restoration will ultimately foster the survival of seedlings needed to ensure the next generation of valley oaks.

—Suzanne Goode

Members of the California Conservation Corps transplant purple needlegrass into a valley savanna at Malibu Creek State Park. SUZANNE GOODE

CHAPTER SIX

EXPLORING CALIFORNIA'S OAK LANDSCAPES

THE CENTURY-LONG HISTORY OF WILDLAND preservation in California has yielded a remarkable legacy of state parks, national forests, and other public lands that harbor native oak communities. From Oregon oak woodlands in Redwood National Park in the north, to mixed evergreen forests in Cuyamaca Rancho State Park in the south, outstanding examples of California's oak heritage have been set aside for recreation, resource conservation, and research. Parks and preserves provide vital access to oak landscapes, especially since most of the state's oak woodlands and savannas are privately owned. As California's once-vast acreage of oaks continues to shrink and remaining oak communities are further fragmented, the biological and recreational significance of these protected lands will steadily increase.

This chapter describes 110 of the best places for viewing oaks and native oak communities in California. Most of the destinations are located on public land and encompass large, relatively pristine oak communities. The text also introduces a number of botanic gardens and nature centers that feature native oaks and provide opportunities for learning about oak ecology. The selection of destinations is far from comprehensive; instead, it presents a variety of choices for exploration and discovery among the oaks, including rural and urban sites, hiking trails and country roads, mountain and coastal parks. The sites are divided into five regions, with each region reflecting its characteristic oak landscapes.

Information for this chapter was compiled with the generous assistance of individuals from many organizations and agencies; among them were the U.S. Forest Service, Bureau of Land Management, National Park Service, California Department of Parks and Recreation, various county and regional park districts, and The Nature Conservancy. When recommending these sites, the rangers, naturalists, and foresters who helped select them took into account various criteria, such as quality of the oak community, ease of access, and proximity to museums, nature trails or other interpretive facilities. The tree oak species and oak communities found at each site are noted whenever possible. Directions to the destination, the name of its managing agency, and a telephone number for information appear with each listing. For general reference, each site appears on one of seven maps that accompany the text.

Above: A country road heads through oak woodlands in the Sierra Nevada foothills. FRANK BALTHIS
Opposite: Basaltic rock and valley oaks in foothills near the Sacramento Valley. CARR CLIFTON

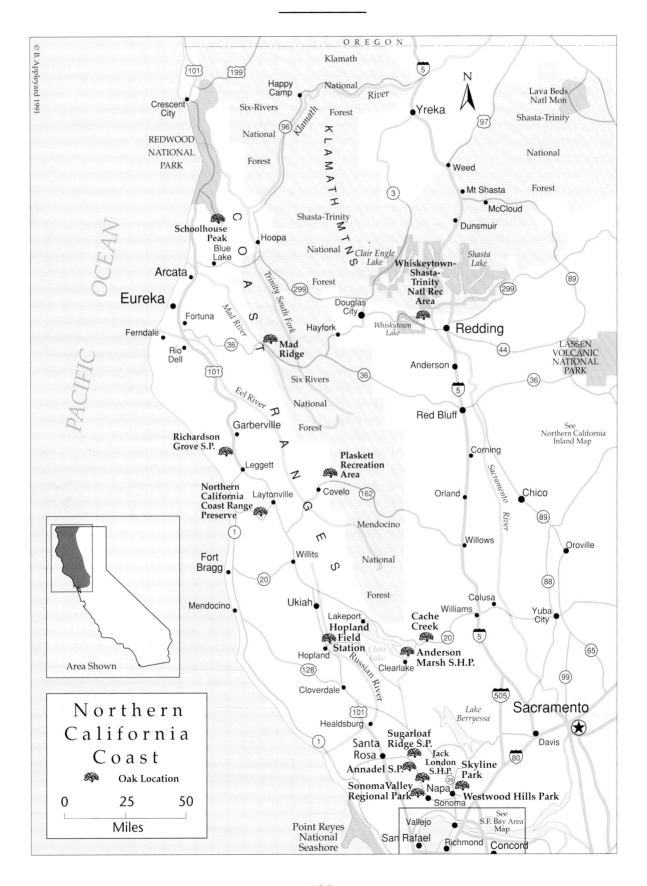

OREGON

Klamath

Happy
Camp

National   River

Six-Rivers   Yreka

Crescent
City

REDWOOD
NATIONAL
PARK

National   Lava Beds
Natl Mon

Forest   Shasta-Trinity

Weed

Mt Shasta   National

McCloud   Forest

Dunsmuir

Schoolhouse
Peak

Blue
Lake   Hoopa

Shasta-Trinity

Clair Engle
Lake

Whiskeytown-
Shasta-
Trinity
Natl Rec
Area

Shasta
Lake

Arcata

Eureka   National   Forest

Douglas
City

Whiskytown
Lake

Redding

LASSEN
VOLCANIC
NATIONAL
PARK

Fortuna   Hayfork   Anderson

Ferndale

Rio
Dell   Mad
Ridge   Six Rivers   Red Bluff

Eel River   National   Corning

Garberville   Forest

Richardson
Grove S.P.   Orland   Chico

Leggett   Plaskett
Recreation
Area   Willows   Oroville

Northern
California
Coast Range
Preserve   Laytonville

Covelo

Mendocino

Colusa   Yuba
City

Fort
Bragg   Willits   National   Williams

Mendocino   Forest   Cache
Creek

Ukiah   Lakeport   Anderson
Marsh S.H.P.

Hopland
Field
Station   Clear
Lake   Clearlake

Hopland

Cloverdale   Russian River   Lake
Berryessa   Sacramento

Healdsburg   Davis

Sugarloaf
Ridge S.P.

Santa
Rosa   Jack
London
S.H.P.   Skyline
Park

Annadel S.P.   Napa

SonomaValley
Regional Park   Westwood Hills Park

Sonoma

Vallejo

Point Reyes
National
Seashore   San Rafael   Richmond   Concord

See
Northern California
Inland Map

See
S.F. Bay Area
Map

© B. Appleyard 1991

PACIFIC   OCEAN

Area Shown

Northern California Coast

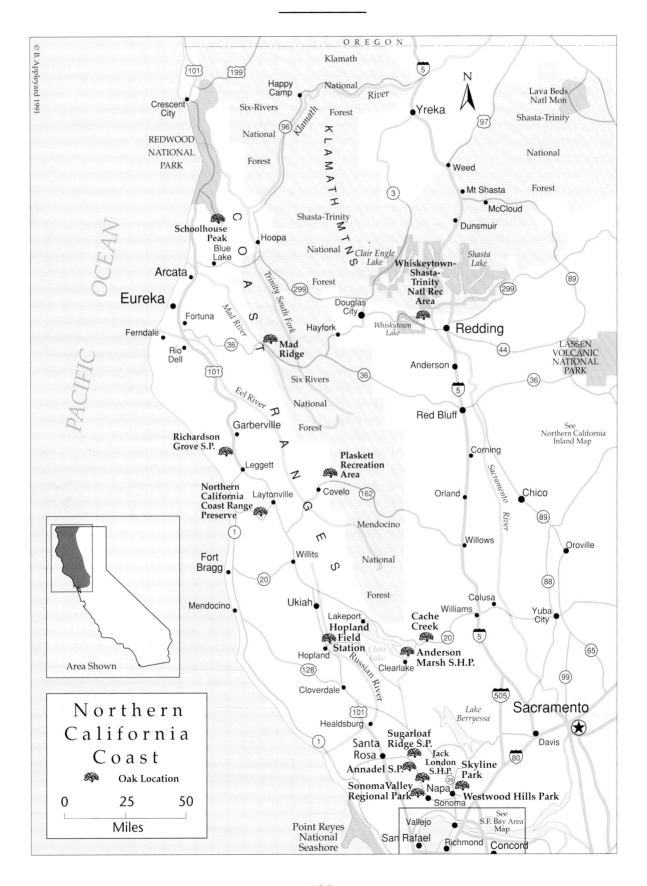 Oak Location

0   25   50

Miles

Northern California Coast

. . . one day, on coming out on a prairie, we beheld a great sight. The prairie seems [sic] a large one; scattered all over it were big oak trees, giving it the appearance of an old orchard in the Eastern States, and, grazing quietly were hundreds of elk, that seemed to take no more notice of us than so many tame cattle grazing in their pastures at home.
— JOHN CARR, CROSSING THE BALD HILLS ON TRINIDAD TRAIL, 1891

North Coast Ranges

Schoolhouse Peak
Although famous for its magnificent coast redwood forests, Redwood National Park also preserves outstanding examples of Oregon oak woodland. Some of the largest oak groves are located near Schoolhouse Peak, in the southern part of the park. Oregon oak, along with canyon and black oak, appears with bigleaf maple, madrone, Douglas fir, and grand fir. From U.S. 101, one mile north of Orick, follow Bald Hills Rd. for 13 miles; the road passes through redwood forest, then small patches of oak as it ascends to Schoolhouse Peak. Redwood National Park (707) 488-3461

Mad Ridge
Oak Grove Campground, located on an east-facing slope below Mad Ridge, comprises about 30 acres of majestic black oak; many specimens boast trunk diameters as large as five feet. Oregon oak, canyon oak, Douglas fir, and ponderosa pine also grow in this northern mixed evergreen forest. There are no established trails in the vicinity. To reach the site, take Highway 36 approximately one mile west of the town of Mad River. Proceed south on Forest Rd. 1N03 (gravel, good condition) for about 4.25 miles. The grove is located just east of the road, on the left side.

Another good oak-viewing destination in the same general area is found near historic Becker Cabin. An extensive stand of Oregon oak is located one mile up Pilot Creek from the cabin. Black oak, Douglas fir, and ponderosa pine are scattered throughout the area, and grassy meadows, or "balds" are interspersed with Oregon oak woodlands. There are no maintained camping facilities nearby. To reach Becker Cabin, go ½ mile east on Highway 36 from the town of Mad River, turn left (north) on Forest Highway 1 and go

approximately 23 miles on this paved road. Turn left (south) on Forest Rd. 3N10 (gravel) and continue for 4.8 miles. Six Rivers National Forest (707) 574-6233

Richardson Grove State Park
Richardson Grove State Park is noted primarily as a redwood park, but visitors here can also see black, canyon, and Oregon oak in the park's northern mixed evergreen forest. The riverside meadow at Oak Flat Campground contains fine examples of black oak. The park is eight miles south of Garberville on U.S. 101. California Department of Parks & Recreation (707) 247-3318

Covelo to Plaskett Recreation Area
Six species of tree and shrub oak can be viewed along a beautiful backcountry route (Highway 162) that crosses the North Coast Range east of Covelo. Magnificent specimens of valley and blue oak are found in Round Valley near Covelo. The pavement ends at Eel River Work Center, the last place to buy gas and groceries before entering the National Forest.

As the road enters the mountains, it climbs past blue, Oregon, and canyon oak, which are often intermixed with ponderosa pine, Douglas fir, and white fir. Fine groves of black oak occur near Surveyor Camp. Beyond the summit of 5,000-foot Mendocino Pass, the hilltops are covered with Brewer oak, a shrubby form of Oregon oak. Look for low-growing huckleberry oak on the south side of the road as you climb to Telephone Camp. Three miles beyond Telephone Camp is Plaskett Recreation Area, a lovely montane setting offering developed campgrounds and lake fishing. It is 29 winding miles one way from Covelo to the Plaskett Recreation Area. The road is normally open from May through October. Mendocino National Forest (916) 934-3316 or (707) 983-6119

Northern California Coast Range Preserve

The Northern California Coast Range Preserve is the largest protected tract of forested coastal land remaining in Northern California. Pristine old-growth conifer forest, abundant oak woodland and meadow habitat, and the magnificent South Fork of the Eel River combine to make this a very worthwhile destination. Canyon, Oregon, black, and interior live oak are all found within the 7,800 acres of the preserve. This is the only Nature Conservancy preserve with significant numbers of Oregon oak. Oregon oaks are most impressive along the road after the Elder Creek bridge by the Angelo homesite; canyon and interior live oak flourish along meadow margins near Wilderness Lodge. Canyon oaks attain impressive size in the canyons along the preserve's five major streams.

Take U.S. 101 north from San Francisco to Laytonville (about 150 miles); turn left on Branscomb Rd., drive west about 20 minutes, and turn right on Wilderness Lodge Rd. Drive north about 10 minutes, bearing right at the only fork. Visitors are asked to make reservations, and overnight camping is available for educational or research groups only. Please sign in at the preserve headquarters on the right side of the road. The Nature Conservancy and the University of California (707) 984-6653

Hopland Field Station

Located in the Russian River watershed, the University of California's Hopland Field Station emphasizes oak regeneration and studies management of trees for harvest as well as for landscape beauty and wildlife needs. Interior live, blue, and black oak are abundant in the field station's woodlands and savannas; seven other tree and scrub species also occur here. For drive-through viewing of managed oak habitat, take Highway 175 east from U.S. 101 for one mile. Turn left on East Side Rd. (Rd. 201) for one block, then turn right on University Rd. Continue four miles to the Field Station. Off-road access is prohibited, but educational tours for groups can be arranged. University of California (707) 744-1424

Anderson Marsh State Historic Park

Located on the southeast shore of Clear Lake off Highway 53, Anderson Marsh State Historic Park offers a short hike on Cache Creek Trail through valley oak woodland. A return by way of Ridge

Trail will take you through a blue oak woodland and past a reconstructed Pomo Indian village. Large valley oak are present near the visitor center and historic ranch buildings where Cache Creek Trail begins. From Redwood Valley on U.S. 101, take Highway 20 southeast to Highway 53. Take Highway 53 south to the park entrance.

Nearby Clear Lake State Park features the Indian Nature Trail with self-guiding brochure describing the Pomo Indian use of valley oak, blue oak, and other native plants. Clear Lake State Park is 3.5 miles from Kelseyville, off Highway 29. Telephone for Clear Lake State Park is (707) 279-4293. California Department of Parks & Recreation (707) 994-0688 or (707) 279-2267

Cache Creek

Visitors can hike through undisturbed valley oak woodlands in the Cache Creek corridor on these Bureau of Land Management lands. Blue oak grows on the hillsides and valley oak on the flats. This protected area is a wintering site for bald eagles and a year-round home to tule elk. To reach the trailhead, follow Highway 20 about eight miles east from the town of Clearlake Oaks; it is located on the south side of the highway where the road bends at North Fork crossing. BLM Clearlake Resource Area (707) 462-3873

Tule elk inhabit the Cache Creek area in the BLM's Clearlake Resource Area B. "MOOSE" PETERSON

Sonoma and Napa Counties

Sugarloaf Ridge State Park

This 2,373-acre park contains seven different tree oak species. Over 25 miles of trails wind through shady canyons and traverse open ridges, providing a myriad of oak-viewing opportunities. The easily accessible Creekside Nature Trail begins near the campground and features coast live and Oregon oak. The park is located seven miles east of Santa Rosa off Highway 12; take Adobe Canyon Rd. three miles north to the park entrance. California Department of Parks & Recreation (707) 833-5712

Annadel State Park

The 35 miles of hiking and riding trails in this popular day-use park pass through numerous plant communities, including beautiful oak woodlands. The slopes of Bennett Mountain offer fine examples of northern mixed evergreen forest. A five-mile loop hike to Lake Ilsanjo passes through woodlands and savannas of Oregon, black, and coast live oak. Begin this hike by taking the Warren Richardson Trail (the old Lake Trail) from the parking lot at the end of Channel Dr. to the lake. Return from the lake on Live Oak Trail and North Burma Trail. The park is located 60 miles north of San Francisco on the eastern edge of Santa Rosa. Take Highway 12 east from Santa Rosa. Turn right on Mission Blvd., left on Montgomery Dr., and right on Channel Dr. to the parking lot. California Department of Parks & Recreation (707) 938-1519 or (707) 539-3911

Jack London State Historic Park

Five different species of oak are represented in Jack London State Historic Park. Trails and unpaved roads crisscross coast live oak woodlands in this 800-acre park. A particularly large specimen of coast live oak grows next to London's Cottage, near the parking area. This day-use-only park is located off Highway 12 in Glen Ellen. California Department of Parks & Recreation (707) 938-5216

Sonoma Valley Regional Park

Pristine oak woodlands and savannas dominate this 162-acre day-use park. Four different tree oak species are represented here, and a paved 1.4-mile bicycle and hiking trail makes viewing them easy and pleasurable. This trail winds through stands of mistletoe-laden oaks, madrone, buckeye, manzanita, and toyon. Picnic tables are situated along this

Black oak leaves emerge during spring, Annadel State Park. CHARLES KENNARD

route. Two additional miles of unpaved footpaths traverse the hills of the park. April is a good month to enjoy wildflowers among the oaks here; bird-watching is excellent year-round. The park is five miles north of the Valley of the Moon off Highway 12, just south of Glen Ellen. Sonoma County Parks & Recreation (707) 527-2041

Skyline Park

A surprisingly large number of different oak species grow in this 850-acre wilderness park within the city limits of Napa. Six species of oak thrive in the park's varied terrain of meadows, creeks, and woodlands. The Oakleaf Trail makes a good choice for hiking among outstanding oak specimens. Skyline Park is located in the southeast corner of Napa. From Highway 121 in Napa, take Imola East Rd. approximately one mile to the park entrance. Oakleaf Trail begins on Lake Marie Rd. City of Napa (707) 257-9529

Westwood Hills Park

Valley and coast live oak shade portions of the Oak Knoll Trail which ends atop a hill with vistas of Napa Valley. This city-owned and -operated park has 110 acres of hills, ridges, and canyons accessible by an extensive system of fire roads and trails. The Carolyn Parr Nature Museum near the park entrance is open on weekends. This is a day-use-only park. It is located at 3105 Browns Valley Rd. in the city of Napa, about one mile west of Highway 29. City of Napa (707) 257-9529

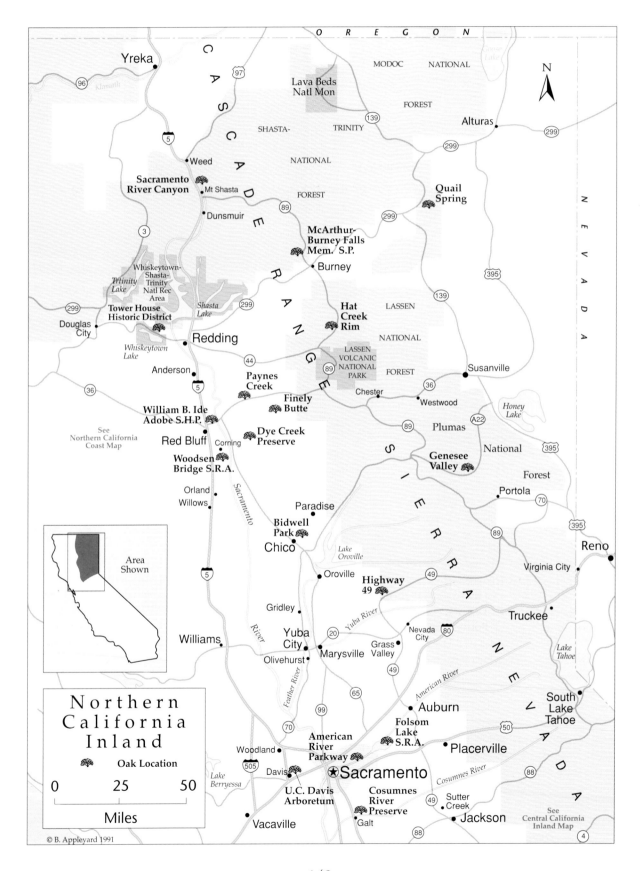

O R E G O N

Yreka

C A S C A D E

96

Klamath

97

MODOC   NATIONAL

Lava Beds
Natl Mon

139

FOREST

Alturas

299

299

N

5

Weed

SHASTA-

TRINITY

89

Sacramento
River Canyon

Mt Shasta

NATIONAL

Quail
Spring

N

Dunsmuir

FOREST

299

E

McArthur-
Burney Falls
Mem. S.P.

V

3

Burney

395

A

Whiskeytown-
Shasta-
Trinity
Natl Rec
Area

Trinity
Lake

LASSEN

139

D

Tower House
Historic District

299

Shasta
Lake

299

Hat
Creek
Rim

NATIONAL

A

Douglas
City

Whiskeytown
Lake

Redding

44

LASSEN
VOLCANIC
NATIONAL
PARK

FOREST

Susanville

36

Anderson

5

89

Paynes
Creek

Chester

89

Westwood

Honey
Lake

A22

395

William B. Ide
Adobe S.H.P.

Finely
Butte

Plumas

See
Northern California
Coast Map

Dye Creek
Preserve

Red Bluff   Corning

89

National

Genesee
Valley

Woodsen
Bridge S.R.A.

Orland

Forest

Willows

Sacramento

Portola

70

Paradise

395

Area
Shown

5

Bidwell
Park

Lake
Oroville

89

Reno

Chico

Virginia City

Oroville

Highway
49

49

Truckee

Gridley

Yuba River

80

Lake
Tahoe

Williams

River

Yuba
City

20

Nevada
City

Grass
Valley

N

Olivehurst   Marysville

49

E

South
Lake
Tahoe

Feather River

65

American River

V

Northern
California
Inland

99

70

Auburn

A

50

Oak Location

American
River
Parkway

Folsom
Lake
S.R.A.

Placerville

D

0   25   50

Woodland

Sacramento

Cosumnes River

88

Miles

505

Davis

A

Lake
Berryessa

U.C. Davis
Arboretum

Cosumnes
River
Preserve

49

Sutter
Creek

See
Central California
Inland Map

© B. Appleyard 1991

Vacaville

Galt

Jackson

4

NEVADA

SIERRA

© B. Appleyard 1991

Northern California Inland

From the upland we descended into broad groves on the river, consisting of the evergreen, and a new species of white oak. . . . Among these was no brushwood; and the grassy surface gave to it the appearance of parks in an old settled country. We made an acorn meal at noon, and hurried on; the valley being gay with flowers, and some of the banks being absolutely golden with the California poppy. . . . Here the grass was smooth and green, and the groves very open; the large old oaks throwing a broad shade among sunny spots.
— John C. Frémont, along the American River, 1844

Upper Sacramento Valley / Cascade Range

Sacramento River Canyon
Fine stands of black oak are accessible along a scenic portion of the Sacramento River Canyon near the community of Mount Shasta. The oaks grow in association with a mixed conifer forest. The nearest campground is Lake Siskiyou County Campground. Take Forest Service Rd. 26 off I-5 at Mount Shasta. Shasta-Trinity National Forest (916) 246-5222

Tower House Historic District
A significant stand of valley oak graces the Tower House Historic District in the Whiskeytown Unit. Valley oak, along with black oak and black walnut, are easily viewed by taking the Historic District's self-guided tour that begins near the parking area. Ranger-guided tours are offered during summer months. There are no facilities for picnicking or camping at the Historic District, but camping is available nearby at Oak Bottom Campground. Tower House Historic District is in the northwest corner of the Whiskeytown Unit, situated on Highway 299 off I-5 west of the town of Redding. Whiskeytown-Shasta-Trinity National Recreation Area (916) 241-6584

McArthur-Burney Falls Memorial State Park
This is one of the few state parks in which Oregon oak is the dominant tree oak. Black and Oregon oak are identified on the one-mile Self-Guiding Nature Trail that begins at the Burney Falls Overlook. Large stands of Oregon oak are found on the north side of the Pit River at Lake Britton Bridge (just outside the park) and put on brilliant displays of fall color. The park is located six miles north of the junction of Highways 299 and 89. California Department of Parks & Recreation (916) 335-2777

Quail Spring
Black oak is the only oak with significant populations in Modoc County. Scattered over the Big Valley Ranger District, black oak mixes with ponderosa pine, Jeffrey pine, incense cedar, and white fir; especially good viewing is found along Highway 299 between McArthur and Nubieber. Quail Spring Rd., located about 7.5 miles north of Adin on 299, also features black oak in a mixed conifer setting; campgrounds are situated nearby at Rush Creek. Modoc National Forest (916) 299-3215

Hat Creek Rim
A volcanic slope with perhaps the northeastern-most large stand of interior live oak rises 1,000 feet above the valley of Hat Creek. The road winds through valley brushlands and ascends past blue oak woodlands before arriving at the rim's dramatic view of Lassen Peak. Several campgrounds and picnic areas are nearby. Hat Creek Rim is located about 50 miles east of Redding via Highways 44 and 89. Lassen National Forest (916) 257-2151

Paynes Creek
Approximately seven miles northeast of Red Bluff, between the Sacramento River and Paynes Creek, are 3,000 acres of prime blue oak woodlands amidst steep bluffs and low, rolling plains. Smaller stands of valley and interior live oak are intermixed. Closed to motor vehicles, this area offers good opportunities

The Nature Conservancy's Dye Creek Preserve encompasses vast woodlands of blue oak. GEORGE STROUD

for hiking, horseback riding, and fishing. Drive 3.5 miles north of Red Bluff on I-5 to Jellys Ferry Rd. Continue north three miles to Bend Ferry Rd., then two miles northeast from Bend. BLM Redding Resource Area (916) 246-5325

Finley Butte
This area's blue oak woodland is especially scenic in spring when bulbs are in bloom and grasses are still green. Follow Highway 36 about 20 miles northeast from Red Bluff. About eight miles east of Paynes Creek take Ponderosa Way southeast to Shakehouse, then head south toward Finley Butte. There are good views from roads and hiking trails throughout the area. Lassen National Forest (916) 258-2141

Gray Davis Dye Creek Preserve
The Gray Davis Dye Creek Preserve has the largest acreage of protected blue oak in California and comprises both woodland and savanna communities. The entire watershed of Dye Creek is within this 37,540-acre preserve. Rolling hills, woodlands, ponds, and streams create ideal wintering grounds for the state's largest herd of mule deer. The Nature Conservancy, manager of the preserve, allows strictly controlled seasonal grazing to minimize the impact of livestock on oak regeneration.

The preserve is only accessible to visitors who attend guided tours (announced in The Nature Conservancy's quarterly newsletter) or who receive special permission. The preserve is 12 miles southeast of Red Bluff in Tehama County. Inquiries may be sent to: Gray Davis Dye Creek Preserve, 11010 Foothill Rd., Los Molinos, CA 96055. The Nature Conservancy (415) 777-0487

Genesee Valley
Genesee Valley provides a lovely backcountry drive through Sierran mixed conifer forest where stands of black and interior live oak grow in association with pine and incense cedar. A dramatic backdrop of Sierra Nevada peaks to the south enhances views along this route. Genesee Valley is located about 20 miles southeast of Lake Almanor in Plumas County; take the paved road from Taylorsville (off Highway 89) towards Antelope Lake. The section of road where the oaks are abundant begins about three miles beyond Taylorsville and extends along Genesee Valley for about six or seven miles. The nearest campground is at Antelope Lake. Plumas National Forest (916) 283-2050

William B. Ide Adobe State Historic Park
A very large specimen valley oak grows next to the historic adobe structure featured in this day-use park. The park is located two miles northeast of the town of Red Bluff on Adobe Rd. California Department of Parks & Recreation (916) 527-5927

Woodson Bridge State Recreation Area
Situated on the Sacramento River, Woodson Bridge State Recreation Area is home to beautiful and large valley oaks. The oaks are the prominent tree species in the park, and they share the rich riparian habitat with California walnut, Oregon ash, black cottonwood, sycamore, and willow. Fishing, boating, hiking, bird-watching, and camping are offered in this natural setting. The Nature Trail featured in the park brochure provides access to the oaks. Woodson Bridge State Recreation Area is off Highway 99 between Chico and Red Bluff. Located on South Ave., the park is three miles west of Highway 99 at Vina, or six miles east of I-5 at Corning. California Department of Parks & Recreation (916) 839-2112

Bidwell Park
Bidwell Park preserves some of northern California's finest acreage of valley oak woodland. At 2,250 acres, it is one of the largest municipal parks in the U.S. Oak communities range from a valley oak woodland along Big Chico Creek to blue oak woodlands in the park's upland areas. Bidwell Park contains developed recreational areas and miles of quiet backcountry hiking trails. The park is in Chico at Highway 99 and Woodland Ave. City of Chico (916) 895-4872

Sacramento Area

Highway 49 / South Yuba River Project

Highway 49, the Gold Country Highway, extends 300 miles through the heart of California's historic Mother Lode mining region. Running from Mariposa to Vinton, this highway is one of the state's premier oak-viewing routes: it winds through foothills dotted with blue oak, crosses gorges filled with canyon and interior live oak, and traverses ridgetops covered with black oak and pine. Near the north end of the highway, two state parks in the Grass Valley area feature trails that visit outstanding oak woodlands. The Osborn Hill Trail at Empire Mine State Historic Park leads ½ mile to a grove of black oak managed for optimum oak regeneration. At South Yuba River Project, Independence Trail provides easy access to stands of canyon and black oak. California Department of Parks & Recreation (916) 273-8522

Folsom Lake State Recreation Area

This 17,000-acre recreation area contains developed campgrounds and many miles of hiking trails. Blue oak woodlands surround much of the lake. Some of the best and most accessible of these woodlands are around the Nimbus Flat and Lake Natoma sites. Entrance to the area is at 7806 Folsom-Auburn Rd. California Department of Parks & Recreation (916) 988-0205

American River Parkway

The 30-mile-long, 6,000-acre American River Parkway is home to three species of oak and contains over 200 heritage-size trees. The parkway extends from Folsom Dam to the confluence of the Sacramento and American rivers in Sacramento; bike, foot, and horse paths run the entire length. Fine specimens of valley oak grow in the Sacramento Bar area near San Juan Rapids; the parkway's Rossmoor Bar and Ancil Hoffman Park also feature nice stands of valley oak. Closer to Folsom Dam, interior live and blue oak are more prevalent.

The Effie Yeaw Nature Center in Ancil Hoffman Park interprets local riparian habitats and Indian culture and hosts nature walks. The center's address is 6700 Tarshes Dr. in Carmichael; phone: (916) 489-4918. Sacramento County Parks & Recreation (916) 456-7423

Peter J. Shields Oak Grove

This 15-acre grove located in the University of California, Davis Arboretum contains an outstanding selection of oaks from around the world; more than 80 species are represented. The excellent booklet for the self-guided tour locates and describes 24 different oak species. The native California oaks represented here include coast live, canyon, interior live, Engelmann, Oregon, blue, valley, and island oak. Many valley oaks in the arboretum are native to the site. Take the University of California, Davis exit from I-80. Go north to central campus; get map and directions to the arboretum at the entrance kiosk. University of California, Davis (916) 752-4880

Cosumnes River Preserve

This preserve features one of California's finest remnants of valley oak riparian forest and is the site of an ambitious reforestation project. The Nature Conservancy is enlarging the natural oak community by planting valley oak, Oregon ash, and willow on adjacent pastures and fields that are no longer farmed; these lands will eventually be covered with oak forest. (See "Restoration of a Valley Oak Riparian Forest" in Chapter Five.) To visit both natural and restored oak forest, hike the day-use Willow Slough Nature Trail. Take I-5 south from Sacramento or north from Stockton to Twin Cities Rd.; turn east on Twin Cities Rd. for one mile to Franklin Blvd.; proceed south 1.25 miles to the preserve and Willow Slough trailhead. Guided tours are offered monthly. The Nature Conservancy (916) 684-2816

Valley oak riparian forest grows up to the water's edge at the Cosumnes River Preserve. BOB WALKER

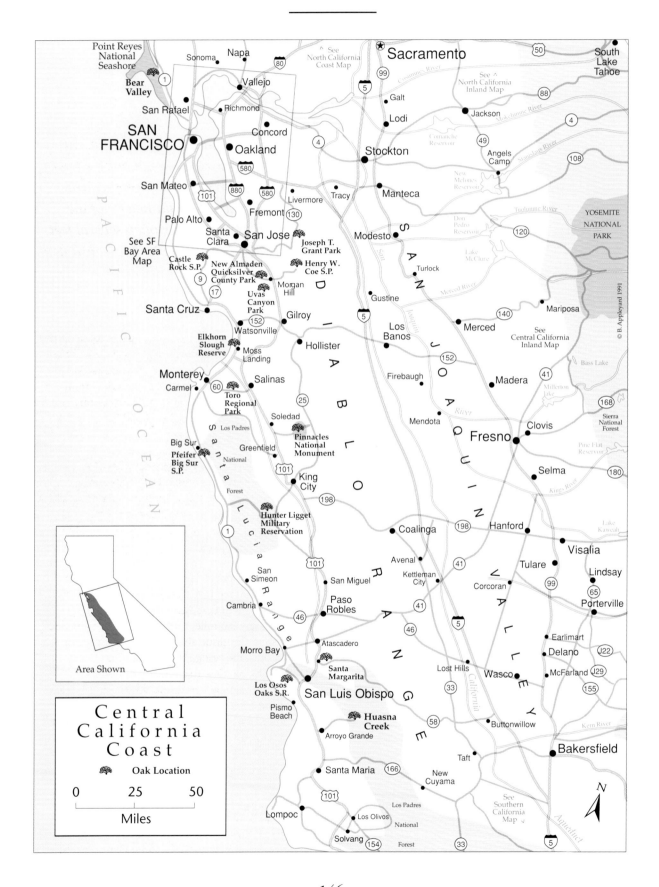

Point Reyes
National
Seashore

Sonoma

Napa

Bear
Valley

Vallejo

San Rafael

Richmond

SAN
FRANCISCO

Concord

Oakland

San Mateo

580

880 580

101

Palo Alto

Fremont 130

Santa
Clara

San Jose

See SF
Bay Area
Map

Castle
Rock S.P.

New Almaden
Quicksilver
County Park

9

17

Joseph T.
Grant Park

Henry W.
Coe S.P.

Morgan
Hill

Uvas
Canyon
Park

Gilroy

Santa Cruz

152

Watsonville

Elkhorn
Slough
Reserve

Moss
Landing

Hollister

Monterey

Carmel

60

Toro
Regional
Park

Salinas

25

Soledad

Los Padres

Big Sur

Pfeifer
Big Sur
S.P.

National

Greenfield

Pinnacles
National
Monument

101

Forest

King
City

198

Hunter Ligget
Military
Reservation

1

San
Simeon

101

San Miguel

Cambria

Paso
Robles

46

Atascadero

Morro Bay

Santa
Margarita

Los Osos
Oaks S.R.

San Luis Obispo

Pismo
Beach

Huasna
Creek

Arroyo Grande

58

Santa Maria

166

101

New
Cuyama

Lompoc

Los Padres

Los Olivos

National

Solvang 154

Forest

33

See ^
North California
Coast Map

80

99

5

★ Sacramento

Galt

Lodi

4

Stockton

Manteca

Cosumnes River

See ^
North California
Inland Map

Jackson

Mokelumne River

Comanche
Reservoir

Angels
Camp

Stanislaus River

New Melones
Reservoir

50

South
Lake
Tahoe

88

4

49

108

S
A
N

Livermore

Tracy

Modesto

Turlock

Gustine

Los
Banos

Firebaugh

Mendota

D
I
A
B
L
O

152

J
O
A
Q
U
I
N

Don
Pedro
Reservoir

Lake
McClure

Merced River

River

Tuolumne River

120

YOSEMITE
NATIONAL
PARK

Mariposa

140

Merced

Madera

41

See
Central California
Inland Map

Bass Lake

168

Millerton
Lake

Sierra
National
Forest

R
A
N
G
E

Fresno

Clovis

Selma

Pine Flat
Reservoir

180

Kings River

© B. Appleyard 1991

Coalinga

Avenal

Kettleman
City

198

41

Hanford

Corcoran

Tulare

99

Lake
Kaweah

Visalia

Lindsay

65

Porterville

Lost Hills

Wasco

33

5

Earlimart

Delano

J22

McFarland J29

155

Buttonwillow

Kern River

Taft

Bakersfield

166

See
Southern
California
Map ↓

Aqueduct

5

33

N

Area Shown

Central
California
Coast

Oak Location

0   25   50

Miles

PACIFIC

OCEAN

Santa

Lucia

Range

San

J O A Q U I N

V A L L E Y

California

California

D I A B L O

R A N G E

146

Central California Coast

On passing the Santa Lucia the entire aspect of the country changed. It was as if we had passed into another land and another clime. . . The soil is already dry and parched, the grass already as dry as hay, except along streams, the hills brown as a stubble field. But scattered over these hills and in these valleys are trees every few rods—great oaks, often of immense size, ten, twelve, eighteen, and more feet in circumference, but not high; their wide-spreading branches making heads often over a hundred feet in diameter—of the deepest green foliage—while from every branch hangs a trailing lichen, often several feet long and delicate as lace. In passing over this country, every hill and valley presents a new view of these trees.

    —WILLIAM H. BREWER, NEAR ATASCADERO, 1861

San Francisco Bay Area

Bear Valley

Although 100 years of ranching and grazing have reduced the woodlands of coast live oak at Point Reyes National Seashore, there remain several areas that offer fine oak-viewing. Perhaps the best locale is the San Andreas fault zone along Bear Valley Rd. A canopy of tall oaks shades a two-mile section of this road as it winds through hillside pastures. Another area of interest is along Limantour Rd. near the Miwok Village interpretive site; some large, mature coast live oaks grow here. This day-use-only park has a superb visitor center and system of trails. From U.S. 101 at Greenbrae, take Sir Francis Drake Blvd. west to the intersection with Highway 1. Turn right (north) on Highway 1, travel ¼ mile, and then turn left on Bear Valley Rd. Point Reyes National Seashore (415) 663-1092, ext. 0193

Mount Burdell

Coast live oak is the most common oak species at Mount Burdell Open Space Preserve; valley and black oak are also found here, as well as buckeye and bay laurel. A series of fire roads and trails provide access to 1,558 acres of oak-dominated savannas, woodlands, and chaparrals. Horses and hikers are allowed on the trails; bicycles are allowed on fire roads only. The San Andreas Dr. entrance leads to fire roads heading both north and south; the southern road will take you to the Michako Trail. The preserve has no facilities or parking lots;

camping is by permit only. Turn west on San Marin Dr. off of U.S. 101 just north of Novato. San Marin Dr. skirts its southern border. Turn north at San Andreas Dr. and continue to the preserve boundary where there is on-street parking. Marin County Open Space Preserves (415) 499-6387

Oakwood Valley Trail

The Oakwood Valley Trail within the Marin Headlands District of Golden Gate National Recreation Area traverses a coast live oak riparian forest that is surrounded by grassland and coastal scrub communities. Bay laurel, willow, and blue gum eucalyptus also thrive along this valley route. Unfortunately, the encroaching eucalyptus threatens the survival of the oaks and other native species here. From U.S. 101 north of San Francisco, take the Muir Woods/Stinson Beach exit. After approximately 0.6 mile, turn left at the "Tennessee Valley" sign. Continue about one mile farther to where a one-lane bridge spans Oakwood Valley. From a small parking area located beyond the bridge, the trail heads south down the valley. Look for oaks on the east side of the path, about ⅓ mile beyond the trailhead. The Marin Headlands Visitor Center, a group campground, and a hike-in site known as Hawk Camp are nearby. Golden Gate National Recreation Area (415) 331-1540

Strybing Arboretum and Botanical Gardens

Strybing Arboretum's California section offers a chance to compare 11 varieties of California native oak right in San Francisco's Golden Gate Park. In addition to well-known oaks such as coast live, interior live, and black oak, the botanic garden also grows less common varieties, such as deer and island oak. Tours, plant sales, and a horticultural library are available. Paths lead through various climate sections and out to the Steinhart Aquarium and other museums. From Highway 1 in San Francisco, take Lincoln Way east to 9th Ave. City of San Francisco (415) 661-1316

Black Diamond Mines Regional Preserve

The dominant oak species in the preserve is blue oak, with large groves covering many of the north- and east-facing slopes. To see excellent specimens of blue oak and enjoy some of the best views of the Sacramento-San Joaquin Delta, go to the staging area one mile south of park headquarters and take the Stewartville Trail southeast to its intersection with the Ridge Trail; continue due east on the Ridge Trail. Maps are available at headquarters, which is 2.5 miles south of Highway 4 on Somersville Rd. in Antioch. There are no campgrounds in this day-use park. East Bay Regional Park District (510) 531-9300

Briones Regional Park

Briones is a 5,834-acre park with very little development, an extensive trail system, and an abundance of oak species, including coast live, blue, interior live, black, and valley oak. Almost any of the higher trails takes hikers through blue oak woodland and scattered stands of black oak. Valley oak is found in lower-elevation alluvial flats, and coast live and canyon oak grow along or near riparian corridors. Group camping is available by reservation. There are five major access points, but the two most easily reached are Alhambra Creek Valley Staging Area off Reliez Valley Rd. near Martinez, and the Bear Creek Rd. Staging Area off Bear Creek Rd. near Orinda. Trail maps are available at both sites. East Bay Regional Park District (510) 531-9300

Tilden Regional Park / Wildcat Canyon Regional Park

Tilden is one of the oldest of the district's parks and has been heavily planted with non-native vegetation. Wildcat is a later addition to the park system, and together the two contiguous parks comprise about 4,500 acres of the upper watershed of Wildcat Creek. There is an extensive trail system in the parks, and the portions that follow Wildcat

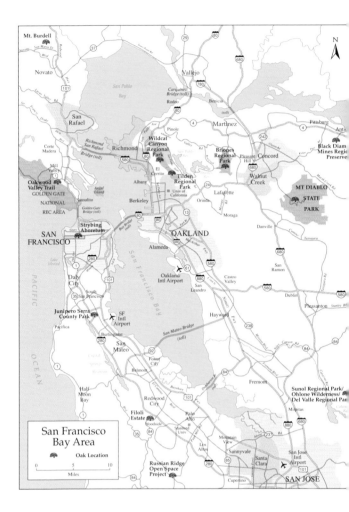

Creek and its tributaries take hikers through coast live oak riparian forest where fine specimens of coast live and canyon oak can be seen. Youth group camping is available by reservation at both parks. Tilden Park is reached via Canon Dr., Shasta Rd., or South Park Dr. off Grizzly Peak Blvd. in the city of Berkeley. Access to the west side of Wildcat Park is from the east end of McBryde Ave. in Richmond. East Bay Regional Park District (510) 531-9300

Regional Parks Botanic Garden

The 10-acre Botanic Garden in Charles Lee Tilden Regional Park hosts representatives of nearly every type of California native oak, with outstanding specimens of huckleberry, Engelmann, Oregon, black, and coast live oak. The garden is devoted to the preservation of native plants of California and displays them in respective climatic sections. A visitor center offers lectures and slide shows on Saturdays, November through February; a plant sale is held during the spring. From Highway 24 in Oakland, take Fish Ranch Rd. north, go right on Grizzly Peak Blvd., and right again on South Park Dr. East Bay Regional Park District (510) 841-8732

Mount Diablo State Park
Many different oak species can be seen along the park's Pine Canyon Trail, from Barbeque Terrace down to Pine Pond; coast live, interior live, canyon, blue, and valley oak are all represented. From Danville on Interstate 680, take Diablo Rd. five miles east. The park can also be reached from Walnut Creek by taking Ignacio Valley Rd. north to Walnut Ave. California Department of Parks & Recreation (510) 837-2525

Sunol Regional Park / Ohlone Wilderness / Del Valle Regional Park
These three contiguous parks encompass the largest publicly-owned open space area in southern Alameda County. A 28-mile hiking trail extends from the Sunol Regional Park entrance through the Ohlone Wilderness and Del Valle Regional Park, traversing a variety of oak-dominated communities, including blue oak woodland and coast live oak riparian forest. Blue and black oak are abundant at the higher elevations while valley oak can be seen at lower elevations. The trail from Sunol can be reached from Calaveras Rd. off I-680. Del Valle Regional Park is accessible from Livermore by taking Mine Rd. and Del Valle Rd. to the park entrance. Some camping is allowed. East Bay Regional Park District (510) 531-9300

Junipero Serra County Park
Fra Junipero Serra held mass under coast live oaks in 1770 and, appropriately, Junipero Serra County Park is home to some outstanding specimens of live oak. Well known for its spring wildflowers, the 100-acre property also features arroyo willow, madrone, and buckeye. The park offers the self-guiding Live Oak Nature Trail, and contains a visitor center and picnic facilities. In San Bruno take Crystal Springs Rd. exit east from Highway 280. San Mateo County Parks & Recreation (415) 589-5708

Filoli Estate
Deeded to the National Trust for Historic Preservation in 1975, Filoli Estate preserves an important example of country house architecture and features lavish gardens amid naturally growing oak woodlands. A small grove of valley oak is found near the estate entrance. A 200- to 300-year-old coast live oak grows near the house. The property's 600 acres of rolling hills, accessible only by docent-led tours, comprise coast live oak woodland, mixed evergreen forest, and a small area of scrub oak chaparral. Reservations are recommended. Filoli is open mid-February through October. The estate is in Woodside on Cañada Rd. National Trust for Historic Preservation (415) 364-2880

Russian Ridge Open Space Preserve
Three open space preserves in the foothills west of Palo Alto offer excellent oak-viewing: Skyline Ridge, Long Ridge, and Russian Ridge. Russian Ridge is particularly notable for its large specimens of canyon oak. This 1,500-acre preserve is located in the Santa Cruz Mountains. Six miles of trails traverse hilly terrain that includes the highest point in San Mateo County. This is a day-use area; there are no campsites. Take Skyline Blvd. north from Highway 9. The main entrance is at the intersection of Alpine Rd and Skyline Blvd. Midpeninsula Regional Open Space District (415) 949-5500

San Jose Area

Joseph T. Grant Park
Located in the Diablo Range east of the Santa Clara Valley, this 10,000-acre park hosts a variety of oak species. Shaded areas of the west ridge have stands of black oak, while blue oak is scattered along the more exposed ridges. Valley oak, coast live oak, and sycamore grow near bottomlands and drainages. More than 20 miles of hiking, bicycling, and riding trails are available for exploring this large park. Used as a cattle ranch since the late 1880s, large areas of this park are still leased for grazing. The visitor center is in the old ranch house. The park is east of San Jose on Hamilton Rd., eight miles east of Alum Rock Ave. Santa Clara County Department of Parks & Recreation (408) 274-6121

New Almaden Quicksilver County Park
This 3,600-acre park occupies the eastern foothills of the Santa Cruz Mountains next to Almaden Valley. It comprises extensive blue oak woodlands as well as savanna and chaparral communities. Blue, valley, and coast live oak are the tree oaks that

occur here. This parkland and adjacent New Almaden National Historic Landmark District contain the site of North America's first and most productive quicksilver (mercury) mining operation. Mine Hill Trail, accessible from the parking area just southwest of the community of New Almaden, traverses many of the park's oak communities. New Almaden Quicksilver County Park is about 10 miles south of San Jose on Almaden Rd. Santa Clara County Department of Park & Recreation (408) 268-3883

Castle Rock State Park

Steep canyons and unusual rock formations provide a dramatic background for viewing coast live and black oak at Castle Rock State Park. Outstanding black oak savanna may be seen along a two-mile section of the Saratoga Gap Trail, a route that passes through plant communities ranging from chaparral to redwood forest. Primitive backpacking campsites are the only overnight facilities. The park is located on Highway 35, about 2.5 miles southeast of the junction with Highway 9. The Saratoga Gap Trail starts at the parking area on the east side of the park. California Department of Parks & Recreation (408) 867-2952 or (408) 335-9145

Uvas Canyon Park

Fine examples of canyon oak grow along the road approaching Uvas Canyon and in the developed portion of the park. An especially picturesque specimen is found at the park entrance. Uvas Canyon also contains black oak along with madrone, redwood, knobcone pine, Douglas fir, and tanbark. This quiet canyon features waterfalls and streams; facilities include interpretive trails, a campground, and picnic areas. Call ahead to arrange guided walks or folk botany interpretations. From Morgan Hill, go south on Monterey Highway (Highway 82), right on Watsonville Rd., right on Uvas Rd., and left on Croy. Santa Clara County Department of Parks & Recreation (408) 779-9232

Henry W. Coe State Park

Oak woodlands dominate this 70,000-acre state park where six different tree oak species are represented. A 10-mile loop trail to Madrone Soda Springs passes through several distinct oak communities, including blue oak woodland. The trail to Madrone Soda Springs begins at park headquarters; return by way of Poverty Flat, Middle

Ridge Trail, and Fish Trail to complete the circular route. From U.S. 101 in Morgan Hill, take Dunne Ave. 13 miles east to the park entrance. California Department of Parks & Recreation (408) 779-2728

Monterey / Salinas Valley Area

Elkhorn Slough National Estuarine Research Reserve

Elkhorn Slough is one of the few places in the country where you can stand in the shade of an oak while watching sharks cut through the water's surface. The reserve's 4,000-plus acres of tidelands encompass the largest coastal wetland between Morro Bay and San Francisco Bay. The Long Valley Loop Trail leads into a fine stand of coast live oak. Other trails in the reserve pass through groves of Monterey pine and introduced eucalyptus, and down to marshlands and view points. A visitor center with exhibits and bookstore is found near the reserve entrance. The Elkhorn Slough Foundation, a local nonprofit organization, supports research and education projects at the slough. From Highway 1 in Moss Landing, take Dolan Rd. east for three miles, then left on Elkhorn Rd. for two miles. The Nature Conservancy, California Department of Fish & Game, National Oceanic and Atmospheric Administration (408) 728-2822 or (408) 728-5939

Pfeiffer Big Sur State Park

Coast live oak are numerous along the Oak Grove Trail in Pfeiffer Big Sur State Park. This trail requires about 60 to 90 minutes to hike and takes visitors through coast live oak riparian forest, redwood groves, and chaparral. The park has developed campsites, rental cabins, and many other hiking trails. It is located 26 miles south of Carmel on Highway 1. California Department of Parks & Recreation (408) 667-2315

Toro Regional Park

Coast live, valley, and interior live oak are found in Monterey County's 5,000-acre Toro Regional Park. There are about 20 miles of fire roads and hiking and riding trails. The Self-Guided Nature Trail, which begins at the upper parking lot, provides good oak-viewing. The route passes by the Youth Overnight Area, nestled in a native oak environment, where non-profit youth groups camp. Toro Regional Park is located about 6 miles west

Valley oak woodlands shade a country road near Mission San Antonio. JOHN EVARTS

of Salinas and 13 miles east of Monterey on Highway 68. Monterey County Department of Parks (408) 755-4899

Pinnacles National Monument
The Bench Trail that parallels Highway 146 on the east side of Pinnacles National Monument passes lovely specimens of coast live and valley oak. Blue oak, gray pine, cottonwood, and sycamore also grow along this fairly level hiking route. The trail borders Pinnacles Campground, a private facility adjacent to the monument. The campground is situated in a stand of valley oak. Blue oak woodlands and scrub oak chaparral are accessible by road on both the east and west sides of the monument. Westside access is from Highway 146 at the U.S. 101 junction in Soledad. Eastside access is via Highway 146 at the junction with Highway 25, south of Hollister. (Highway 146 does not extend through the monument; the east and west segments are not connected.) Use the east-side entrance for Bench Trail. There is a visitor center at Bear Gulch on the east side of the park. Pinnacles National Monument (408) 389-4485

Mission San Antonio / Hunter-Liggett
Outstanding examples of valley oak savanna and woodland are found in the upper San Antonio River Valley on Hunter-Liggett Military Reservation. A good area for oak-viewing is along Del Venturi and Milpitas roads, between Mission San Antonio and the northern edge of the military reservation. From Highway 101 in King City, take G14 south to Jolon (about 20 miles). In Jolon, take Mission Rd. to Del Venturi Rd. which heads northwest through this remote valley. Just north of the reservation border,

Milpitas Rd. passes through distinct groves of blue, coast live, and valley oak. Santa Lucia Memorial Park Campground is located on Milpitas Rd. about five miles north of the reservation. Call ahead to find out if the gates at Hunter-Liggett are open. Hunter Liggett Military Reservation/ Los Padres National Forest (408) 385-2403 or (408) 385-5434

San Luis Obispo Area

Santa Margarita / Cuesta Ridge
The Santa Margarita region features some of the best stands of valley oak in San Luis Obispo County. For a country drive through oak woodlands and savannas, exit U.S. 101 at Highway 58 and turn south on Pozo Rd. just east of Santa Margarita. Pozo Rd. swings east about 10 miles beyond town, passing groves of blue oak. To see leather oak, Sargent cypress, and several species of rare plants, visit the nearby Cuesta Ridge Botanical Area in Los Padres National Forest. Return to 101, head south three miles and exit west (right) at TV Tower Rd. at the top of Cuesta Grade. Continue 2.5 miles on a narrow, winding road to the botanic area. Los Padres National Forest (805) 925-9538

Los Osos Oaks State Reserve
The reserve's one mile self-guided trail winds through a dramatic grove of gnarled, ancient coast live oaks; it also leads through an area of sandy soil covered with small, moss-covered oaks that are no larger than 10 feet high. The 85-acre reserve is for day use only; there is a parking area, but no other facilities. The reserve is located eight miles west of San Luis Obispo on Los Osos Valley Rd. The self-guided trail starts at the parking area. California Department of Parks & Recreation (805) 528-0513

Huasna Road
Good examples of coast live oak woodland border Huasna Rd. southeast of Arroyo Grande. After crossing the Huasna River, the road passes stands of blue and coast live oak. Further east, as you approach National Forest lands and Agua Escondido Campground, blue oak predominates along the route. From Highway 101 in Arroyo Grande, follow signs to Lopez Lake (Grand Ave. to Branch to Lopez Dr.) for two miles. Turn right on Huasna Rd. Los Padres National Forest (805) 925-9538

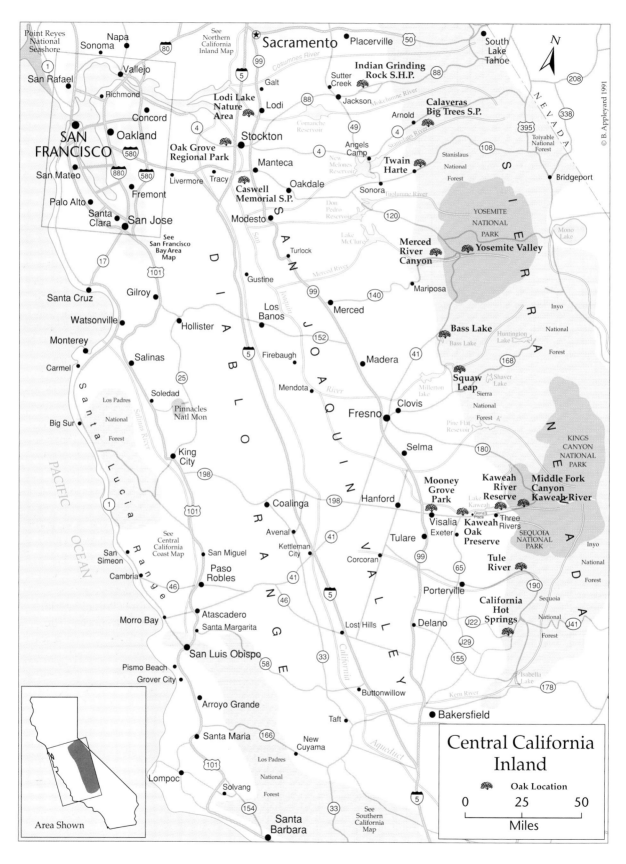

Central California Inland

. . . I forded the San Joaquin, and I at once left the road, determined to follow a mountain trail which led toward Mariposa. The trail proved a good one to travel. . . with rambling curves which led through open regions of brown hills, whose fern and grass were ripened to a common yellow-brown, then among park-like slopes, crowned with fine oaks, and occasional pine woods, the ground frequently covering itself with clumps of such shrubs as chaparral, and the never-enough-admired manzanita.
—CLARENCE KING, IN MADERA COUNTY, 1872

Northern Sierra / Yosemite

Indian Grinding Rock State Historic Park
Large specimens of valley oak grow near this famous acorn grinding rock. The rock's surface is pitted with more than 1,000 mortar holes, which were used by many generations of Miwok Indians for acorn-pounding. The park's Chaw'se Regional Indian Museum includes information on Native American use of oaks; a nature trail passes through Sierran mixed conifer forest where valley, black, and canyon oak can be seen. Developed and primitive walk-in campsites are available. This 135-acre park is located 11 miles northeast of Jackson, 1.4 miles from Highway 88 on Pine Grove-Volcano Rd. California Department of Parks & Recreation (209) 296-7488

Calaveras Big Trees State Park
Best known for its groves of giant sequoia trees, this 6,000-acre park is also home to nice specimens of black oak in a Sierran mixed conifer forest. The River Trail provides access to black oaks and is an especially good route for viewing fall color. The Lava Bluffs Trail leads past black and canyon oak. Park facilities include a visitor center and family and walk-in campsites. Calaveras Big Trees State Park is located three miles northeast of Arnold, on Highway 4. California Department of Parks & Recreation (209) 795-2334

Twain Harte
North of the town of Twain Harte, a maintained dirt and gravel road within the Stanislaus National Forest takes you through a large area of mixed oak, conifer, and chaparral plant communities. The South Fork Road (2N63) north from Twain Harte to the Knight Creek drainage traverses valleys and ridges where interior live, canyon, and black oak grow. Associated conifers here are ponderosa pine, gray pine, and incense cedar. Primitive camping is available at several sites. From Highway 99 at Modesto, take Highway 108 northeast to Twain Harte. Use the Stanislaus National Forest, Pacific Southwest Region map to avoid confusion when navigating the area's vast network of back country roads. This map is available at the Mi-Wok Ranger District Office, a few miles north of Twain Harte on Highway 108. Stanislaus National Forest (209) 586-3234

Merced River Canyon
Canyon oak flourishes along the steep walls of the Merced River canyon, from El Portal to Yosemite Valley. Some of the woodlands are almost pure canyon oak, while others contain ponderosa pine, gray pine, and incense cedar. In the extensive recreation areas downriver from El Portal, interior live oak is the predominant tree oak species. The campground nearest the oak-viewing area is Indian Flat Campground (Stanislaus National Forest), about four miles below El Portal on Highway 140. Take Highway 140 east from Mariposa for access to the upper Merced River. Yosemite National Park; Stanislaus National Forest (209) 966-3638

Yosemite Valley
Yosemite National Park personnel are currently involved in comprehensive restoration projects for Yosemite Valley's once-extensive black oak woodlands. (See "Expanding Yosemite's Black Oak Woodlands" in Chapter Five.) Several impressive

black oak groves are found on the valley floor. The most accessible black oaks are the majestic specimens growing near the visitor center in Yosemite Village. A more extensive stand is within easy walking distance, situated between the visitor center and the base of Yosemite Falls. Black oak acorns were a dietary staple of the Ahwaneechee Indians of Yosemite Valley, and the park's Indian Culture Museum occasionally sponsors programs on preparing acorn meal. Three highways lead to Yosemite: Highway 41 (Wawona Rd.) north from Fresno, Highway 140 northeast from Merced, and Highway 120 from San Francisco to the west, and Nevada to the east. Yosemite National Park (209) 372-0529

Fresno to Bass Lake Loop

This loop trip from Fresno to Bass Lake traverses a variety of oak landscapes and provides an opportunity to learn about the ways California Indians used oaks and other native plants. Allow a full day for a leisurely drive. Heading north from Fresno on Highway 41, you will see blue oak savannas and woodlands; valley oaks are scattered through the lowland and foothill areas. As you ascend from Oakhurst to Bass Lake, canyon and black oak occur within a Sierran mixed conifer forest. Return to Fresno via North Fork and O'Neals.

There are three sites along the route that introduce different aspects of regional Native American heritage. A short side trip from Oakhurst to Ahwahnee, about five miles north on Highway 49, brings you to Wassama Roundhouse State Historic Park; phone (209) 683-3631. This is one of the few surviving ceremonial roundhouses in California that is still in use. The spacious, oak-shaded grounds include rock outcroppings where acorns were pounded into meal. Another educational stop along this loop drive is the Mono Interpretive Trail at Bass Lake; a trail brochure provides information on how Monache Indians prepared acorn. A third worthwhile stop is the Sierra Mono Museum in North Fork. Built and run by the local Mono Indians, this museum houses a superb collection of Native American baskets and artifacts. Sierra National Forest (209) 487-5155

Squaw Leap

Squaw Leap Management Area in the San Joaquin River Gorge offers a scenic riverside hiking and riding trail through blue oak woodlands and savanna. The oaks are interspersed with gray pine along the four-mile-long southern portion of the Squaw Leap Trail, which leads to Millerton Lake. A primitive campsite (no water) is found at the trailhead, located five miles northwest of Auberry, off Highway 168. Take Power House Road north from Auberry to Small Road, which leads to the trailhead and campsite. BLM Hollister Resource Area (408) 637-8183

San Joaquin Valley

Lodi Lake Nature Area

This 58-acre nature area along the Mokelumne River supports both riparian and grassland habitats. Interior live is the predominant oak species here, and is joined by valley oak, willow, black locust, and cottonwood. A 1.2-mile loop trail offers natural history interpretation, and docent-led walks can be arranged. Exit Highway 99 at Turner Rd. and head west two miles to the Lodi Lake Park gate where you can get directions to the nature area. Another approach is to take the Turner Rd. exit off I-5 and head east about six miles to Lodi Lake Park. City of Lodi (209) 369-1251

Oak Grove Regional Park

As a cattle ranch in the late 1800s, the valley oaks of Oak Grove Park were spared the saws. The southern half of Oak Grove's 170 acres is kept as an oak preserve with hiking trails winding through it. The recreational northern portion of the park offers picnic facilities, pedal boat rentals, sand volleyball courts, and horseshoe courts. A nature center (open weekends only) features native plant and animal displays. Oak Grove is in Stockton at 4520 West Eight Mile Rd. Take the Eight Mile Rd. exit off I-5. San Joaquin County Department of Parks & Recreation (209) 953-8800

Caswell Memorial State Park

A small but outstanding remnant of valley oak riparian forest is preserved in this 250-acre state park. Some of the trees here are more than 60 feet high, with girths of over 17 feet. The one-mile Oak Forest Nature Trail passes through portions of a lovely closed-canopy forest along the Stanislaus River. A variety of birds and other wildlife are found in this lush riverside habitat. Facilities include developed and walk-in campsites. Take Austin Rd. off Highway 99, six miles south of the town of Ripon. California Department of Parks & Recreation (209) 599-3810

Mooney Grove Park

Mooney Grove Park was established in 1909 when Visalia residents, alarmed over the rapid destruction of the area's magnificent oak forest, persuaded Tulare County to buy this prime tract of valley oak. (See "Visalia, City of Oaks" in Chapter Five.) Picnic areas, a lagoon, and the Tulare County Museum are set amid the park's 100 acres of huge old oaks. A 10-year program of park renovation was completed in 1990 to enhance protection of Mooney Grove's trees. The park is located two miles south of Visalia on Highway 63 (Mooney Blvd.). Tulare County Department of Buildings and Parks (209) 738-6612

Kaweah Oaks Preserve

This preserve protects one of California's finest examples of valley oak riparian forest. Valley oaks and some very large specimens of sycamore form an open forest along two tributaries of the Kaweah River. The 324-acre preserve also features native herbaceous meadow habitat. The Self-Guided Nature Trail begins near the main entrance. A volunteer group offers guided tours by appointment. Take Highway 198 east from Visalia towards Sequoia National Park. In about seven miles, turn north on Road 182 and continue ½ mile to the entrance of the preserve. The Nature Conservancy (209) 992-2833

Southern Sierra / Sequoia Area

Kaweah River Ecological Reserve

The Kaweah River Ecological Reserve features blue, canyon, and interior live oak in a 98-acre woodland setting. Just outside Sequoia National Park, the reserve is nine miles southeast of Three Rivers and Highway 198 on South Fork Road. Access is by foot via the well-maintained Salt Creek Fire Road. California Department of Fish and Game (209) 222-3761

Middle Fork Canyon of Kaweah River

The middle fork canyon of the Kaweah River in Sequoia National Park offers some of the finest oak-

viewing on national park land in California. Four species of tree oak are visible from the Generals Highway (198) between Ash Mountain and Hospital Rock. The route begins in blue oak savannas and woodlands, crosses patches of mixed evergreen forest with extensive stands of interior live and canyon oak, and, at higher elevations, enters Sierran mixed conifer forest with black oak. Two oak-shaded campgrounds, Potwisha and Buckeye Flat (¼ mile off the highway), are found along the way. A visitor center is located at Ash Mountain, 35 miles east of Visalia on Highway 198. Sequoia National Park (209) 565-3341

Tule River

The drive on Highway 190 along the Tule River from Porterville to Camp Nelson provides views of four different types of tree oaks. Scattered valley oak is found at lower elevations around Lake Success. Beyond the lake, blue, interior live, and valley oak are found. Blue oak savanna is predominant near the community of Springville. Blue and interior live oak provide shade at the Coffee Camp Day Use Area and Campground. (This popular riverside destination can be crowded.) As you continue up Highway 190, more canyon oak is found, beginning at about 4,000 feet. Take Highway 190 east from Porterville into Sequoia National Forest and continue to Camp Nelson. Sequoia National Forest (209) 539-2607

California Hot Springs Area

A scenic drive on Mountain Rd. 56 from the community of Fountain Springs to the town of California Hot Springs will take you through several oak-dominated plant communities. Blue oak savanna predominates at the lower elevations and makes a transition to blue oak woodland as the road gains elevation. Interior live oak appears as the route climbs out of the valley. Black oak, incense cedar, and gray pine appear along the approach to California Hot Springs. A privately operated resort offers day use of pools filled by the waters of the hot springs. At nearby Leavis Flat Campground, shade is provided by interior live oak, canyon oak, and sycamore. California Hot Springs is 35 miles southeast of Porterville. From Fountain Springs (about 15 miles south of Porterville), take Mountain Rd. 56 east to California Hot Springs, which is just inside the boundary of Sequoia National Forest. Sequoia National Forest (805) 548-6503

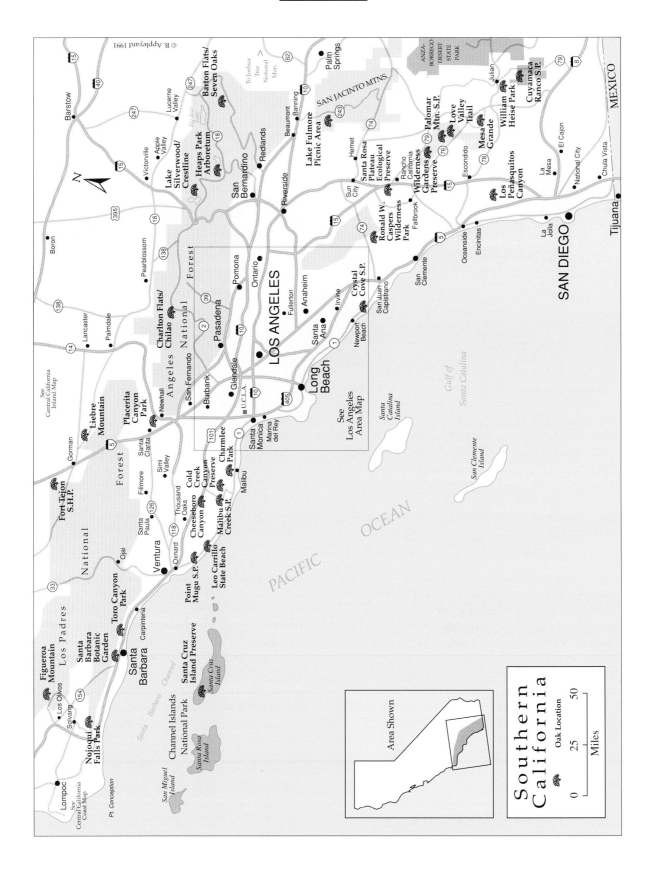

© B. Appleyard 1991

Southern California

🌳 Oak Location

Miles

0   25   50

Area Shown

Southern California

Emerging from a particularly tedious breadth of chaparral, I found myself . . . in a beautiful park-like grove of Mountain Live Oak [canyon oak], where the ground was planted with aspidiums and brier-roses, while the glossy foliage made a close canopy overhead, leaving the gray dividing trunks bare to show the beauty of their interlacing arches. . . . Tracing the dry channel about a mile farther down . . . I at length discovered a lot of boulder pools, clear as crystal, brimming full, and linked together by glistening streamlets just strong enough to sing audibly. Flowers in full bloom adorned their margins . . . while a noble old Live Oak spread its rugged arms over all. Here I camped, making my bed on smooth cobblestones.
—JOHN MUIR, IN THE SAN GABRIEL MOUNTAINS, 1882

Santa Barbara Area

Figueroa Mountain
Several distinct oak communities are encountered during a drive to the 4,500-foot summit of Figueroa Mountain. This wooded peak is renowned for its spring wildflowers and panoramic views of the rugged Santa Barbara backcountry. From U.S. 101 in Santa Barbara, take Highway 154 to Los Olivos and turn right (north) on Figueroa Mountain Rd. After leaving the highway, the route takes you through valley oak savanna. About seven miles from Los Olivos, where the road crosses the creek and begins its winding ascent into the mountains, the route enters blue oak woodland; it then climbs past serpentine rock outcrops and scrub oak chaparral.

One mile past Figueroa Station, head left on to unpaved Figueroa Lookout Rd. and continue two miles to the mountaintop where you'll find ponderosa and Coulter pine, bigcone spruce, coast live oak, and canyon oak. A paved nature trail begins at the Pino Alto Picnic Area near the summit. Return by the same route (15 miles one way to Los Olivos) or continue east on Figueroa Mountain Rd. (past Figueroa Campground) to Happy Canyon Rd. for a scenic loop trip back to Highway 154. Los Padres National Forest (805) 688-3017

Nojoqui Falls Park
This popular 82-acre oak woodland contains one of Santa Barbara County's tallest waterfalls. Coast live oak, sycamore, and bay laurel shade creekside paths

and picnic areas. For pleasant backroad oak-viewing, head east from the park toward the town of Solvang (six miles) on Alisal Road; the route winds beneath a canopy of lichen-draped oaks. From the junction of U.S. 101 and Highway 1, drive two miles north, turn right onto Old Coast Rd. at the summit of the grade, and continue to Alisal Rd. Santa Barbara County (805) 568-2461

Santa Barbara Botanic Garden
The Santa Barbara Botanic Garden is devoted to the study, display, and preservation of native California plants. More than 1,000 species, including over 20 varieties of oak, are grown on the 65-acre grounds. The Woodland Trail features coast live oak woodland with its natural understory of coastal wood fern, redberry, lemonade berry, and toyon. The native vegetation along the Pritchett Trail includes stands of native scrub oak and coast live oak, along with other chaparral species indigenous to the region. The Island Section displays several large specimens of island oak, a handsome tree endemic to Southern California's Channel Islands.

For information on plant identification and landscaping under oaks, the garden provides classes and literature. A well-stocked bookstore, library (non-circulating), and native plant nursery are located on the grounds; docent tours, children's workshops, and field trips are offered throughout the year. The botanic garden is in Santa Barbara at 1212 Mission Canyon Rd. (805) 682-4726

Toro Canyon Park

Toro Canyon County Park includes two distinct oak communities: scrub oak chaparral and coast live oak woodland. The woodland, found on north-facing slopes, supports species such as coast live oak, bay laurel, toyon, and gooseberry. There are picnic and playground areas, and a trail extends east from the park into Los Padres National Forest. From northbound U.S. 101 take Toro Canyon Rd. north for three miles and watch for a park sign on the right. Santa Barbara County (805) 568-2461

Santa Cruz Island Preserve

Numerous stands of the rare island oak are found on Santa Cruz Island, located about 25 miles off the Santa Barbara County coastline. At least seven other species of oak plus two hybrid oaks grow on the island, including coast live, canyon, MacDonald (a hybrid), and island scrub oak. The fascinating and diverse flora of Santa Cruz Island comprises a number of plants endemic to the Southern California Islands, such as island ceanothus, island manzanita, and Santa Cruz Island ironwood. The Nature Conservancy owns and manages 90% of the island and offers one-day field trips April through November.

For information about how to visit the island, stop by the Conservancy's Southern California Field Office and Visitor Center on Stearns Wharf in Santa Barbara. The Channel Islands National Park Visitor Center at 1901 Spinnaker Dr., Ventura Harbor, (805)-644-8262, also provides visitor information for Santa Cruz Island and neighboring Santa Rosa Island. The Nature Conservancy (805) 962-9111

Santa Monica Mountains

Cheeseboro Canyon

Encompassing several hundred acres, Cheeseboro Canyon contains one of the last undisturbed examples of valley oak savanna in Los Angeles County. Coast live oak woodland covers slopes above the savanna, and scrub oak chaparral occurs near the canyon's upper end. Large specimens of sycamore and desert willow also flourish here. From U.S. 101 just west of Agoura Hills, take the Chesebro exit and head west on Driver Ave. Make a right turn at the Cheeseboro Canyon sign. The Santa Monica Mountains National Recreation

Visitor Center is located in nearby Agoura Hills at 30401 Agoura Rd. Santa Monica Mountains National Recreation Area (818) 597-1036

Point Mugu State Park

Coast live oak grows throughout Point Mugu State Park, and oak woodlands are accessible from many of the park's 70 miles of hiking trails. Sycamore Canyon Campground is located in a woodland of sycamore and coast live oak. Beautiful and large specimens of both species are growing along the Sycamore Canyon Trail. The La Jolla Valley Natural Preserve contains excellent stands of native bunch-grass. It is accessible via a strenuous hike from La Jolla Canyon, located about one mile northwest of the park's entrance. The park is located 15 miles southeast of Oxnard on Highway 1 (Pacific Coast Highway). Sycamore Canyon Trail and Campground are at Point Mugu's southeastern corner near park headquarters. California Department of Parks & Recreation (805) 488-1872 or (818) 706-1310

Leo Carrillo State Beach

A small savanna with coast live oak and native grass overlooks the ocean from Nicholas Flat, a day-use area within Leo Carrillo State Beach. Campgrounds near the main entrance are situated among coast live oak and sycamore. Leo Carrillo State Beach is 21 miles southeast of Oxnard at the intersection of Highway 1 (Pacific Coast Highway) and Mulholland Highway. Nicholas Flat is reached by going north on Decker Canyon Rd., about one mile east of the State Beach entrance. Turn left on Decker School Rd. which ends at Nicholas Flat. California Department of Parks & Recreation (213) 457-6589 or (818) 706-1310

Malibu Creek State Park

Malibu Creek State Park preserves fine examples of coast live oak riparian forest and valley oak savanna. The park contains California's southernmost valley oaks. A beautiful pocket of valley oak savanna in Liberty Canyon is the site of an innovative native grass restoration program conducted by state park staff to help improve valley oak regeneration. (See "Planting Bunchgrass in a Valley Oak Savanna" in Chapter Five.) The park entrance is located on the Las Virgenes-Malibu Canyon Rd. about three miles south of U.S. 101. Ask at the entrance for directions to Liberty Canyon. California Department of Parks & Recreation (818) 706-8809 or 706-1310

Cold Creek Canyon Preserve

This undeveloped 650-acre canyon, owned by the nonprofit Mountains Restoration Trust, features a riparian habitat and a variety of plant species. A 1.6-mile trail into the preserve winds through coast live oak woodland and leads to waterfalls along the canyon's year-round stream. Hikers will pass fine specimens of redshank and manzanita in the chaparral; they can also view some of the five species of ferns that are found on the canyon's cool, north-facing slopes. Cold Creek Canyon Preserve is located between Malibu and Calabasas. Mountains Restoration Trust requests that you call for reservations and directions. Mountains Restoration Trust (213) 456-5627 or 456-5625

Charmlee Park

Known for its wildflowers and panoramic views of the Pacific, this 520-acre ocean bluff park hosts coast live oak, scrub oak, and sycamore. The park features trails, picnic areas, group programs, and a nature center with live animals. Charmlee Park is three miles off Highway 1 (Pacific Coast Highway), at 2577 N. Encinal Canyon Rd., Malibu. Los Angeles County (213) 457-7247

Topanga State Park

Topanga State Park contains large areas of coast live oak woodland interspersed with chaparral. One of the loveliest woodlands, with majestic oak specimens, is on a hill south of Trippet Ranch. Although one primitive walk-in campground exists, this is primarily a day-use park, offering picnic areas and 35 miles of hiking and riding trails. Take Entrada Rd. off Highway 27 (Topanga Canyon Blvd.), about five miles north of Highway 1 (Pacific Coast Highway). Entrada Rd. leads directly to Trippet Ranch. The park can also be reached from San Fernando Valley by taking Highway 27 south from U.S. 101. California Department of Parks & Recreation (213) 455-2465 or (818) 706-1310

Los Angeles / Orange County Area

Theodore Payne Foundation

Established in 1963, the Theodore Payne Foundation was the first California organization dedicated solely to the propagation and preservation of native California flora. Today, the foundation features a 21-acre retail nursery stocked with over 600 species of California native plants, including nine species of oak. The property also has a bookstore and library that offer horticultural and botanical literature. The foundation is located at 10459 Tuxford St. in Sun Valley. Take the Sunland Blvd. exit from I-5. (818) 768-1802

Descanso Gardens

Known for its extensive rose and camellia gardens, Descanso Gardens is also a good location for viewing three oak species. The world-famous camellia garden is nestled in a 30-acre woodland of coast live oak. The native plant garden contains examples of Engelmann and valley oak. A network of paths and hiking trails traverse 60 acres of manicured botanic gardens; tram tours are available. Descanso Gardens is in La Cañada Flintridge at 1418 Descanso Dr. Los Angeles County (818) 952-4400

Eaton Canyon Nature Center

Eaton Canyon Nature Center's 184 acres contain several plant communities, including scrub oak chaparral, coastal sage scrub, and coast live oak woodland. Scattered groves of coast live oak and a stand of Engelmann oak (north of the Meadow Trail) occur on the property. The brochure for the self-guiding Oak Terrace Nature Trail includes a section on oak tree ecology. Eaton Canyon Park is situated at the base of Mount Wilson in the San Gabriel Mountains, at 1750 N. Altadena Dr. in Pasadena. Los Angeles County (818) 794-1866

Los Angeles State and County Arboretum

This arboretum and botanic garden cover 127 acres and feature collections of plants from around the world. The arboretum promotes scientific and educational work in its park-like setting. Seven species of California oak are represented here. A native grove of Engelmann oak near the Southwestern Native Plant Section comprises the last remaining intact stand of Engelmann oak woodland in Los Angeles County. The arboretum is at 301 N. Baldwin Ave. in Arcadia. Los Angeles County (818) 821-3222

Rancho Santa Ana Botanic Garden

One of the best places in the state for oak tree information, this 86-acre garden is primarily a botanical research and educational facility devoted to study and preservation of California native flora. Among its collection of over 1,500 native plants, all nine major oak tree species are represented. A display case on the grounds compares leaves and acorns of the various species. The Woodland Trail passes beneath a shady canopy of coast live oak, Engelmann oak, and California walnut. Volunteer docents give group tours focusing on the oaks of the garden; general public tours are offered on weekends in spring. The botanic garden is in Claremont at 1500 North College Ave. (714) 625-8767

Fullerton Arboretum

Fullerton Arboretum, which opened in 1979, has 10 species of native California shrub and tree oak in its collection. Coast live, canyon, blue, black, and interior live oak have been planted with other native vegetation on and in the vicinity of Chaparral Hill as part of the Arid Zone botanical collection. The arboretum offers an excellent self-guiding tour brochure that features the historic Heritage House as well as the botanical collections and cultivated gardens. The arboretum is located at the northeast corner of the California State University, Fullerton campus. Take Yorba Linda Blvd. west off Highway

57. Turn south on Associated Rd. to the entrance. California State University, Fullerton (714) 773-3579

Irvine Regional Park

This 477-acre park features one of the oldest stands of coast live oak in Orange County. The William Harding Nature Area has self-guided nature trails meandering through scrub oak chaparral and coast live oak woodland. This day-use park includes picnic areas, hiking and riding trails, horse rentals, and the Orange County Zoo. It is located in Santiago Canyon, six miles east of the city of Orange. Take the Newport Freeway (55) to the Chapman offramp. Head east on Chapman for about five miles to Jamboree Rd. Turn left on Jamboree Rd. to the park entrance. Orange County (714) 633-8072

Crystal Cove State Park

This 2,700-acre park features three miles of beach and extends inland to protect fine examples of coast live oak woodland and scrub oak chaparral. El Moro Canyon Trail provides access to the oak woodlands and leads to scenic viewpoints

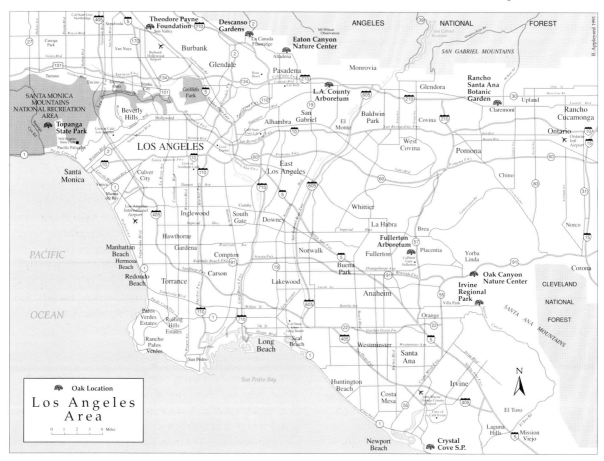

overlooking the Pacific. Three hike-in campsites are located in the upland portion of the park. It is situated between Corona del Mar and Laguna Beach on Highway 1. California Department of Parks & Recreation (714) 494-3539

Oak Canyon Nature Center
Coast live oak growing in association with black walnut and sycamore can be seen along six miles of trails in this 58-acre day-use park. The drier canyon slopes support chaparral plant communities. A riparian oak woodland flourishes along the short, paved Heritage Trail, which has information plaques about the plants and animals of Oak Canyon. By making reservations, groups can enjoy guided nature walks. There is also an interpretive and resource center in the park. Oak Canyon Nature Center is located near Anaheim Hills Golf Course off Nohl Ranch Rd. at 6700 Walnut Canyon Rd. City of Anaheim Recreation Department (714) 998-8380 or (714) 999-5191

Ronald W. Caspers Wilderness Park
This 7,600-acre park in the western Santa Ana Mountains is one of the last true wilderness areas of Orange County. Thirty miles of trails provide access to oak groves, streamside habitats, and ridgetops. The Live Oak Grove Campground is situated in a lovely riparian oak woodland. Because of previous attacks on children by mountain lions, minors (under 18 years of age) are restricted to designated day-use areas of the park. All campgrounds are for adults only. Take San Diego Freeway (I-5) to the Ortega Highway (74) exit at San Juan Capistrano. Turn due east (inland) along Ortega Highway and continue 7.5 miles to the park entrance. Orange County (714) 728-0235 or (714) 831-2174

Tehachapi, San Gabriel, and San Bernardino Mountains

Placerita Canyon Park and Nature Center
This 350-acre park is one of the best places in Southern California to learn about native oak species. Three types of tree oak occur naturally here: coast live, valley, and canyon oak. A network of hiking and equestrian trails winds through oak woodlands and chaparral-covered slopes and ridgetops. The ½-mile self-guiding Ecology Trail

features majestic coast live oak, sycamore, and numerous chaparral species. The nature center contains exhibits on oak ecology and wildlife of the oak woodland. The "Oak of the Golden Dream," a California historical landmark, grows near the park's west entrance. The legend is that in 1842 a vaquero took a nap under this coast live oak and dreamt of gold, then woke and found gold while digging up wild onions for lunch. The park facilities include a picnic area, group campground, playground, nature center, and museum. Placerita Canyon Park is in Newhall at 19152 W. Placerita Canyon Rd. Los Angeles County (805) 259-7721

Fort Tejon State Historic Park
The main feature of this day-use park is the historic army fort (ca. 1854) and museum. Immense valley oaks shade the edges of the parade grounds; one specimen measures eight feet in diameter. The upper canyon stands of both valley and blue oak are accessible by foot. The historic Peter Lebeck Oak is also located on park property. (See "California's Historic Oaks" in Chapter Four.) California Department of Parks & Recreation (805) 248-6692

Liebre Mountain
The north slope of Liebre Mountain in Angeles National Forest contains some of the largest pure stands of black oak in Southern California. These woodlands occur between 5,000 and 5,700 feet and encompass some 5,000 acres. A mixture of oaks are found at lower elevations and include black, canyon, blue, and Oregon oak in association with buckeye. The Pacific Crest Trail traverses this area and provides good hiking access to the oak woodlands. From I-5 just south of Gorman, take Highway 138 east towards Lancaster. Go about three miles; just past Quail Lake, turn right on Forest Road 8N04. After 5.5 miles, turn left on Forest Road 7N22, then left again on 7N23 which takes you over Liebre Ridge and through the upper stands of black oak. Bear Camp on Forest Road 7N23 is the nearest campground (bring your own water). Angeles National Forest (818) 574-1613

Charlton Flats and Chilao
Canyon oak is the most common oak species in the San Gabriel Mountains. It is widespread in southern mixed evergreen forests, where it is associated with Jeffrey pine, Coulter pine, and bigcone spruce. Large specimens of canyon oak shade the Charlton

Flats Picnic Area; the nearest overnight campground is at Chilao where there is also a visitor center. In La Cañada, take Highway 2 northeast into Angeles National Forest. Charlton Flats and Chilao are on this highway beyond the Mount Wilson turnoff. Angeles National Forest (818) 796-1151

Lake Silverwood and Crestline
South of Lake Silverwood, Highway 138 traverses slopes covered with interior live oak and crosses drainages lined with canyon oak. A beautiful drive continuing up Highway 138 to Crestline will take you through stands of the above-mentioned oaks, as well as black oak in association with mixed stands of large old conifers. There is a campground at Silverwood Lake State Park. From Victorville or San Bernardino, take I-15 and head east on Highway 138. San Bernardino National Forest (714) 337-2444

Heaps Peak Arboretum
Black oaks in a mixed conifer community are easily accessible along a ¾-mile self-guided nature trail at Heaps Peak Arboretum. Situated at 6,421 feet, the arboretum is found on the "Rim of the World National Scenic Byway." Take Highway 138 east off I-15. San Bernardino National Forest (714) 337-2444

Barton Flats and Seven Oaks
The campgrounds, nature trails, and visitor center at Barton Flats Recreation Area are found within a black oak and mixed conifer forest. A fine oak-viewing route near Barton Flats is a loop drive at Seven Oaks; extensive stands of canyon oak grow here and include some very large specimens at the river crossings. Black oak, white fir, and ponderosa pine intermingle on the Glass Rd. portion of the loop. There is a private campground at Seven Oaks. To reach Barton Flats, take Highway 38 off I-10. Seven Oaks is located off Highway 38, between Barton Flats and Angeles Oaks. Take Middle Control Rd. 1N07 or Glass Rd. 1N86 for the loop drive. San Bernardino National Forest (714) 794-1123

Riverside and San Diego Counties

Lake Fulmore Picnic Area
Black, canyon, and interior live oak are growing in and around this day-use picnic area. The oaks exist within mixed conifer stands of white fir, sugar pine,

Coulter pine, ponderosa pine, and Jeffrey pine. The nearest campground is at Black Mountain. Take Highway 243 off I-10 at Banning, towards Idyllwild. San Bernardino National Forest (714) 659-2117

Santa Rosa Plateau Ecological Reserve
The best destination for viewing Engelmann oak savanna is the 6,925-acre Santa Rosa Plateau Ecological Reserve. Coast live oak and sycamore also flourish in this ecologically diverse area of streambeds, native prairie, and chaparral-covered hillsides. The Oak Tree Trail is a self-guiding trail that introduces the visitor to Engelmann oak and other features of the reserve. Use the Trans-Preserve Trail to see the largest specimens of Engelmann oak; this route follows Sycamore Creek upstream through riparian oak woodlands, turns south through chaparral, and eventually reaches Mesa de Colorado where the largest Engelmann oaks are found. Hours are dawn to dusk; no dogs allowed.

The reserve is off I-15 between Lake Elsinore and Murrieta. Exit I-15 on Clinton Keith Rd., continue about four miles southwest to the preserve entrance and visitor center, located on the left side of the road. (For more information, see the text in Chapter Five: "Conserving Engelmann Oaks on the Santa Rosa Plateau.") The reserve is managed by the following agencies: The Nature Conservancy, Riverside County Parks and Open Space District, California Department of Fish and Game, U.S. Fish and Wildlife Service, and the Metropolitan Water District. (714) 677-6951

Wilderness Gardens Preserve
Wilderness Gardens' 584 acres along the San Luis Rey River preserve a fine example of coast live oak riparian forest. Opened in 1983 as a walk-in facility, this education-oriented park offers bird walks, historical tours, and seminars. The preserve is 45 miles north of San Diego on I-15, then 10 miles east on Highway 76. San Diego County Department of Parks & Recreation (619) 267-7323

Palomar Mountain State Park
Five species of oak, often intermixed with a variety of conifers, are found in Palomar Mountain State Park. An excellent location for viewing large specimens of canyon oak is the Doane Valley Campground and adjacent Lower Doane Meadow area; fine examples of canyon oak also grow along the Oak Grove Trail. A huge boulder containing

over 200 mortar holes once used by Luiseño Indians for pounding acorns is located near Silver Crest Picnic Area. Take Highway 76 east from Pauma Valley and turn left on Route S6 (the "Highway to the Stars" built for Palomar Observatory). Follow S6 to a junction near the top of the mountain, where you turn left on State Park Rd. California Department of Parks & Recreation (619) 765-0755 or (619) 742-3462

Love Valley Trail

The Love Valley Trail in Cleveland National Forest passes through stands of Engelmann and coast live oak in a lovely meadow setting. As the trail descends to Love Valley there are excellent views of Lake Henshaw. The oak-dominated meadow is a day-use picnic destination; there are no camping facilities. From Santa Ysabel, head north on Highway 79. At Morettis Junction, take Highway 76 along the shores of Lake Henshaw. Pass the Henshaw Forest Service Guard Station, and turn on County Highway S-7 towards the Palomar Observatory. Climb the grade for 2.5 miles, and look for the "Love Valley Trailhead" sign on the left. Cleveland National Forest (619) 557-5050

Mesa Grande

This scenic drive passes through the natural communities of several species of oak and is probably the best motor route in California for viewing native Engelmann oak habitat. Take Highway 76 east from I-15 at Escondido and head to San Luis Rey Picnic Grounds in the Cleveland National Forest, where lovely specimens of coast live oak flourish. Continue southeast on Highway 76; two miles south of the Lake Henshaw Work Center, turn right on Scholder Creek Rd. Continue on this road for about three miles, passing through the Santa Ysabel Indian Reservation, then turn left on Mesa Grande Rd. Along Mesa Grande Rd., Engelmann oaks mix with coast live oaks.

Continue on Mesa Grande Rd., then turn right on Highway 79 towards Santa Ysabel. About one mile south of Santa Ysabel on Highway 79 is Inaja Memorial Park, which honors 11 firefighters killed in a 1953 wildfire. The park has an excellent interpretive nature trail that passes through groves of coast live oak. To complete this scenic tour, continue south on Highway 79 to the town of Julian where fine specimens of black oak occur. Cleveland National Forest (619) 557-5050

William Heise Park

The 2.5-mile Canyon Oak Trail at William Heise County Park displays canyon oak in its natural steep, rocky habitat. Heise Park highlights the beauty of canyon oak as it blends with black oak, Coulter pine, and incense cedar in this southern mixed evergreen forest. The 311-acre park offers several other loop trails and contains picnic and overnight facilities. From Highways 78/79 (merged here) west of Julian, take Pine Hills Road south to Frisius Drive. San Diego County Department of Parks & Recreation (619) 565-3600

Cuyamaca Rancho State Park

Cuyamaca Rancho State Park contains a diversity of oak and conifer species unequaled in Southern California. The park's 110 miles of hiking and riding trails provide opportunities to see up to seven types of oak. A mixed woodland of black oak, coast live oak, and conifers surrounds the park headquarters and Indian Museum. Very large specimens of canyon oak shade the Paso Picacho Group Camp. Bedrock mortars which were used for acorn preparation by the Kumeyaay Indians are found throughout the park. (It is illegal to remove any native American artifacts that you find.) Park Headquarters is 12 miles north of I-8 on Highway 79, which exits the freeway 30 miles east of San Diego. California Department of Parks & Recreation (619) 765-0755

Los Peñasquitos Canyon Preserve

This riparian corridor through Peñasquitos Canyon supports one of the finest oak woodlands in metropolitan San Diego. The best oak viewing is found in the eastern portion of this 3,000-acre preserve. Large coast live oaks and sycamores shade riding and hiking trails on the canyon floor; scrub oak chaparral forms dense thickets on adjacent north-facing slopes. A popular six-mile roundtrip hike from the east entrance to small waterfalls near the middle of the preserve winds through lovely oak groves and meadows. Native plants that flourish in the canyon are introduced along a short nature trail loop at the east end staging area. This is a day-use only park, open from 8 a.m. to sunset; dogs must be leashed. Exit I-15 at Mercy and proceed west to the junction with Black Mountain Rd., and continue straight through the intersection to reach the east entrance staging area. San Diego City and County (619) 533-4067 or 484-7504

Appendix A

California Topography

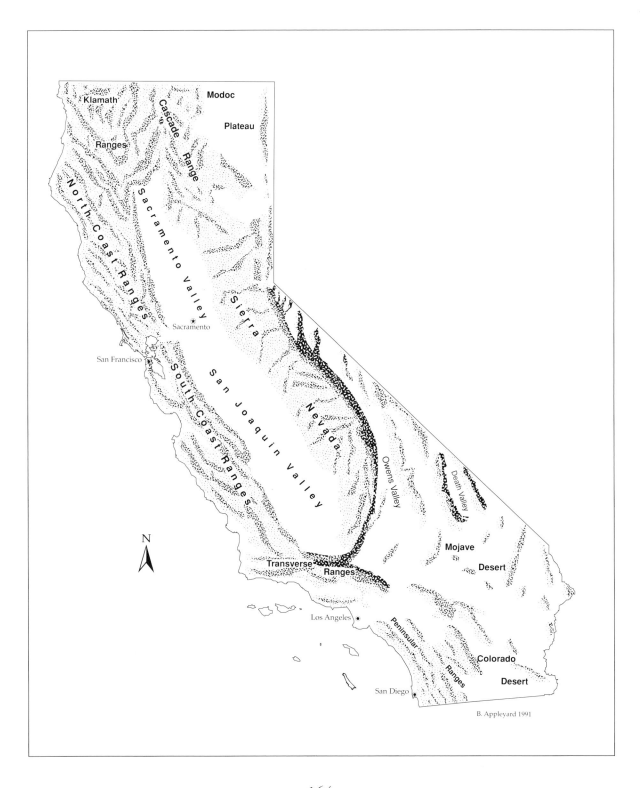

Klamath
Modoc
Cascade Range
Plateau
Ranges
North Coast Ranges
Sacramento Valley
Sierra
Sacramento
San Francisco
South Coast Ranges
San Joaquin Valley
Nevada
Owens Valley
Death Valley
Mojave
N
Transverse Ranges
Desert
Los Angeles
Peninsular
Colorado
Ranges
Desert
San Diego

B. Appleyard 1991

Appendix B

Tribal Areas of California

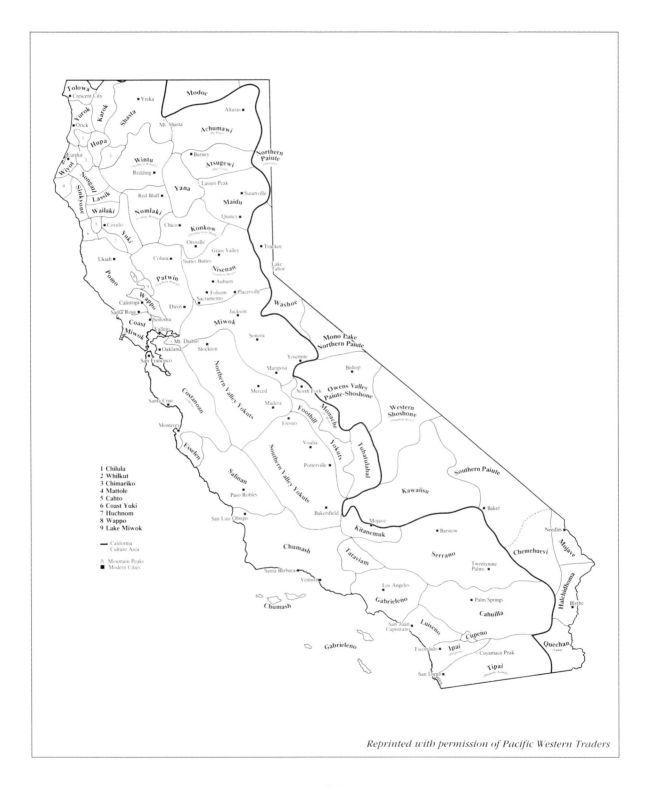

1 Chilula
2 Whilkut
3 Chimariko
4 Mattole
5 Cahto
6 Coast Yuki
7 Huchnom
8 Wappo
9 Lake Miwok

— California Culture Area
∧ Mountain Peaks
■ Modern Cities

Reprinted with permission of Pacific Western Traders

Appendix C

Index to Common and Scientific Plant Names

CALIFORNIA OAKS

Tree Oaks

black oak *(Quercus kelloggii)*
blue oak *(Quercus douglasii)*
canyon oak *(Quercus chrysolepis)*
coast live oak *(Quercus agrifolia)*
Engelmann oak *(Quercus engelmannii)*
interior live oak *(Quercus wislizenii)*
island oak *(Quercus tomentella)*
Oregon oak *(Quercus garryana)*
valley oak *(Quercus lobata)*

Shrub Oaks

Brewer oak *(Quercus garryana* var. *breweri)*
coastal scrub oak *(Quercus dumosa)*
deer oak *(Quercus sadleriana)*
desert scrub oak *(Quercus turbinella)*
huckleberry oak *(Quercus vaccinifolia)*

Shrub Oaks, cont.

island scrub oak *(Quercus parvula)*
shrub interior live oak *(Quercus wislizenii* var. *frutescens)*
leather oak *(Quercus durata)*
Muller oak *(Quercus cornelius-mulleri)*
Palmer oak *(Quercus palmeri)*
scrub oak *(Quercus berberidifolia)*
shin oak *(Quercus garryana* var. *semota).*

Hybrid Oaks

Alvord oak *(Quercus* X *alvordiana)*
Chase oak *(Quercus* X *chasei)*
Epling oak *(Quercus* X *eplingii)*
MacDonald oak *(Quercus* X *macdonaldii)*
oracle oak *(Quercus* X *morehus)*

OTHER PLANTS

Alaska yellow cedar *(Chamaecyparis nootkatensis)*
alder *(Alnus* sp.*)*
almond *(Prunus* sp.*)*
Arizona white oak *(Quercus arizonica)*

barley *(Hordeum* sp.*)*
bay laurel *(Umbellularia californica)*
bean *(Phaseolus vulgaris)*
beech *(Fagus* sp.*)*
bigcone spruce *(Pseudotsuga macrocarpa)*
bigleaf maple *(Acer macrophyllum)*
black cottonwood *(Populus trichocarpa)*
black locust *(Robinia pseudoacacia)*
black walnut *(Juglans hindsii)*
blue clover *(Medicago* sp.*)*
box elder *(Acer negundo* ssp. *californicum)*
bromegrass *(Bromus* sp.*)*
buckbrush *(Ceanothus* sp.*)*
buckeye *(Aesculus californica)*
buckwheat *(Eriogonum fasiculatum)*
bush monkeyflower *(Mimulus longiflorus)*

California blackberry *(Rubus* sp.*)*
California brome *(Bromus carinatus)*
California juniper *(Juniperus californica)*
California poppy *(Eschscholzia californica)*
California redbud *(Cercis occidentalis)*
California walnut *(Juglans californica)*
Catalina cherry *(Prunus lyonii)*
Catalina ironwood *(Lyonothamnus floribundus)*
ceanothus *(Ceanothus* sp.*)*
cedar *(Thuja plicata)*
chamise *(Adenostoma fasciculatum)*
chestnut *(Castanea* sp.*)*
chinquapin *(Chrysolepis chrysolepis)*
Chinese houses *(Collinsia heterophylla)*

coastal wood fern *(Dryopteris arguta)*
coffeeberry *(Rhamnus californica)*
Congdon's silktassel *(Garrya congdoni)*
corn *(Zea mays)*
cottonwood *(Populus fremontii)*
Coulter pine *(Pinus coulteri)*
coyotebush *(Baccharis pilularis* ssp. *consanguinea)*

dogwood *(Cornus* sp.*)*
Douglas fir *(Pseudotsuga menziesii)*
dwarf chinquapin *(Castanopsis sempervirens)*

fan palm *(Washingtonia filifera)*
filaree *(Erodium* sp.*)*
fir *(Abies* sp.*)*
foothill ash *(Fraxinus dipetala)*

giant sequoia *(Sequoiadendron giganteum)*
gooseberry *(Ribes* sp.*)*
gooseberry *(Ribes speciosum)*
grand fir *(Abies grandis)*
grasses *(species in the family Poaceae)*
gray pine *(Pinus sabiniana)*
greenleaf manzanita *(Arctostaphylos patula)*

hazelnut *(Corylus cornuta* var. *californica)*

incense cedar *(Calocedrus decurrens)*
ironwood *(Olneya tesota)*
island bush poppy *(Dendromecon harfordii)*
island ceanothus *(Ceanothus insularis)*
island manzanita *(Arctostaphylos insularis)*

Jeffrey pine *(Pinus jeffreyi)*
Jepson's ceanothus *(Ceanothus jepsonii)*
juniper *(Juniperus* sp.*)*

OTHER PLANTS, cont.

knobcone pine *(Pinus attenuata)*

laurel sumac *(Rhus laurina)*
lemonade berry *(Rhus integrifolia)*

madrone *(Arbutus menziesii)*
manzanita *(Arctostaphylos* sp.*)*
mesquite *(Prosopis juliflora* var. *torreyana)*
Mexican blue oak *(Quercus oblongifolia)*
mountain mahogany *(Cercocarpus betuloides)*
mountain whitethorn *(Ceanothus cordulatus)*

nettles *(Urtica* sp.*)*

oats *(Avena* sp.*)*
olive *(Olea* sp.*)*
opuntia *(Opuntia* sp.*)*
Oregon ash *(Fraxinus latifolia)*

pear *(Pyrus communis)*
pine *(Pinus* sp.*)*
pinemat manzanita *(Arctosaphylos nevadensis)*
pink globe lilly *(Calochortus amoenus)*
poison oak *(Toxicodendron diversilobum)*
ponderosa pine *(Pinus ponderosa)*
Port Orford cedar *(Chamaecyparis lawsoniana)*
purple needlegrass *(Stipa pulchra)*
purple nightshade *(Solanum xantil)*

red fir *(Abies magnifica)*
redberry *(Rhamnus crocea)*
redshank *(Adenostoma sparsifolium)*
redwood *(Sequoia sempervirens)*

sagebrush *(Artemesia californica)*
sandbar willow *(Salix hindsiana)*
Santa Cruz Island ironwood *(Lyonothamnus floribundus* var. *asplenifolius)*
Santa Cruz Island pine *(Pinus remorata)*
Santa Lucia fir *(Abies bracteata)*
sargent cypress *(Cupressus sargentii)*
sedge *(Carex* sp.*)*
silktassel *(Garrya* sp.*)*
snowberry *(Symphoricarpos rivularis)*
squawbush *(Rhus trilobata)*
succulent lupine *(Lupinus succulentus)*
sugar pine *(Pinus lambertiana)*
sycamore *(Plantanus racemosa)*

tanbark *(Lithocarpus densiflorus)*
toyon *(Heteromeles arbutifolia)*

western azalea *(Rhododendron occidentale)*
western juniper *(Juniperus occidentalis)*
western white pine *(Pinus monticola)*
white fir *(Abies concolor)*
white sage *(Salvia apiana)*
whiteleaf manzanita *(Arctostaphylos viscida)*
wild grape *(Vitis californica)*
wild rose *(Rosa californica)*
wild rye *(Elymus glaucus)*
willow *(Salix* sp.*)*
wormwood *(Artemisia douglasiana)*

yucca *(Yucca whipplei*)

Appendix D

Insect Species Associated With California Oaks

Leaf Consumers
California oak moth *(Phryganidia californica)*
fruit tree leafroller *(Archips argyrospilus)*
tent caterpillars *(Malacosoma* sp.*)*
western tussock moth *(Orgyia gulosa)*

Borers
California prionus *(Prionus californicus)*
carpenterworm *(Prionoxystus robiniae)*
dry-wood termites *(Kalotermes* sp.*)*
nautical borer *(Xylotrechus nauticus)*
oak bark beetles *(Pseudopityophthorus* sp.*)*
pacific flatheaded borer *(Chyrsobothris mali)*
roundheaded oak twig borer *(Styloxus fulleri)*
western sycamore borer *(Synanthedon resplendens)*

Girdlers
oak twig girdler *(Agrilus angelicus)*
other buprestid beetles *(species in the family Buprestidae)*

Sucking Insects
aphids *(species in the family Aphididae)*
crown whitefly *(Aleuroplatus coronatus)*
leafhoppers *(species in the family Cicadellidae)*
oak pit scales *(Asterolecanium* sp.*)*
treehoppers *(species in the family Membracidae)*
whiteflies *(species in the family Aleyrodidae)*

Acorn Consumers
filbert weevils *(Curculio* sp.*)*
filbertworm *(Melissopus latiferreanus)*

Others
California oak gall wasp *Andricus californicus)*
gall wasps *(species in the family Cynipidae)*
oak gall chalcid *(Torymus californicus)*
proturans *(species in the order Protura)*
springtails *(species in the order Collembola)*
springtail-stalking ant *(Smithistruma reliquia)*

Appendix E

Vertebrate Species Associated With California Oaks

Amphibians

arboreal salamander *(Aneides lugubris)*
black-bellied slender salamander *(Batrachoseps nigriventris)*
California newt *(Taricha torosa)*
California slender salamander *(Batrachoseps attenuatus)*
California tiger salamander *(Ambystoma californiense)*
ensatina *(Ensatina eschscholtzi)*
foothill yellow-legged frog *(Rana boylei)*
Pacific treefrog *(Hyla regilla)*
relictual slender salamander *(Batrachoseps pacificus)*
rough-skinned newt *(Taricha granulosa)*
Tehachapi slender salamander *(Batrachoseps stebbinsi)*
western spadefoot toad *(Scaphiopus hammondi)*
western toad *(Bufo boreas)*

Reptiles

blue racer *(Coluber constrictor mormon)*
California kingsnake *(Lampropeltis getulus californiae)*
California legless lizard *(Anniella pulchra)*
Gilbert's skink *(Eumeces gilberti)*
gopher snake *(Pituophis melanoleucus)*
northern alligator lizard *(Elegaria coeruleus)*
ringneck snake *(Diadophis punctatus)*
sharp-tailed snake *(Contia tenuis)*
southern alligator lizard *(Elegaria multicarinata)*
striped racer *(Masticophis lateralis)*
western fence lizard *(Sceloporus occidentalis)*
western rattlesnake *(Crotalus viridis)*
western skink *(Eumeces skiltonianus)*
western whiptail *(Cnemidophorus tigris)*

Birds

acorn woodpecker *(Melanerpes formicivorus)*
American goldfinch *(Carduelis tristis)*
American kestrel *(Falco sparverius)*
Anna's hummingbird *(Calypte anna)*
ash-throated flycatcher *(Myiarchus cinerascens)*
band-tailed pigeon *(Columba fasciata)*
barn owl *(Tyto alba)*
Bewick's wren *(Thyromanes bewickii)*
black-chinned hummingbird *(Archilochus alexandri)*
black-headed grosbeak *(Pheucticus melanocephalus)*
black-shouldered kete *(Elanus caeruleus)*
black-throated gray warbler *(Dendroica nigrescens)*
blue-gray gnatcatcher *(Polioptila caerulea)*
bushtit *(Psaltriparus minimus)*
California condor *(Gymnogyps californianus)*
California quail *(Callipepla californica)*
California thrasher *(Toxostoma redivivum)*
California towhee *(Pipilo crissalis)*
chipping sparrow *(Spizella passerina)*

Birds, cont.

Cooper's hawk *(Accipiter cooperii)*
European starling *(Sturnus vulgaris)*
golden eagle *(Aquila chrysaetos)*
great horned owl *(Bubo virginianus)*
greater road runner *(Geococcyx californianus)*
house finch *(Carpodacus mexicanus)*
house wren *(Troglodytes aedon)*
Hutton's vireo *(Vireo huttoni)*
lark sparrow *(Chondestes grammacus)*
Lawrence's goldfinch *(Carduelis lawrencei)*
lesser goldfinch *(Carduelis psaltria)*
Lewis' woodpecker *(Melanerpes lewis)*
merlin *(Falco columbarius)*
mourning dove *(Zenaida macroura)*
Nashville warbler *(Vermivora ruficapilla)*
northern flicker *(Colaptes auratus)*
northern oriole *(Icterus galbula)*
northern pygmy-owl *(Glaucidium gnoma)*
Nuttall's woodpecker *(Picoides nuttallii)*
orange-crowned warbler *(Vermivora celata)*
Pacific-slope flycatcher *(Empidonax difficilis)*
phainopepla *(Phainopepla nitens)*
plain titmouse *(Parus inornatus)*
red-shouldered hawk *(Buteo lineatus)*
red-tailed hawk *(Buteo jamaicensis)*
Say's phoebe *(Sayornis saya)*
scrub jay *(Aphelocoma coerulescens)*
Steller's jay *(Cyanocitta stelleri)*
Swainson's hawk *(Buteo swasoni)*
turkey vulture *(Cathartes aura)*
violet-green swallow *(Tachycineta thalassina)*
western bluebird *(Sialia mexicana)*
western kingbird *(Tyrannus verticalis)*
western screech-owl *(Otus kennicottii)*
western wood-pewee *(Contopus sordidulus)*
white-breasted nuthatch *(Sitta carolinensis)*
wild turkey *(Meleagris gallopavo)*
wood duck *(Aix sponsa)*
wrentit *(Chamaea fasciata)*
yellow warbler *(Dendroica petechia)*
yellow-billed magpie *(Pica nuttalli)*

Mammals

Audubon's cottontail *(Sylvilagus audubonii)*
badger *(Taxidea taxus)*
big brown bat *(Eptesicus fuscus)*
black bear *(Ursus americanus)*
black-tailed jackrabbit *(Lepus californicus)*
bobcat *(Lynx rufus)*
Botta's pocket gopher *(Thomomys bottae)*
broad-footed mole *(Scapanus latimanus)*
brush mouse *(Peromyscus boylii)*
brush rabbit *(Sylvilagus bachmani)*
California ground squirrel *(Spermophilus beecheyi)*
California kangaroo rat *(Dipodomys californicus)*
California mouse *(Peromyscus californicus)*

Mammals, cont.
California myotis *(Myotis californicus)*
California pocket mouse *(Perognathus californicus)*
California vole *(Microtus californicus)*
coyote *(Canis latrans)*
deer mouse *(Peromyscus maniculatus)*
dusky-footed woodrat *(Neotoma fuscipes)*
feral pig *(Sus scrofa)*
gray fox *(Urocyon cinereoargenteus)*
Heermann's kangaroo rat *(Dipodomys heermanni)*
hoary bat *(Lasiurus cinereus)*
mountain lion *(Felis concolor)*
mule deer *(Odocoileus hemionus)*
ornate shrew *(Sorex ornatus)*

Mammals, cont.
pallid bat *(Antrozous pallidus)*
pinyon mouse *(Peromyscus truei)*
raccoon *(Procyon lotor)*
red bat *(Lasiurus borealis)*
ring tail *(Bassariscus astutus)*
silver-haired bat *(Lasionycteris noctivagans)*
striped skunk *(Mephitis mephitis)*
tule elk *(Cervus elaphus nannodes)*
Virginia opposum *(Didelphis virginiana)*
western gray squirrel *(Sciurus griseus)*
western harvest mouse *(Reithrodontomys megalotis)*
western pipistrelle *(Pipistrellus hesperus)*
western spotted skunk *(Spilogale putorius)*

Appendix F

Endangered Species Associated With California Oaks

Oak forests, woodlands, savannas, and chaparrals harbor many species that are at risk of going extinct in the near future. Although there are as many causes for extinction as there are endangered species, by far the common cause is habitat modification by humans. Protection under federal and California state endangered species acts requires that species facing extinction (officially called endangered species) and species that may become endangered in the near future (officially called threatened species) enter a formal review process. If the review establishes the need for protection, the species may be listed as endangered (E) or threatened (T) under federal (F) or state (S) law. California state law has an additional category known as rare (R) for plants that could become threatened or endangered if conditions worsen.

Presented below are the animals and plants associated with oaks in California that, as of January 1991, are listed under the federal and/or state endangered species acts. These are species that would benefit from protection of oaks and oak habitats within their ranges of distribution. Many more species could be added to this list if time, money, and politics did not slow or interfere with the listing process.

Plants
Camatta canyon amole *(Chlorogalum purpureum* var. *reductum)* SR
Clara Hunt's milk vetch *(Astragalus clarianus)* ST
Congdon's lewisia *(Lewisia congdonii)* SR
Congdon's woolly sunflower *(Eriophyllum congdonii)* SR
El Dorado bedstraw *(Galium californicum* ssp. *sierrae)* SR
Laguna Mountains aster *(Machaeranthera lagunensis)* SR
large-flowered fiddleneck *(Amsinckia grandiflora)* SE, FE
Layne's butterweed *(Senecio layneae)* SR
Mariposa lupine *(Lupinus deflexus)* ST
Merced clarkia *(Clarkia lingulata)* SE
Mexican flannelbush *(Fremontodendron mexicanum)* SR
Milo Baker's lupine *(Lupinus milo-bakeri)* ST
Parish's checkerbloom *(Sidalcea hickmanii* ssp. *parishii)* SR
Pine Hill ceanothus *(Ceanothus roderickii)* SR
Pine Hill flannelbush *(Fremontodenron decumbens)* SR
Roderick's fritillary *(Fritillaria roderickii)* SE
Santa Catalina Island mountain mahogany *(Cercocarpus traskiae)* SE
Santa Lucia mint *(Pogogyne clareana)* SE
Springville clarkia *(Clarkia springvillensis)* SE
striped adobe lily *(Fritillaria striata)* ST
tree anemone *(Carpenteria californica)* ST

Amphibians and Reptiles
Alameda whipsnake *(Masticophis lateralis euryxanthus)* ST
Santa Cruz long-toed salamander *(Ambystoma macrodactylum croceum)* FE, SE
Tehachapi slender salamander *(Batrachoseps stebbinsi)* ST

Birds
bald eagle *(Haliaeetus leucocephalus)* SE, FE
California condor *(Gymnogyps californianus)* SE, FE
least Bell's vireo *(Vireo bellii pusillus)* SE, FE
northern spotted owl *(Strix occidentalis caurina)* FT
Swainson's hawk *(Buteo swainsoni)* ST
western yellow-billed cuckoo *(Coccyzus americanus occidentalis)* SE

Mammals
island fox *(Urocyon littoralis)* ST

Insects
valley elderberry longhorn beetle *(Desmocerus californicus dimorphus)* FT

Glossary

Acorn cup. The scaly or knobby cap that attaches an acorn to a branch.

Acorn hull. The outer shell or fruit wall of an acorn; husk.

Acorn. The nut-like fruit of an oak that contains a single, large seed.

Alluvial soil. A soil formed from sand, gravel, silt, or other material that has been deposited by running water, usually a river.

Arboreal oak. An oak that grows in the form of a tree rather than a shrub.

Architecture. The structure of vegetation; the number and height of canopy layers, the vertical distribution of leaf and branch material, the spatial distribution of trunks or stems.

Autecology. The study of a single species and its relationships to the environment.

Bifacial leaves. Leaves whose upper and lower surfaces are distinctly different, usually with reference to color, hairiness, or venation patterns.

Broadleaf trees. Trees with wide, flat leaves as opposed to needle-like or scaly leaves.

Browse. Portion of trees and shrubs, such as leaves, twigs, and young shoots, that animals feed on (noun). To consume leaves, twigs, young shoots of trees and shrubs (verb).

Buds. Growing points, protected by thin, woody scales, that usually lie dormant on stems until stimulated to produce leafy branches or flowers.

Cambium. A continuous sheath of dividing cells between the bark and wood of stems and roots. Growth of the cambium increases the diameter of stems and roots and contributes to the formation of bark.

Catkins. Dense clusters of male (pollen-producing) flowers along a small, linear stem.

Cellulose. The primary building material of a plant's body. Herbaceous and woody tissues are largely composed of cellulose that has come from photosynthesis.

Chaparral. A dense, shrub-dominated vegetation of fire-adapted, drought-tolerant plants.

Close-grained wood. Wood composed of dense annual growth rings with fine variations in color, hardness, and texture.

Conifers. Cone-bearing, non-flowering trees and shrubs that have needle- or scale-like leaves. Pines, firs, and redwoods are examples.

Cotyledons. The plant embryo's first leaves, present in the seed and on the young seedling. They store or make the seedling's first food.

Cross-pollination. The transfer of pollen from the stamens of one plant to the stigma (female receptor) of another plant of the same species.

Detritus. Fresh or decomposing materials of plant or animal origin.

Disjunct population. A population that is geographically separated from other populations of the same species.

Drought-deciduous. A perennial plant that loses its leaves during periods of drought and becomes dormant.

Ecosystem. Organisms or communities in relation to their physical environment, characterized by the exchange of energy and materials.

Embryo. The dormant, undeveloped plant within a seed.

Endemic. Native to a particular geographic area or set of ecological conditions.

Epidermis. The outer covering of cells on leaves and herbaceous stems and roots.

Estivate. To enter a state of dormancy during summer.

Evergreen. A perennial plant that retains a canopy of leaves throughout the year. Evergreen leaves are usually thick, leathery, and drought tolerant.

Floodplain. The relatively flat area beside a river or stream that is inundated with water and sediment during a flood; characterized by rich, fertile soil.

Flora. A list of the plants native to a particular area.

Foliage. Leaves.

Food chain. The array of organisms that produce food energy through photosynthesis (plants), consume food energy by ingestion (animals), or scavenge food energy from dead plant and animal bodies (fungi and bacteria) in a community.

Food web. Interconnecting relationships among food chains.

Forest. A tree-dominated vegetation in which the overstory canopies overlap to form continuous cover over the land.

Gall. A swelling of leaf or stem tissue caused by the egg-laying activities of certain kinds of parasitic wasps. The swelling provides shelter and food for the larvae that hatch from the eggs with no benefit to the plant.

Genus. A level in the taxonomic hierarchy indicating a group of related species. *Quercus* is the genus of oaks and contains the related species *agrifolia, lobata*, etc.

Grassland. A vegetation dominated by grasses and other herbaceous plants in which woody trees and shrubs are absent or uncommon.

Hardwood forest. A vegetation dominated by broadleaved, flowering trees such as oak, maple, and bay. The species may be evergreen or deciduous.

Haustoria. Modified roots of parasitic plants or modified hyphae of parasitic fungi that invade the living tissues of their host organisms.

Heartwood. Wood in the center of a trunk that is usually darker in color than the outer sapwood. Heartwood no longer conducts water and minerals to the canopy.

Herbaceous. The soft, green, non-woody tissues of a plant. Herbaceous plants are those composed entirely of soft stems, roots and leaves.

Herbivory. The phenomenon of plant-eating, as opposed to meat-eating.

Herpetofauna. The reptiles of a given area; also known as herps.

Insectivorous. Insect-eating animals and plants.

Lateral vein. A vein that branches off of the main, central vein of a leaf.

Leaf canopy. The three-dimensional distribution of leaves among branches of a shoot, or within a layer of vegetation.

Leaf margin. The edge of a leaf.

Lignin. A hardening chemical that gives strength to wood and other supportive tissues of a plant.

Lineage. Ancestry, usually with reference to long, evolutionary time scales.

Lobed leaves. Leaf margins that are incised to form sinuses that separate rounded or pointed subdivisions of the blade.

Mast. A large crop of acorns or other nuts.

Midrib. The central vein of a leaf.

Mistletoe. A green, leafy flowering plant (often of the genus *Phoradendron*) that is parasitic on the stems of oaks and other kinds of trees.

Mixed coniferous forest. A vegetation where several species of conifers share dominance of the overstory. It is the principle mid-elevation forest of the Sierra Nevada.

Mixed Evergreen Forest. A vegetation where several species of non-deciduous, broadleaf trees are dominant. Best developed in the Coast Ranges.

Montane. Associated with high elevations and abrupt topographic relief.

Needleleaf tree. A tree, usually coniferous, with long, whisker-like leaves.

Non-native grasses. Grasses, usually annuals, first brought to California by European explorers and settlers.

Oak regeneration. The replacement of old oaks by new, young oaks in a population through sexual reproduction (acorn production, germination, and seedling establishment).

Overstory. The uppermost layer of foliage and branches in a piece of vegetation; the highest canopy.

Parasites. Animals or plants that obtain food, water, minerals, and/or shelter at the expense of another living organism (the host).

Phloem. The food-conducting tissues of plants, which extend from the leaves to stems, roots, flowers, and fruit.

Photosynthesis. The process by which plants make food from water, sunlight, and carbon dioxide.

Plant community. The physical structure and biological interactions of all plant species in a particular area; synonymous with vegetation. Grassland, woodland and forest are general types of plant communities that have different kinds of architecture and life forms.

Pollen. The dormant male gametes of flowering and coniferous plants. Each grain is enclosed in a hard coat and can form two sperm with which to fertilize an egg.

Predator. An organism that captures and feeds on other live organisms.

Relict species. A species that was once widespread but is now restricted to a smaller geographic or ecological area.

Riparian forest. A tree-dominated vegetation found along rivers and streams.

Riparian. Associated with the margins of running water (e.g. river and stream banks).

Root crown. The woody, often enlarged junction between stem and root that often contains many buds.

Root hairs. Single-cell extensions of the root epidermis that protrude into soil and greatly enhance the absorption of water and minerals.

Sapling. Young, established trees not yet four inches in diameter.

Sapwood. The lighter-colored, outer wood of a trunk which conducts water and minerals to the canopy.

Savanna. A grassland with scattered trees as a sparse overstory. The tree canopies do not cover more than 30% of the ground surface.

Scientific Name. A standardized Latin binomial consisting of the genus name (e.g. *Quercus*) and species name (e.g. *garryana*).

Seedlings. Young, yet-to-be established plants that may still depend on the food reserves stored in the seed or cotyledons.

Serpentine. An unusual green mineral that contains large amounts of magnesium, chromium and nickel. The soils derived from serpentine are reddish and infertile.

Shoots. The above-ground portions of a plant. Often used to refer to new, vigorously growing stems.

Shrub. A woody plant that is smaller than a tree and usually branches at or near ground level.

Shrublands. An area where shrubs are the dominant plant growth form.

Smooth margin. The edge of a leaf that is not toothed, lobed, or otherwise incised; also referred to as an entire margin.

Snags. Trees that are dead but standing.

Species. The basic biological unit which includes all morphologically and ecologically similar populations.

Stamens. The pollen-producing structures found in flowers.

Stomata. Regulated openings on the surface of leaves that determine the inward flux of carbon dioxide for photosynthesis and the outward flux of water as transpiration.

Stump-sprouting. The ability to produce new shoots from buds on woody stems near the base of the plant. New shoots develop from buds off of the ground, on the stump of the former trunk.

Subgenus. A level in the taxonomic hierarchy below genus, which indicates a relationship between some but not all species in the genus. The subgenus *Erythrobalanus* within the genus *Quercus* includes the species *agrifoila*, *kelloggi* and *wislizenii*, but not the species *lobata*, *chrysolepis*, etc.

Subtropical oaks. Oak species that are found in subtropical regions, particularly in the highlands of Mexico.

Summer drought. An absence of rainfall usually associated with a Mediterranean climate during the period from May to October.

Synecology. The study of multiple species assemblages and their relationships to the environment and to each other. Used with reference to the study of biological communities.

Tannic acids. Tannins.

Tannins. Astringent, bitter tasting chemicals that protect a plant against decaying or being injured by animals or insects.

Tap root. The main, undivided vertical root of a plant that produces smaller lateral roots.

Timber tree. A tree that can be used for lumber.

Toothed leaves. Leaves whose margins are serrated, or saw-edged.

Toothed margin. The edge of a leaf that is regularly serrated with pointed teeth.

Understory plants. Plants that live in the shade of others, forming one of the lower canopy layers in a plant community.

Ungulate. A mammal with hooves.

Vegetation structure. Same as "Architecture."

Vegetation type. The kind of plant community in an area (mixed evergreen forest, chaparral, etc.).

Vegetation. The plant community of a particular geographic area, with all species and their architecture considered together. The living, green "cloth" over the land.

Waxy cuticle. A layer of wax secreted over the outer leaf surface that prevents water from escaping uncontrollably through the stomata.

Winter-deciduous. A plant which loses its leaves in winter and appears barren of foliage.

Woodland. An open, tree-dominated vegetation with more tree cover than a savanna but less than a forest. Tree canopies contribute more than 30% cover but seldom overlap.

Xylem. The water- and mineral-conducting tissue of plants, which extends from the roots, through the stems, and into the leaves, fruits, and flowers. It contains vessel cells that function like pipes in trees and shrubs. The xylem make up most of the wood.

Bibliography

Chapter One: The Diversity of California Oaks

Aizen, M. A. and W. A. Patterson III. 1990. "Acorn Size and Geographical Range in the North American Oaks (*Quercus L.*)." *Journal of Biogeography* 17: 327-332.

Axelrod, D. I. "Geologic History of the Californian Insular Flora." In: Philbrick, R. N., ed. 1967. *Proceedings of the Symposium on the Biology of the California Islands.* Santa Barbara: Santa Barbara Botanic Garden.

Barbour, M. G. and J. Major, eds. 1977. *Terrestrial Vegetation of California.*

Brewer, W. H. 1930. *Up and Down California in 1860-1864.* New Haven: Yale University Press.

California Native Plant Society, Oak Hardwood Committee. 1989. *Oak Action Kit: Resources for Preservation and Conservation of Oak Habitats.* Sacramento: California Native Plant Society.

Carrol, M. 1989. *Native Oak Species of Southern California.* Informational Bulletin #6. Santa Barbara: Santa Barbara Botanic Garden.

Faber, P. M., ed. 1990. "Year of the oak." *Fremontia* 18 (3). Sacramento: California Native Plant Society. (Numerous articles by some of the leading authorities on California oaks.)

Farquhar, F. P. 1965. *History of the Sierra Nevada.* Berkeley: University of California Press.

Griffin, J. R. 1977. "Oak woodland." In: Barbour, M. G. and J. Major, eds. *Terrestrial Vegetation of California.* J. Wiley and Sons. Reprint. Sacramento: California Native Plant Society.

Griffin, J. R. and P. C. Muick. 1990. "California Native Oaks: Past and Present." *Fremontia* 18 (3): 4-12.

Griffin, J. R. and W. B. Critchfield. 1972. *The Distribution of Forest Trees in California.* Berkeley: Pacific SW Forest and Range Experiment Station, Forest Service, U.S. Department of Agriculture.

Harlow, W. M. and E. S. Harrar. 1969. *Textbook of Dendrology.* New York: McGraw-Hill.

Holland, R. F. 1986. *Preliminary Descriptions of the Terrestrial Natural Communities of California.* Sacramento: State of California, Dept. of Fish and Game.

Jepson, W. L. 1910. "The Silva of California." In: *Memoirs of the University of California,* Volume 2. Berkeley: University of California Press.

Matsuda, K. and J. R. McBride. 1986. "Difference in Seedling Growth Morphology As a Factor in the Distribution of Three Oaks in Central California." *Madroño* 33: 207-216.

Minnich, R. A. 1987. "The Distribution of Forest Trees in Northern Baja California, Mexico." *Madroño* 34: 98-127.

Muir, J. 1894. *The Mountains of California.* Garden City: Doubleday Anchor Books.

Muir, J. 1912. *The Yosemite.* Garden City: Doubleday Anchor Books.

Muller, C. H. 1967. "Relictual Origins of Insular Endemics in *Quercus.*" In: Philbrick, R. N., ed. *Proceedings of the Symposium on the Biology of the California Islands.* Santa Barbara: Santa Barbara Botanic Garden.

Munz, P. A. and D. D. Keck. 1968. *A California Flora and Supplement.* Berkeley: University of California Press.

Nixon, K. 1989. "Phylogeny and Systematics of the Oaks." *New York's Food and Life Science Quarterly* 19 (2): 7-10.

Nixon, K. C. and K. P. Steele. "A New Species of *Quercus* (Fagaceae) From Southern California." *Madroño* 28: 210-219.

Orcutt, C. R. 1887. "The Oaks of Southern and Baja California." *W. Amer. Sci.* 3: 135-139.

Pavlik, B. M. 1976. *A Natural History of Southern California Oaks.* Los Angeles: West Los Angeles County Resource Conservation District.

Peattie, D. C. 1953. *A Natural History of Western Trees.* New York: Bonanza Books.

Plumb, T. R. and A. P. Gomez. 1983. *Five Southern California Oaks: Identification and Postfire Management.* Berkeley: Pacific SW Forest and Range Experiment Station, Forest Service, U.S. Department of Agriculture.

Plumb, T. R. and N. H. Pillsbury, tech. coords. 1987. *Proceedings of the Symposium on Multiple-Use Management of California's Hardwood Resources.* Gen. Tech. Rep. PSW-100. Berkeley: Pacific SW Forest and Range Experiment Station, Forest Service, U.S. Department of Agriculture. (Numerous papers by many authors were consulted.)

Plumb, T. R., tech. coord. 1980. *Proceedings of the Symposium on the Ecology, Management, and Utilization of California Oaks.* Gen. Tech. Rep. PSW-44. Berkeley: Pacific SW Forest and Range Experiment Station, Forest Service, U.S. Department of Agriculture. (Numerous papers by many authors were consulted.)

Roberts, N. C. 1989. *Baja California Plant Field Guide.* La Jolla: Natural History Publishing Company.

Scott, T. A. 1991. "The Distribution of Engelmann Oak (*Quercus engelmanii*) in California." In: Standiford, R., tech. coord. *Proceedings of the Symposium on Oak Woodlands and Hardwood Rangeland Management.* Gen. Tech Rep. PSW-126. Berkeley: Pacific SW Research Station, Forest Service, U.S. Department of Agriculture.

Snow, G. E. 1972. *Some Factors Controlling the Establishment and Distribution of* Quercus agrifolia *and* Quercus engelmannii *in Certain Southern California Woodlands.* Ph.D. dissertation. Oregon State University, Corvalis.

Sudworth, G. B. 1908. *Forest Trees of the Pacific Slope.* Washington, D.C.: U.S. Dept. of Agriculture, Forest Service, Government Printing Office.

Sugihara, N. G., L. J. Reed and J. M. Lenihan. 1987. "Vegetation of the Bald Hills Oak Woodlands, Redwood National Park, California." *Madroño* 34: 193-208.

Tucker, J. M. 1953. "The Relationship Between *Quercus dumosa* and *Quercus turbinella.*" *Madroño* 12: 49-60.

Tucker, J. M. 1980. "Taxonomy of California Oaks." In: Plumb, T. R., tech coord. *Proceedings of the Symposium on the Ecology, Management and Utilization of California Oaks.* Berkeley: Pacific SW Forest and Range Experiment Station, Forest Service, U.S. Department of Agriculture.

Tucker, J. M. 1990. "Hybridization in California Oaks." *Fremontia* 18 (3): 13-19.

Chapter Two: The Oak Landscapes of California

Allen-Diaz, B. H. and B. A. Holzman. 1991. "Blue Oak Communities in California." *Madroño* 38: 90-95.

Barbour, M. G. and J. Major, eds. 1977. *Terrestrial Vegetation of California*. J. Wiley and Sons. Reprint. Sacramento: California Native Plant Society.

Borchert, M. I., F. W. Davis, J. Michaelsen and L. D. Owyler. 1989. "Interactions of Factors Affecting Seedling Establishment of Blue Oak (*Quercus douglasii*) in California." *Ecology* 70: 389-404.

Bolsinger, C. L. 1988. *The Hardwoods of California's Timberlands, Woodlands and Savannas*. Portland: U.S. Department of Agriculture, Forest Service, Pacific NW Research Station.

California Native Plant Society, Oak Hardwood Committee. 1989. *Oak Action Kit: Resources for Preservation and Conservation of Oak Habitats*. Sacramento: California Native Plant Society.

Faber, P. M., ed. 1990. "Year of the Oak." *Fremontia* 18 (3). Sacramento: California Native Plant Society. (Numerous articles by some of the leading authorities on California oaks.)

Griffin, J. R. 1977. "Oak Woodland." In: Barbour, M. G. and J. Major, eds. *Terrestrial Vegetation of California*. J. Wiley and Sons. Reprint. Sacramento: California Native Plant Society.

Griffin, J. R. and W. B. Critchfield. 1972. *The Distribution of Forest Trees in California*. Berkeley: Pacific SW Forest and Range Experiment Station, Forest Service, U.S. Department of Agriculture.

Griffin, J. R., P. M. McDonald and P. C. Muick. 1987. *California Oaks: A Bibliography*. Berkeley: Pacific SW Forest and Range Experiment Station, Forest Service, U.S. Department of Agriculture.

Holland, R. F. 1986. *Preliminary Descriptions of the Terrestrial Natural Communities of California*. Sacramento: California Department of Fish and Game.

Mayer, K. E. and W. F. Laudenslayer Jr., eds. 1988. *A Guide to Wildlife Habitats of California*. Sacramento: California Department of Forestry and Fire Protection, State of California.

McBride, J. R. 1974. "Plant Succession in the Berkeley Hills, California." *Madroño* 22: 137-380.

McClaran, M. P. and J. W. Bartolome. 1989. "Effect of *Quercus douglasii* (Fagaceae) on Herbaceous Understory Along a Rainfall Gradient." *Madroño* 36: 141-153.

Plumb, T. R. and N. H. Pillsbury, tech. coords. 1987. *Proceedings of the Symposium on Multiple-Use Management of California's Hardwood Resources*. Gen. Tech. Rep. PSW-100. Berkeley: Pacific SW Forest and Range Experiment Station, Forest Service, U.S. Department of Agriculture. (Numerous papers by many authors were consulted.)

Plumb, T. R., tech. coord. 1980. *Proceedings of the Symposium on the Ecology, Management, and Utilization of California Oaks*. Gen. Tech. Rep. PSW-44. Berkeley: Pacific SW Forest and Range Experiment Station, Forest Service, U.S. Department of Agriculture. (Numerous papers by many authors were consulted.)

Snow, G. E. 1972. *Some Factors Controlling the Establishment and Distribution of* Quercus agrifolia *and* Quercus engelmannii *in Certain Southern California Woodlands*. Ph.D. dissertation. Oregon State University, Corvalis.

Sugihara, N. G., L. J. Reed, and J. M. Lenihan. 1987. "Vegetation of the Bald Hills Oak Woodlands, Redwood National Park, California." *Madroño* 34: 193-208.

Warner, R. E. and K. M. Hendrix. 1985. *Riparian Resources of the Central Valley and California Desert*. Sacramento: California Department of Fish and Game.

Chapter Three: Oaks and Wildlife

Ashcraft, G. 1981. "Deer Use Under Black Oaks With and Without Mistletoe." *California Fish and Game* 67 (7): 257-260.

Avery, M. L. and C. van Riper III. 1990. "Evaluation of Wildlife-Habitat Relationships Data Base for Predicting Bird Community Composition in Central California Chaparral and Blue Oak Woodlands." *California Fish and Game* 76 (2): 103-117.

Barrett, R. 1990. "Pigs and Oaks." *Fremontia* 18 (3): 82.

Beedy, E. C. and S. L. Granholm. 1985. *Discovering Sierra Birds*. Yosemite Natural History Association and Sequoia Natural History Association.

Behler, J. L. and F. W. King. 1979. *The Audubon Society Field Guide to North American Reptiles and Amphibians*. New York: Alfred A. Knopf.

Benyus, J. M. 1989. *The Field Guide to Wildlife Habitats of the Western United States*. New York: Simon & Schuster.

Berry, W. D. and E. Berry. 1959. *Mammals of the San Francisco Bay Region*. Berkeley: University of California Press.

Bishop, S. C. 1943. *Handbook of Salamanders*. Ithaca: Cornell University Press.

Block, W. M., M. L. Morrison, and J. Verner. 1990. "Wildlife and Oak-Woodland Interdependency." *Fremontia* 18 (3): 72-76.

Borchert, M. 1990. "From Acorn to Seedling: A Perilous Stage." *Fremontia*. 18 (3): 36-37.

Borchert, M. I., F. R. Davis, J. Michaelsen, and L. D. Oyler. 1989. "Intereactions of Factors Affecting Seedling Recruitment of Blue Oak (*Quercus douglasii*) in California." *Ecology* (70) 2: 389-404.

Borror, D. J. and R. E. White. 1970. *A Field Guide to the Insects of America North of Mexico*. Boston: Houghton Mifflin Company.

Borror, D. J., D. M. DeLong, and C. A. Triplehorn. 1976. *An Introduction to the Study of Insects*. 4th ed. New York: Holt, Rinehart and Winston.

Brown, L. R. and C. O. Eads. 1965. *A Technical Study of Insects Affecting the Oak Tree in Southern California*. Berkeley: California Agricultural Experiment Station, Bulletin 810.

Burt, W. H. and R. P. Grossenheider. 1976. *A Field Guide to the Mammals*. 3rd ed. Boston: Houghton Mifflin Company.

California Nature Conservancy. 1991. "Wonderland for Rare Ants." *California Nature Conservancy Newsletter*. Summer: 4-5.

Chapman, J. A. and G. A. Feldhamer, eds. 1982. *Wild Mammals of North America*. Baltimore: John Hopkins University Press.

Fremont, J. B. 1890. *Far West Sketches*. Boston: D. Lathrop Co.

Gaines, D. 1988. *Birds of Yosemite and the East Slope*. Lee Vining: Artemisia Press.

Griffin, J. R., P. M. McDonald, and P. C. Muick. 1987. *California Oaks: A Bibliography*. Berkeley: Pacific SW Forest and Range Experiment Station, Forest Service, U.S. Department of Agriculture.

Grinnell, J. 1936. "Up-hill Planters." *Condor* 38 (2): 80-82.

Hoffman, E. 1985. "Wild Hog in the Woods". *Pacific Discovery* July-Sept.: 22-30.

Ingles, L. G. 1965. *Mammals of the Pacific States*. Stanford: Stanford University Press.

Ingles, L. G. "Ecology and Life History of the California Gray Squirrel." *California Fish and Game* 33 (3): 139-158.

Jameson, E. W., Jr. and H. J. Peeters. 1988. *California Mammals*. Berkeley: University of California Press.

Kee, V. 1982. "Structure, Ecology, and Wildlife Use of Five Southern California Black Oak and Canyon Live Oak Communities." Masters thesis. California State Polytechnic University, Pomona.

Kelly, P. A. 1990. "Population Ecology and Social Organization of the Dusky-footed Woodrat, *Neotoma fuscipes*." Ph.D. dissertation. University of California, Berkeley.

Keter, T. S. 1988. "A Diachronic Catchment Model for the North Fork of the Eel River Basin." Paper presented to the Society for California Archaeology. Redding, CA.

Koehler, C. S., L. R. Brown, and C. O. Eads. 1980. *Pit Scales on Oak*. U.S.D.A. Cooperative Extension Leaflet 2543. Berkeley: University of California.

Koenig, W. 1990. "Oaks, Acorns, and the Acorn Woodpecker." *Fremontia* 18 (3): 77-79.

Lathrop, E. W. and C. D. Osborne. 1990. "From Acorn to Tree: Ecology of the Engelmann Oak." *Fremontia* 18 (3): 30-35.

Linsdale, J. M. 1936. "California Quail Feeding Upon Acorns." *Condor* 38 (3):126.

Loft, E. R., T. S. Burton, J. W. Menke, and G. E. Peterson. 1988. "Characterization of Black-tailed Deer Habitats in a Northern California Oak-Conifer Zone." *California Fish and Game* 74 (3): 154-171.

Longhurst, W. M., G. E. Connolly, B. M. Browning, and E. O. Garton. "Food Interrelationships of Deer and Sheep in Parts of Mendocino and Lake Counties, California." *Hilgardia* 47 (6): 191-247.

Mayer, K. E. and W. F. Laudenslayer, Jr., eds. 1988. *A Guide to Wildlife Habitats of California*. Sacramento: California Department of Forestry and Fire Protection.

McCreary, D. D. 1990. "Native Oaks—The Next Generation." *Fremontia* 18 (3): 44-47.

Milne, L. and M. Milne. 1980. *The Audubon Society Field Guide to North American Insects & Spiders*. New York: Alfred A. Knopf.

Moffett, M. W. 1989. "Life in a Nutshell." *National Geographic* June 175: 782-96.

Novick, H. J. and G. R. Stewart. 1982. "Home Range and Habitat Preferences of Black Bears in the San Bernardino Mountains of Southern California." *California Fish and Game*. 68 (1): 21-35.

Novick, H. J., J. M. Siperek, and G. R. Stewart. 1981. "Denning Characteristics of Black Bears, *Urus Americanus*, in the San Bernardino Mountains of Southern California." *California Fish and Game* 67 (1): 52-61.

Opler, P. A. 1973. "Fossil Lepidopterous Leaf Mines Demonstrate the Age of Some Insect-Plant Relationships." *Science* 179 (4080): 1321-1323.

Opler, P. A. 1974. "Oaks as Evolutionary Islands for Leaf-Mining Insects." *American Scientist* 62 (1): 67-73.

Opler, P. A. 1974. "Biology, Ecology, and Host Specificity of Microlepidoptera Associated with *Quercus agrifolia* (Fagaceae)." University of California Publications in Entomology 75: 1974a.

Pavlik, B. M. 1976. *A Natural History of Southern California Oaks*. Los Angeles: West Los Angeles County Resource Conservation District.

Peterson, R. T. 1990. *A Field Guide to Western Birds*. 3rd ed. Boston: Houghton Mifflin Company.

Plumb, T. R., tech. coord. 1980. *Proceedings of the Symposium on the Ecology, Management, and Utilization of California Oaks*. Gen. Tech. Rep. PSW-44. Berkeley: Pacific SW Forest and Range Experiment Station, Forest Service, U.S. Department of Agriculture. (Numerous papers by many authors were consulted.)

Powell, J. and C. L. Hogue. 1979. *California Insects*. Berkeley: University of California Press.

Quinn, R. 1990. "Habitat Preferences and Distribution of Mammals in California Chaparral." *USDA Forest Service Research Paper PSW-202*. Berkeley: Pacific SW Research Station.

Robbins, C. S., B. Bruun, and H. S. Zim. 1983. *Birds of North America*. New York: Golden Press.

Russo, R. 1990. "Blue Oak: A Gall Wasp Nursery." *Fremontia* 18 (3) 68-71.

Smith, W. A. 1968. "The Band-tailed Pigeon in California". *California Fish and Game* 54 (1): 4-16.

Smith, W. A. and B. Browning. 1967. "Wild Turkey Food Habits in San Luis Obispo County, California." *California Fish and Game*. 53 (4): 246-253.

Standiford, R., tech. coord. 1991. *Proceedings of the Symposium on Oak Woodlands and Hardwood Rangeland Management*. Gen. Tech Rep. PSW-126. Berkeley: Pacific SW Research Station, Forest Service, U.S. Department of Agriculture. (Numerous papers by many authors were consulted.)

Stebbins, R. C. 1972. *California Amphibians and Reptiles*. Berkeley: University of California Press.

Stebbins, R.C. 1966. *A Field Guide to Western Reptiles and Amphibians*. Boston: Houghton Mifflin Company.

Stienecker, W. E. 1977. "Supplemental Data on the Food Habits of the Western Gray Squirrel." *California Fish and Game* 63 (1): 11-21.

Storer, T. I. and L. P. Tevis, Jr. 1955. *California Grizzly*. Berkeley: University of California Press.

Sunset Books and Sunset Magazine. eds. 1988. *Sunset Western Garden Book*. 5th ed. Menlo Park: Lane Publishing Co.

Swiecki, T. J. 1990. "Oak Diseases and Insects: A Delicate Balance." *Fremontia* 18 (3): 58-63.

Swiecki, T. J., E. A. Bernhardt, and R. A. Arnold. 1990. *Impacts of Diseases and Arthropods on California's Rangeland Oaks*. Sacramento: California Department of Forestry and Fire Protection.

Tietje, W. 1990. "Acorns: Planning for Oak-Woodland Wildlife." *Fremontia* 18 (3): 80-81.

Udvardy, M. D. F. 1977. *The Audubon Society Field Guide to North American Birds*. New York: Alfred A. Knopf.

Villee, C. A., W. F. Walker, Jr. and R. D. Barnes. 1973. *General Zoology*. 5th ed. Philadelphia: W. B. Saunders Company.

Wallmo, O. C., ed. 1981. *Mule and Black-tailed Deer of North America*. Lincoln: University of Nebraska Press.

Winston, P. W. 1956. "The Acorn Microsere, With Special Reference to Arthropods." *Ecology* 37 (1): 120-132.

Chapter Four: California Oaks and the Human Past

Alvarez, S. H. and D. W. Peri. 1987. "Acorns: The Staff of Life." *News From Native California* 1 Sept.-Oct.: 10-14.

Arno, S. F. 1973. *Discovering Sierra Trees*. Yosemite: Yosemite and Sequoia Natural History Association.

Balls, E. K. 1972. *Early Uses of California Plants*. Berkeley: University of California Press.

Bancroft, H. H. 1890. *History of California*. Volume 7. San Francisco: The History Company.

Barrett, S. A. and E. W. Gifford. 1933. "Miwok Material Culture." *Bulletin of the Public Museum of Milwaukee* 2: 117-376.

Bates, C. D. 1983. "Acorn Storehouses of the Yosemite Miwok." *The Masterkey, Southwest Museum* 57 (1): 19-27.

Bauer, P. 1954. "The Beginning of Tanning in California." *California Historical Society Quarterly* 33: 59-72.

Beck, W. A. and Y. D. Haase. 1974. *Historical Atlas of California*. Norman: University of Oklahoma Press.

Bolsinger, C. L. 1988. *The Hardwoods of California's Timberlands, Woodlands and Savannas*. Portland: U.S. Department of Agriculture, Forest Service, Pacific NW Research Station.

Bolton, H. E., ed. 1966. *Anza's California Expeditions. Font's Complete Diary*. Volume 4. New York: Russell and Russell.

Brooks, G. R., ed. 1977. *The Expedition of Jedediah Smith: His Personal Account of the Journey to California, 1826-27*. Glendale: Arthur H. Clark Co.

Burcham, L. T. 1957. *California Range Land: An Historical-Ecological Study of the Range Resource of California*. Sacramento: Division of Forestry, California Department of Natural Resources.

Burcham, L. T. 1981. "California Rangelands in Historical Perspective." *Rangelands* 3: 95-104.

Caldwell, J. C. 1979. *Carpinteria As It Was*. Carpinteria: Papillon Press.

California Department of Parks and Recreation. 1982. *California Historical Landmarks*. Sacramento: California Department of Parks and Recreation.

Costanso, M. 1769. *The Costanso Narrative of the Portola Expedition*. Translated by R. Brandes, 1970. Newhall: Hogarth Press.

Cullimore, C. 1949. *Old Adobes of Forgotten Fort Tejon*. Bakersfield: Kern County Historical Society.

Dana, Jr., R. H. 1835. *Two Years Before the Mast*. Reprint. 1981. New York: Penguin Books.

Eastwood, A. 1954. "Early Botanical Explorers on the Pacific Coast and the Trees They Found There." In: *The Perennial Adventure: A Tribute to Alice Eastwood, 1859-1953*. S. B. Dakin, ed. San Francisco: California Academy of Sciences.

Fages, P. 1775. *A Historical, Political and Natural Description of California*. Reprint. 1937. H. I. Priestly, ed. Berkeley: University of California.

Farris, G. J. 1980. "A Reassessment of the Nutritional Value of

Pinus monophylla." *Journal of California and Great Basin Anthropology* 2: 132-136.

Frémont, J. B. 1890. *Far-West Sketches*. Boston: D. Lathrop Co.

Frémont, J. C. 1845. *Report of the Second Expedition*. Washington, D.C.: United States Government Printing Office.

Griffin, J. R. and P. C. Muick. 1990. "California Native Oaks: Past and Present." *Fremontia* 18: 4-12.

Griffin, J. R., P. M. McDonald, and P. C. Muick. 1987. *California Oaks: A Bibliography*. Berkeley: Pacific SW Forest and Range Experiment Station, Forest Service, U.S. Department of Agriculture.

Gudde, E. G. 1969. *California Place Names*. 3rd ed. Berkeley: University of California Press.

Hedges, K. and C. Beresford. 1986. *Santa Ysabel Ethnobotany*. San Diego Museum of Man Ethnic Technology Notes, No. 20. San Diego: San Diego Museum of Man.

Heizer, R. F. and A. B. Elsasser. 1980. *The Natural World of the California Indians*. Berkeley: University of California Press.

Heizer, R. F., ed. 1978. *California Handbook of North American Indians*. Volume 8. Washington, D.C.: Smithsonian Institution.

Jepson, W. L. 1910. "The Silva of California." In: *Memoirs of the University of California*, Volume 2. Berkeley: University of California Press.

Kroeber, A. L. 1925. *Handbook of the Indians of California*. Bureau of American Ethnology of the Smithsonian Institution, Bulletin 78. Reprint. 1953. Berkeley: California Book Company.

Merriam, C. H. 1918. "The Acorn, a Possibly Neglected Source of Food." *National Geographic Magazine* Aug.: 129-137.

Muir, J. 1913. *The Mountains of California*. New York: The Century Co.

Ortiz, B. 1988. "It Will Live Forever: Yosemite Indian Acorn Preparation." *News from Native California* 2 Nov.-Dec.: 24-28.

Pavlik, B. M. 1976. *A Natural History of Southern California Oaks*. Los Angeles: West Los Angeles County Resource Conservation District.

Peattie, D. C. 1953. *A Natural History of Western Trees*. New York: Bonanza Books.

Peri, D. W. 1987. "Plant of the Season: Oaks." *News from Native California* 1 Nov.-Dec.: 6-9.

Plumb, T. R. and N. H. Pillsbury, tech. coords. 1987. *Proceedings of the Symposium on Multiple-Use Management of California's Hardwood Resources*. Gen. Tech. Rep. PSW-100. Berkeley: Pacific SW Forest and Range Experiment Station, Forest Service, U.S. Department of Agriculture. (Numerous papers by many authors were consulted.)

Plumb, T. R., tech. coord. 1980. *Proceedings of the Symposium on the Ecology, Management, and Utilization of California Oaks*. Gen. Tech. Rep. PSW-44. Berkeley: Pacific SW Forest and Range Experiment Station, Forest Service, U.S. Department of Agriculture. (Numerous papers by many authors were consulted.)

Rice, R. B., W. A. Bullough, and R. J. Orsi. 1988. *The Elusive Eden: A New History of California*. New York: Alfred A. Knopf.

Robinson, W. W. 1961. *The Story of San Fernando Valley*. Los Angeles: Title Insurance and Trust Co.

Thomson and West. 1961. *History of Santa Barbara and Ventura Counties*. Berkeley: Howell-North.

Twisselman, E. C. 1967. *A Flora of Kern County*. San Francisco: University of San Francisco.

Warner, R. E. and K. M. Hendrix. 1985. *Riparian Resources of the Central Valley and California Desert*. Sacramento: California Department of Fish and Game.

Chapter Five: Preserving Oaks for Future Generations

Bernhardt, E. A. and T. J. Swiecki. 1991. *Guidelines for Developing and Evaluating Tree Ordinances*. Prepared for the California Department of Forestry, Urban Forestry Program. Davis: Plant Science Consulting and Research.

Bolsinger, C. L. 1988. *The Hardwoods of California's Timberlands, Woodlands, and Savannas*. Resource Bulletin PNW-RB-148. Portland: U.S. Department of Agriculture, Forest Service, Pacific NW Research Station.

Borchert, M. I., F. R. Davis, J. Michaelsen, and L. D. Oyler. 1989. "Intereactions of Factors Affecting Seedling Recruitment of Blue Oak (*Quercus douglasii*) in California." *Ecology* (70) 2: 389-404.

Ewing, R. A. 1990. "How Are Oaks Protected? What Are the Issues?" *Fremontia* 18 (3): 83-88.

Forest and Rangeland Resources Assessment Program. 1988. *California's Forests and Rangelands: Growing Conflict Over Changing Uses*. Sacramento: California Department of Forestry and Fire Protection.

Griffin, J. R. 1971. "Oak Regeneration in the Upper Carmel Valley." California. *Ecology* 52 (5): 862-868.

Griffin, J. R. 1973. "Valley Oaks-The End of an Era?" *Fremontia* 1 (1): 5-9.

Griffin, J. R. and P. C. Muick. 1990. California Native Oaks: Past and Present." *Fremontia* 18 (3): 4-10.

Holland, V. L. 1976. "In Defense of Blue Oaks." *Fremontia* 4 (1): 3-8.

Jepson, W. L. 1909. *The Trees of California*. San Francisco: Cunningham, Curtis, & Welch.

Johnson, S. 1989. *Living Among the Oaks*. U.C. Cooperative Extension Publication. Berkeley: University of California, Division of Agriculture and Natural Resources.

Lewis, H. T. 1973. *Patterns of Indian Burning in California: Ecology and Ethnohistory*. Ballena Press Anthropological Papers No. 1. Ramona: Ballena Press.

McClaran, M. P. 1986. "Age Structure of *Quercus douglasii* in Relation to Livestock Grazing and Fire." Ph. D. dissertation, University of California, Berkeley.

McClaran, M. P. and J. W. Bartolome. 1989. "Fire Related Recruitment in Stagnant *Quercus douglasii* Populations." *Canadian Journal of Forest Research* 19: 580-585.

McClaran, M. P. and J. W. Bartolome. 1990. "Comparison of Actual and Predicted Blue Oak Age Structures." *Journal of Range Management* (43) 1: 61-63.

McCreary, D. 1989. "Regenerating Native Oaks in California." *California Agriculture* Jan-Feb.: 4-6.

Mensing, S. 1990. "Blue Oak Regeneration in the Tehachapi Mountains. *Fremontia* 18 (3): 38-41.

Muick, P. C. and J. W. Bartolome. 1987. *An Assessment of Natural Regeneration of Oaks in California*. Prepared for the California Department of Forestry. Berkeley:

University of California, Department of Forestry and Range Management.

Rossi, R. S. 1979. "History of Cultural Influences on the Distribution and Reproduction of Oaks in California." In: Plumb, T. R., tech. coord. 1980. *Proceedings of the Symposium on the Ecology, Management, and Utilization of California Oaks*. Gen. Tech. Rep. PSW-44. Berkeley: Pacific SW Forest and Range Experiment Station, Forest Service, U.S. Department of Agriculture.

Rossi, R. S. 1990. "Oak Ordinances: Do They Help or Hurt?" *Fremontia* 18 (3): 96-98.

Standiford, R., N. McDougald, R. Phillips, and A. Nelson. 1991. "South Sierra Oak Regeneration Weak in Sapling Stage." *California Agriculture* March-April: 12-14.

Standiford, R., tech. coord. 1991. *Proceedings of the Symposium on Oak Woodlands and Hardwood Rangeland Management*. Gen. Tech Rep. PSW-126. Berkeley: Pacific SW Research Station, Forest Service, U.S. Department of Agriculture. (Numerous papers by many authors were consulted.)

Sudworth, G. B. 1908. *Forest Trees of the Pacific Slope*. Washington, D.C.: U.S. Dept. of Agriculture, Forest Service, Government Printing Office.

Twisselman, E. C. 1956. "A Flora of the Temblor Range and Neighboring Part of the San Joaquin Valley." *Wasmann Journal of Biology* 14 (2): 161-300.

Chapter Six: Exploring California's Oak Landscapes

Brewer, W. and F. P. Farquhar, ed. 1966. *Up and Down California in 1860-1864*. Berkeley: University of California Press.

California Department of Parks and Recreation. 1989. *A Visitor's Guide to California State Parks*. Sacramento: California Department of Parks and Recreation.

Carr, J. 1891. *Pioneer Days in California*. Eureka: The Times Publication Company.

Frémont, J. C. 1845. *Report of the Second Expedition*. Washington, D.C.: United States Government Printing Office.

Holing, D. 1988. *California Wild Lands*. San Francisco: Chronicle Books.

King, C. 1874. *Mountaineering in the Sierra Nevada*. Reprint 1989. New York: Penguin Books.

Muir, J. 1894. *The Mountains of California*. Reprint. 1988.

Contributing Authors

BEN ALEXANDER is a revegetation specialist with Yosemite National Park. A graduate of Evergreen State College in Olympia, Washington, he has also worked as a revegetation technician for Olympic National Park in Washington State.

SUZANNE GOODE holds a master of science degree in biology from California State University, Los Angeles. Her Master's research produced a baseline study of the native grassland of La Jolla Valley Natural Preserve in Point Mugu State Park, Ventura County. She has worked for over ten years as a consultant and researcher in grassland, oak woodland, and chaparral communities in the Santa Monica and San Gabriel mountains. She is currently employed as a resource ecologist for the California Department of Parks and Recreation in the Santa Monica Mountains.

TOM GRIGGS received his Ph.D. in ecology from the University of California, Davis where he studied the life histories of vernal pool plants. Tom has worked for the California Nature Conservancy for the past nine years as a restoration ecologist, managing preserves which protect several California oak species: Kaweah Oaks Preserve, Santa Rosa Plateau, and Cosumnes River. Currently, Tom manages The Nature Conservancy's riparian restoration projects along the Sacramento River.

PATRICK A. KELLY received his Ph.D. in zoology from the University of California, Berkeley in 1989 upon filing his dissertation: "Population Ecology and Social Organization of Dusky-footed Woodrats, Neotoma fuscipes." He currently does research at the University of California, Riverside as part of a three-campus team developing a Habitat Conservation Plan for the Stephens' kangaroo rat, Dipodomys stephensi, a federally listed endangered species.

WALTER D. KOENIG received his Ph.D. from the University of California, Berkeley in 1978. He is currently an Associate Research Zoologist at the University of California's Hastings Natural History Reservation in upper Carmel Valley, and an Adjunct Associate Professor in the Department of Integrative Biology at the University of California, Berkeley. He has been studying the bizarre behavior of acorn woodpeckers since 1974.

BEV ORTIZ is a naturalist with the East Bay Regional Park District, ethnographic consultant, and freelance writer. She has been working with, researching, writing, and teaching about California Indians for more than 12 years. Heyday Books recently published her book *It Will Live Forever: Yosemite Indian Acorn Making,* an elegant photographic and textual tribute to Yosemite Indian Cultural Program Supervisor Julia Parker, who still practices the ancient art of acorn preparation with delicacy, reverence, and consummate skill.

ROBERT C. PAVLIK is a State Historian for the San Simeon Region, California Department of Parks and Recreation. He is a graduate of the Public Historical Studies Program at the University of California, Santa Barbara.

GINGER STRONG has been active in oak issues since the early 1980s. She is the Arborist for the City of Visalia and served as President of the Board of Directors of the California Oak Foundation in 1990-91.

RON RUSSO is Chief Naturalist for the East Bay Regional Park District in Oakland. He is the author of *Plant Galls of the California Region* (Boxwood Press, 1979) and a variety of articles on galls in several magazines including *Pacific Discovery* and *Fremontia.* He has also authored three field guides for the Nature Study Guild in Berkeley.

TEDMUND J. SWIECKI received his Ph.D. from the University of California, Davis. He is a plant pathologist and principal of Plant Science Consulting & Research, Vacaville, California. He has recently completed research projects on diseases and insects of California oaks and valley oak restoration.

Index

South Yuba River Project. *See* Highway 49
Southern mixed evergreen forest, 27, 33, 69, 72, 137; where to see, 155, 163
Springtail-stalking ant, 81
Springtails, 81
Squaw Leap Management Area, 154
Stanislaus National Forest, 153
Stanley, Dorothy, 116
State of California, Department of Fish and Game, 113
State of California, Department of Forestry, 113
Steller's jay, 79, 85
Stevenson, Robert Louis, 26
Strybing Arboretum and Botanical Gardens, 147
Stump-sprouting. *See* Oak sprouting
Subtropical oaks, 22
Sudworth, George, B., 121
Sugarloaf Ridge State Park, 141
Sunol Regional Park, 149
Swamp oak, 11
Synecology, 52, 75

Tanbark, 8, 15, 20, 59, 69, 72; acorns of, 8, 97; Indian burning under, 124; use of tanins of, 104
Tanins, 29, 76; leaching of before acorn meal preparation, 99, 117; use of for making dyes, 101; use of for medicine, 101; use of for tanning hides, 104
Tent caterpillar, 76, 80
Tevis, L. P., Jr., 90
The Nature Conservancy, 113, 127; Cosumnes River Preserve of, 132-133, 145, Elkhorn Slough Reserve of, 150, 145; Gray Davis Dye Creek Preserve of, 144; Kaweah Oaks Preserve of, 125, 155; Northern California Coast Range Preserve of, 140; Santa Cruz Island Preserve of, 158; Santa Rosa Plateau Ecological Reserve of, 131-132, 162
Theodore Payne Foundation, 159
Tilden Regional Park, 148
Topanga State Park, 159
Toro Canyon Park, 158
Toro Regional Park, 150
Tower House Historic District, 143
Toxicodendron diversilobum. See Poison oak
Tree oaks, 3, 6, 9, 52, 67
Treehoppers, 80
Trees of the Pacific Slope, 121
True oaks, 8
Tule River, 155
Twain Harte, 153
Twisselman, Ernest, 122
Tyloses, 54

U.S. Forest Service, 113, 126; Pacific Southwest Forest and Range Experimental Station of, 120. *See also* U.S.F.S. National Forest destinations in Chapter 6
University of California, 113, 121, 127; Hastings Natural History Reservation of, 124, Hopland Field Station of, 140; Northern California Coast Range Preserve of, 140; Peter J. Shields Oak Grove of, 145
"Up-Hill Planters," 78-79
Urban forestry, 126, 129
Uvas Canyon Park, 150

Valley oak ant, 81
Valley oak riparian forest, 12, 63-64, 72, 125; habitat restoration in, 127, 132-133; preservation of, 130; where to see, 145, 154, 155; wildlife diversity in, 63
Valley oak savanna, 12; low recruitment rate of valley oak trees in, 125; habitat restoration in, 127, 134-135; where to see, 151, 157, 158
Valley oak woodland, 12, 18, 27, 64, 66, 73, 86; where to see, 140, 144, 151
Valley oak, 10-12, 18, 30, 35, 44, 45, 51, 53, 54, 55, 81, 87, 91, 106, 108, 114, 115, 119, 120, 121, 127, 130, 133; acorns of, 7, 12; bark of, 10, 12, 57; community affiliation of, 12, 62, 64, 72-73; effect of land development on, 111, 125, 130; geographical distribution of, 12; growth form of, 11; habitat of, 12; identifying characteristics of, 11-12; key to, 48; leaves of, 11, 54; poor regeneration of, 122, 124, 125, 134-135 range map of, 46; uses of, 11, 12, 107-108; wood of, 11,12
Valley Yokuts, 99
Vancouver, George, 10
Visalia, oak preservation in, 120, 130. *See also* Mooney Grove Park
Vizcaíno, Sebastián, 103, 114
Walker, Lieutenant Joseph R., 105

Wappo, 97
Wassama Roundhouse State Historic Park, 154
Water oak, 11
Weeping oak, 11
Western bluebird, 78, 82, 85, 86
Western gray squirrel, 58, 76, 78, 79, 88, 89, 124
Western harvest mice, 77
Western tussock moth, 76
Westwood Hills Park, 141
Whiskeytown-Shasta-Trinity National Recreation Area, 143
White oak 11
White oak evolutionary lineage, 11, 36, 78. *See also Lepidobalanus*
Whiteflies, 76, 80
Wildcat Canyon Regional Park, 148
Wilderness Gardens Preserve, 162
Wildfire, 60, 62, 69, 113, 125, 128, 133
Wildflowers in oak landscapes, 66
Wildland management. *See* Oaks, wildland management of
Wildlife and oaks, 75-93, 129
William B. Ide Adobe State Historic Park, 144
William Heise Park, 163
Wintu, 14, 98, 99, 101
Wislizenius, Dr. F. A., 28, 106
Woodland and savanna communities, 72; agricultural clearing of, 111; fire in, 56; livestock grazing in, 128. *See also* Oaks, threats to
Woodland. *See* Oak woodland
Woodrat. *See* Dusky-footed woodrat
Woodson Bridge State Recreation Area, 144

Yosemite Miwok, 14, 116
Yosemite National Park, 153-154
Yosemite Valley, 153-154; habitat restoration in, 127, 133-134
Yuki, 97, 98
Yurok, 97